The Book of Divination

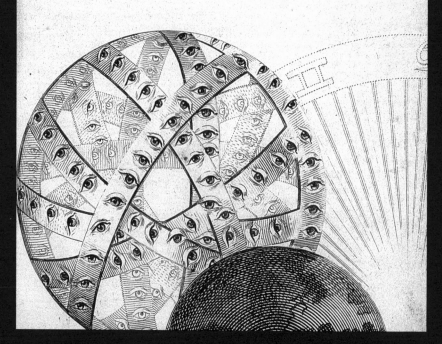

From Des Gottseeligen Hocherleuchteten Jacob Bohmens, *1682.*

THE BOOK OF
DIVINATION

by Ann Fiery

CHRONICLE BOOKS

SAN FRANCISCO

Pages 211–12 are a continuation of the copyright page.

Library of Congress Cataloging-in-Publication Data:
Fiery, Ann.
The book of divination / by Ann Fiery.
    p.   cm.
    Includes bibliographical references and index.
    ISBN 0-8118-1618-4 (hc)
    1. Fortune-telling. I. Title.
BF 1861.F54   1999
133.3—dc21   98-36499
                   CIP

Designed by Pamela Geismar
Composed using Fairfield Light and Engravers Bold Face

Printed in Hong Kong.

Distributed in Canada by
Raincoast Books
8680 Cambie Street
Vancouver, British Columbia V6P 6M9

10 9 8 7 6 5 4 3 2 1

Chronicle Books
85 Second Street
San Francisco, California 94105

www.chroniclebooks.com

CONTENTS

A bevy of fortune-telling Gypsies divest a foolish young man of his property. Georges de La Tour, The Fortune Teller, seventeenth century.

INTRODUCTION

Divination allows us to achieve the great goal of humankind: a practice life. Each of the divinatory systems discussed in this book offers not a sewn-up, completed future but a possible outcome of a certain course of action. This is precisely the information we seek as we career down the freeway of existence: if I make this turn, will my life be better or worse? Divination provides us with a map of the road not taken.

The real benefit of a practice life would be freedom. Practicing, we could fritter away our money, attach ourselves to inappropriate partners, take up impractical professions such as animal taming, and generally seek gratification instead of achievement. Then, having learned of the relative un-gratifyingness of a life devoted to gratification, we could embark upon our real lives, at once wise and humble. Unfortunately, as far as we know, we have only one chance at incarnation. Thus, we are forced by circumstance to take our lives seriously. We want to have plenty of money, we want to find profound love, we want secure and fulfilling professions, and we want to get as much gratification as possible without endangering any of the above. We want more than anything to have made the right choices. Divination is the answer to this dilemma. It offers a cost-benefit analysis of all our innermost desires and wayward impulses in order that we may exercise our wills sagely. What could possibly be more useful than a glimpse into the corridors of the future while one actually remains comfortably slouched on the threshold? Nothing. Clearly, this is the source of the enduring popularity of divination.

"Enduring" is an understatement. Excavations at the sites of the world's oldest civilizations have revealed, in virtually every instance, implements for the management or discernment of the future. These may take the form of blandishments to the gods or, in more sanguine cultures, of amulets that transform their bearers into gods by allowing them to arrange the future to their liking. The impulse is ancient and, apparently, inescapable. We seek high and low for clues as to our future. Mostly we seek high, on the theory that the organizers of the universe must have left evidence of their plans for us in their plans for the cosmos. Such is the stance behind the central tenet of Western divination, "As above, so below." This means, essentially, that the structure of the cosmos is reflected in our own structure. Accordingly, an understanding of celestial organization will lead to an understanding of human organization. This theory is embodied most comprehensively in astrology, which postulates a one-to-one correspondence between the stars and the individual, but it is also integral to the teachings of the Kabbalah. In a less complex way, it is the basis for tarot, tasseomancy (otherwise known as tea-leaf reading), geomancy, and rune casting. The idea in these systems is that the order in which the cards or runes or tea leaves or dots fall is not only divinely ordained but reflective of the cosmic structure. In other words, the forces of gravity and spiritu-

ality that pull the runes toward the earth in a certain pattern contain within them the germ of everything that ever has or ever will happen. Thus, to read the pattern correctly is to know all. Numerology, palmistry, metoposcopy, rhabdomancy (dowsing), haruspicy, phrenology, and oneiromancy (dream interpretation) proceed from the slightly divergent assumption that the creator has left clues to the divine plan in particular spots, such as in the hand or, more disgustingly, in the liver of a goat (haruspicy is divination by entrails). Oracles, talismans, and, in its own weird way, alchemy are bold attempts to bypass the complexities of interpretation and access the power of the gods directly. These methods tiptoe precariously into the waters of magic, and, appropriately, the success of the undertaking depends on the quality of the engineer.

No one was more devoted to finding the macrocosm in the microcosm than the exceedingly strange British occultist Robert Fludd. As you can see in this illustration from his Utriusque cosmi majoris et minoris historia *(1617), God regulates Nature (represented by the woman crowned with stars), and Nature, in turn, regulates mankind and its arts (represented by the monkey). Heretical though this cosmology is, it provides a tidy evaluation of the divinatory project: the grand plan of God is diluted by intervening rulers; thus the aspect of the divine available to us in the form of divinatory systems is but a pale ape of God.*

This introduces an interesting question about the worthiness of the venture as a whole. What *is* the motive of the divinatory impulse? Well, it is hubris and greed—the history of divination is copiously supplied with scoundrels—but it is also something else: curiosity of the highest caliber. In their desire to know the universe within and without themselves, the great diviners searched minute particles of dust as well as the infinite celestial gyre to find evidence of God's hand. Their efforts to create a meaningful cosmology out of a million disparate clues required both magnificent leaps of imagination and incessant calculation, analysis, and experimentation. Almost all the systems of divination employed today were created over centuries from the observations and deductions of inventors, philosophers, scientists, and theologians, and, as you will see, some of the most beautiful art in the Western world was created in the service of divination.

This book is no more than a dabble in the deep waters of Western divination. I have tried to give a sense of the traditions of each of the systems I discuss, but all of them (with the possible exception of haruspicy) would repay further investigation. I have also given instructions for the employment of these practices. However, some of these subjects, notably astrology and tarot, are gloriously complicated and reward plenty of study and practice by yielding more of their secrets. Others, like tea-leaf reading, can be conquered quickly. I am not demure about my opinions; you will undoubtedly notice that I approve of some interpretations and developments more than others. I assure you, though, that everything I disdain has its advocates—even phrenology must have some advocates—and I urge you to follow your inclination in choosing a divinatory method that suits you.

One further warning: you will find that divination reveals as much about the reader as it does about the "readee," or querent. If you hope to become a great diviner, you must first accept what the cards or stars or lines reveal about your own character and future. Only after you have followed their guidance can you become an adept yourself.

—*Ann Fiery*

Signs of the
ZODIAC.

Astrology is the queen of the divinatory arts. Not only is it the oldest method of fortune-telling known to humanity, it is also the most pervasive. Even the grouchiest skeptic can't resist reading his horoscope in the morning paper, and many of us have, at one time or another, sat down for a good long perusal of our sign's attributes according to an authoritative astrologer.

There's a reason for this: astrology is convincing. Virgos are tense, Libras are reasonable, Scorpios are mean. It's almost alarming how consistently correct the characterizations are and strange to think—as is the next logical step—that the stars can determine our personalities and fortunes. But, no matter how vast our knowledge of the world has become, it would be the rare scientist who would claim to know what motivates the universe. In the absence of this certain knowledge, we must take whatever clues we can get.

Astrology is older than history. There is some evidence that Cro-Magnon man may have followed the cycles of the stars, notching bones to aid his substandard memory in creating an almanac. We know that by 3000 B.C., both the Babylonians and the Chaldeans were scanning the night skies and recording the movements of the constellations, though, as usual, the Greeks and Romans get credit for the names and the stories. Until the fifth century B.C., astrologers studied the stars primarily to determine the most auspicious moment to, say, start a war. This became known as *horary astrology* and was distinctly the province of kings and great priests, whose study of the stars gave them divine authority. Although this brand of astrology has fallen into disuse in the twentieth century— starting a war having become a

Above: Your average astrologer, from an early twentieth-century postcard.

more complicated business—the interpretation of birth charts and transits offers the same type of advice on a personal level. A second type of astrology was concerned with predicting the weather and natural disasters, as well as with assigning astrological signs to countries, cities, and ethnicities. Termed *mundane astrology,* this is largely defunct today. The third type of astrology, *natal astrology,* was developed by the Chaldeans around 500 B.C. as they began to notice a consistency of character among individuals born at the same time. After about two hundred years of reflection, they attributed these consistencies to the positions of the stars. This concept forms the theoretical basis for the horoscope, which is, in essence, a picture of the position of the stars and planets at the moment of an individual's birth. Over hundreds of years of observation and, more important, record keeping, the Chaldeans, the Greeks, the Romans, and the great sorcerers and philosophers of the Middle Ages developed interpretations of the thousands of permutations presented by the movements of the planets and the stars across the night sky.

When we say "he's an Aries" or "she's a Capricorn," we are referring to only one, albeit the most important, element of the horoscope: the Sun sign. The Sun sign indicates where in the Zodiac—the band of twelve constellations that girdles the earth—the Sun was located on the day of the querent's birth. But the Sun is just one of the ten planets that are swirling around the skies (okay, it's not really a planet, but for astrological purposes, it's called a planet). The full horoscope shows the placement of all the planets in the signs and in the houses (more about houses later). The astrologer's task is to interpret the forces represented by these planets according to both their position and their relationship to one another. It sounds simple, but it is an outrageously complicated task, for the position of each element bears on every other element, creating a vast number of permutations that have to be interpreted. A full horoscope contains between thirty and one hundred indicators to analyze and then synthesize.

In this chapter, you will learn the basics of reading and interpreting a birth chart (i.e., a natal horoscope). For the sake of your sanity, I will not delve into the subject of chart erection, that is, how to construct a horoscope. It is a hideous task, requiring the conversion of one set of hours and minutes to another set of hours and minutes and an acute understanding of longitude. Any book that claims to be a definitive guide to astrology should include instructions about chart erection, along with an ephemeris, a table of houses, a chart of sidereal times, and a schedule of daylight savings times for the last century throughout the world, all of which would be necessary for your calculations. Another, and to my mind, superior, means of constructing a horoscope is to use a computer. The Io Edition of Time Cycles Research's Graphic Astrology program is a miracle of ease. Simply enter the salient facts—place, date, and hour of birth—and the computer generates the translated figures, a birth chart, and a table of aspects, all ready to be interpreted.

Computer-generated horoscopes rescue you only from the trauma of arithmetic; they do not relieve you of the obligation to understand the theory behind the horoscope. This theory is based on the concept that individual humans are subject to forces exerted by the Sun, Moon, and other planets, rather in the same way that tides are affected by the waxing and waning of the Moon. The early astronomers, studying the night skies, saw the Sun, Moon, Mercury, Venus, Mars, Jupiter, and Saturn apparently revolving around Earth, as is depicted in Figure 1 (Neptune, Uranus, and Pluto were later discoveries). These planets move against a background of stars, and, because all the planets are orbiting in the same plane as Earth, they are always moving against the

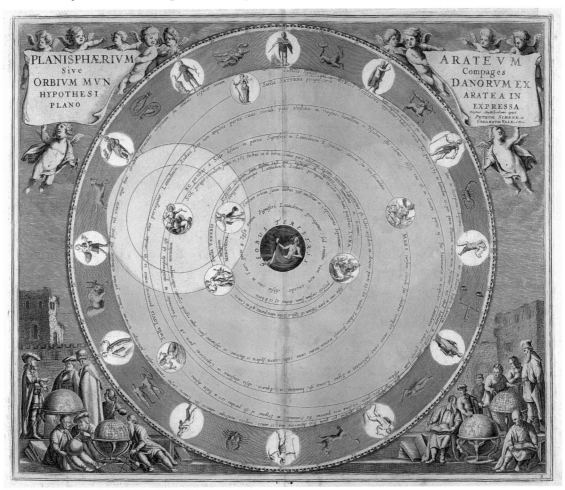

FIGURE 1. *This interesting rendition of the orbits of the planets reveals a Herculean effort to reconcile religion and observation. The Earth remains at the center of the universe, but the orbits of Mercury and Venus around the Sun are also acknowledged. The impossibility of the scheme is not addressed. From Andreas Cellarius's* Harmonia macrosomica.

same series of constellations—the Zodiac. Let us cast our minds back to grammar school. The equator is the belt wrapped around Earth's waist, but Earth tilts on its axis, so that the Sun appears to travel around Earth on a path that lies at an angle to the equator. This path is called the ecliptic. Ranged along the band of the ecliptic are the twelve constellations that form the Zodiac; each occupies 30 degrees of the band (30 x 12 = 360 degrees). The Sun journeys all the way around the ecliptic in a year, spending about a month moving through each constellation. This is where we get the Sun sign designations: if you're born on May 30, when the Sun was moving through the constellation of Gemini, you must be a Gemini, etcetera. Back to the ecliptic. Look at Figure 2. You'll see that the ecliptic and the celestial equator (which is merely the plain equator extrapolated into space) meet at two points. These are the equinoxes, vernal and autumnal. The vernal equinox, which occurs on March 21, marks the beginning of the Zodiacal cycle, when the Sun enters the constellation of Aries.

Two further markers of astrological significance are the midheaven (also called the *medium coeli,* or MC) and the ascendant. The midheaven is calculated using the meridian, which is any one of a nearly infinite number of bands encircling Earth from Pole to Pole, specifically, the one that runs through the birthplace of the querent; that is, the longitude of the place of birth. The midheaven is the point at which the meridian of the place of birth meets the ecliptic. The ascendant is the degree of the sign of the Zodiac that is rising over the eastern horizon at the moment of birth.

So, the position of the Sun on the band of the constellations determines what is popularly known as your sign. Remember, though, that there are nine other planets, all traveling at various speeds around the ecliptic. Your Sun may be, for instance, in Gemini, while your Mercury sits in Cancer and your Moon rests in Aquarius. A full reading of a horoscope must give all the planets their due.

One more thing to keep in mind, before we move on to the characteristics of the planets and the signs, is the issue of degree. As I described above, each sign occupies 30 degrees of the ecliptic band. A planet may, then, occupy the first degree of a sign or the thirtieth, or anything in between. This is not just a fun fact but an essential element of interpretation, for the influence of a sign is weakest at its borders and strongest in the middle. A notation of degree is a standard feature of a horoscope and should be used in analysis. For example, if your querent's Sun is two degrees in Virgo, her Virgoan traits may be muted and she will display plenty of Leonine qualities—in the worst-case scenario, she will be both fussy *and* bossy. Bear in mind, also, that the planets take different lengths of time to move through the signs. Speedy Mercury completes a tour of the ecliptic in a year, while ponderous Jupiter makes the same trip in twelve years. What this means is that Mercury's influence is filtered through Taurus for a month, and then it moves on to act in a Geminian manner. Jupiter, on the other hand, hangs out in Taurus for a year. So, for example, a classroom full of children born in the same year will express their Jovian characteristics in the same way, which will be charming if Jupiter was in Sagittarius that year, but miserable if it was in Gemini.

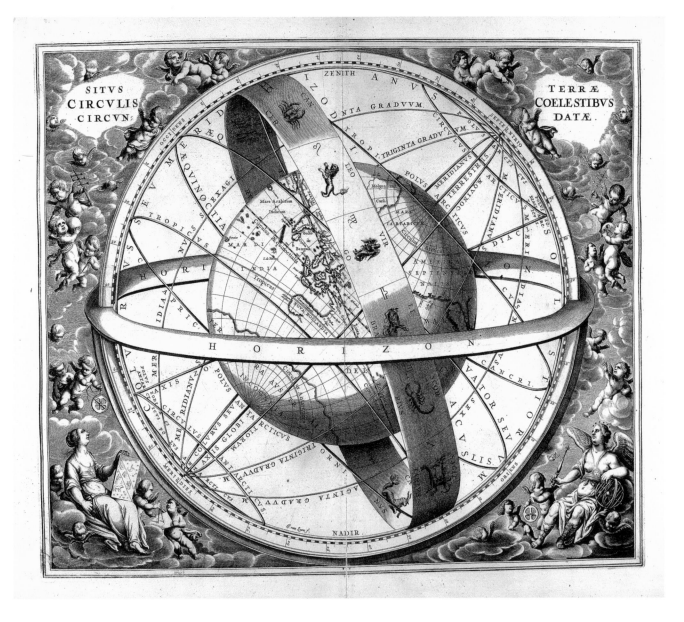

FIGURE 2. *The great seventeenth-century astronomer Andreas Cellarius created this celestial map depicting the relationship of the Earth to the Zodiac. Note the relationship of the equator (designated here as AEQUATOR) to the ecliptic, here portrayed in a wide band of Zodiac signs. The horizon, so firmly defined in this map, is actually a constantly shifting event that depends on your location, but, for purposes of illustration, if you were born in the middle of the Pacific Ocean at the exact time shown on this map, which is, I believe, the actual equinox, your ascendant would be in Libra.*

ASCENDANT: The degree of the sign of the Zodiac rising over the horizon at the moment of birth. This point marks the cusp of the first house and begins the horoscope.

ECLIPTIC: Once thought to be the path of the Sun's orbit around the Earth, the ecliptic is now known to be the path of the Earth's orbit around the Sun, which describes a circle that lies at an angle to the equator. The twelve constellations that appear on this circle are the signs of the Zodiac. Since all planets orbit the Sun in the same plane as the Earth, they appear to us to be moving against the background of the Zodiac.

EQUATOR: The band, or more correctly, the plane, that marks the circumference of the Earth perpendicular to the poles. The extension of this plane into space is called the celestial equator.

EQUINOX: Meaning "equal night," the equinox occurs when the center of the Sun is directly over the equator, which happens twice a year. The vernal equinox takes place around March 21, at zero degrees Aries, and starts the astrological year. The autumnal equinox occurs when the Sun enters zero degrees Libra, around September 21. The days and nights are the same length on the equinoxes.

HOROSCOPE: A schema of the positions of all nine planets against the band of the Zodiac as seen from the exact location of the querent's birth at the exact moment of the querent's birth. This map or picture, which may be thought of as a snapshot of the heavens, usually includes the division of the ecliptic into houses, which represent various spheres of activity, and aspects, which reveal the influences that the elements of the horoscope (e.g., the planets) have upon one another.

MERIDIAN: Any one of the nearly infinite number of bands encircling the Earth from pole to pole, the meridian designates the longitude of the querent's place of birth.

MIDHEAVEN (also called *medium coeli* or MC): The point at which the meridian of the querent's place of birth meets the ecliptic; in the Quadrant house system, the midheaven is on the cusp of the tenth house.

ZODIAC: Among the thousands of constellations, these are the twelve that are arranged around the ecliptic. The planets, all orbiting the Sun on the same plane, appear to travel against the background of these twelve constellations.

THE PLANETS

Now that we have established the composition of the horoscope—the placement of the planets in the signs of the Zodiac—it is time to discuss the qualities and forces that the planets embody.

THE SUN

The Sun is the most important planet in the horoscope because it represents the self, the ego, the life force. Although Sun sign astrology as it appears in the fashion magazines and in the daily papers is considered hopelessly elemental by serious astrologers, a person's character is revealed by the position of the sun to such an extent that its power cannot be overemphasized. The sign occupied by the Sun will reveal the subject's personality traits, his strengths and weaknesses, and his predisposition to certain types of behavior. It is the central emblem of the self—both inner and outer—in the horoscope.

The Sun is masculine and rules Leo.

THE MOON

The Moon is the second most important planet, and its influence should be given a great deal of weight in the analysis of the horoscope. The Moon is a feminine planet; she represents the maternal, the mysterious, the hidden, the receptive, and the intuitive. Less positively, the moon is regarded as changeable, fluctuating, and perhaps narrow-minded. From its position in the chart, the astrologer may deduce the querent's relationship to the feminine, particularly toward his or her mother, and toward family life in general. The querent's level of emotionality may be understood from the placement of the Moon—in a water sign, it may denote strong instincts; in an earth sign, the emotions may be buried.

The Moon is feminine and rules Cancer.

MERCURY

Mercury, named after the mythological messenger of the gods, is, appropriately, the planet of communication, both mental and physical. The life—and liveliness—of the mind is the realm of Mercury, and in its highest manifestation, the knowledge it represents is self-knowledge. All types of travel are represented by Mercury, from the most picayune bus ride to the grandest spiritual journey. Mercury is the only hermaphroditic planet and thus can provide the reconciliation of warring male and female impulses, but its chief role in the birth chart is to represent the manner of the subject's thinking, her intellectual range and expression.

Mercury rules both Gemini, where it is benignly expressed in an active, perceptive, and versatile mind, and Virgo, where the Mercurial influence is expressed more arduously, in analytical and critical powers.

VENUS

As does its mythological counterpart, the planet Venus represents love and all that is feminine. Close relationships of all kinds, but particularly marriage, are ruled by Venus, as are sensual pleasures: most obviously sex itself, but also luxury, beauty, and indulgence. Venus is the planet of union, harmony, and love; in an advantageous position, Venus will promote the qualities necessary to the success of relationships, such as sensitivity and devotion. In a less auspicious situation, Venus can lead to self-indulgence, indecision, and jealousy. In a man's chart, the sign and aspect of Venus portrays his ideal woman. In a woman's chart, the planet's position shows the image of the female she wishes herself to be. Venus is also responsible for money and its fruits, so its situation reveals the querent's prospects for material gain.

Venus is, of course, feminine and rules Taurus and Libra.

Venus, with a discreet star, hovers over the emblems of Taurus and Libra in this fifteenth-century manuscript illumination.

MARS

Mars is the last of the so-called personal planets. (Mercury and Venus are the two others. With Mars, they are deemed to have a particular influence on the life and personality of the querent.) It is the planet of action, energy, assertion, and aggression. Named after the god of war, Mars rules physical actions, but also mental vigor, initiative, and impulses. Gut-level desire, especially when linked to the will to conquer and possess, is associated with Mars. The rawness of Martian aggression may be amplified or mitigated by the sign it occupies; its house will show the arena to which the main thrust of energy will be devoted. Unsurprisingly, Mars represents the male principle and the subject's idea of masculinity. In a woman's chart, Mars shows both her manner of expressing her own male side and the male qualities she seeks in a partner.

Mars is masculine and rules Aries and Scorpio.

JUPITER

As befits the largest planet in the solar system, Jupiter expresses the forces of growth, expansion, and abundance. Its beneficence may be applied to any realm—physical, emotional, moral, intellectual. Its role in the birth chart is positive, showing the realm in which the subject will experience opportunity and good fortune. If badly positioned or aspected, Jupiter may devolve into excess, overindulgence, and waste. Although Mercury rules intelligence, Jupiter rules thought, especially abstract and philosophic thought. It is also associated with religion and higher education.

Jupiter is masculine and rules Sagittarius.

SATURN

Saturn is known as the bad seed among the planets. Of course, this designation is too simplistic: Saturn presents the opposing force to Jupiter's jovial generosity and abundance. Saturn embodies the ideas of limitation and restriction. The area of the chart in which Saturn appears is the area in which the querent experiences the most difficulty and frustration. But Saturn should not be dismissed as an irretrievably negative entity. We have to learn to meet challenges and overcome obstacles, and it is Saturn's role to help us do this. When dealt with positively, Saturn teaches self-discipline and control. In its most negative aspect, it portends incapacitating repression.

It is useful to consider Saturn as a representation of the shadow side of each of us, the place that holds everything we find too repugnant to claim as part of ourselves. In this view, Saturn becomes a sort of anti-Sun, a shadow Sun that must be reconciled with the Sun self for life to be fully integrated and whole.

Saturn's orbit around the Sun takes $29^{1}/_{2}$ years, which means—we are slipping, for a moment here, into predictive astrology—that the planet returns to its original place in the birth chart of any individual every $29^{1}/_{2}$ years. This event, known as Saturn's Return, usually causes an eruption of change and stress (this may be the origin of the universal anxiety about turning thirty). The power of Saturn's Return is so great that many people experience a life-altering event on the exact day that Saturn slips into its original spot.

Saturn is masculine and rules Capricorn.

Saturn's death-dealing scythe, which was derived from his supposedly malefic influence, is the source of the scythe-bearing Old Man Time, who makes his appearance at New Year's. They are related through Capricorn, which rules the new year and is ruled by Saturn. From the fifteenth-century manuscript De sphaera.

URANUS

Uranus is the hippie planet—it moves to disrupt the existing order and replace it with new ideas and attitudes. Uranus is unpredictable, revolutionary, free, original, and antiauthoritarian. Bear in mind that while Uranus generally stands for progress and improvement—i.e., the replacement of the old and bad with the new and good—its primary goal is change itself. Thus, in a progressive era, Uranus may represent the forces of counterrevolution. A querent with a heavily aspected Uranus will be humanitarian and visionary, but may also be a bit too inclined to believe in her own superiority.

It takes Uranus eighty-four years to complete its cycle around the Sun, and it lingers seven years in each sign. Its influence, therefore, is considered to be generational.

Uranus is masculine and rules Aquarius.

NEPTUNE

Neptune's attributes are as elusive and watery as the god for whom it was named. Circling the Zodiac once every 165 years, Neptune represents the intangible, the idealistic, the arcane, and the unknowable. It may denote spiritualism and mysticism, but, equally, it may point toward delusion and escapism. In the birth chart, Neptune reveals the illusions to which the querent subscribes, but the aspects will show whether those illusions will be the source of spiritual development or the source of weak-minded delusions. An extremely afflicted Neptune, such as Neptune conjunct a Libra or Scorpio Ascendant (don't worry, you're not supposed to know yet what conjunct means), may indicate a tendency to become addicted to drugs or alcohol. The generation born between 1942 and 1956—Neptune in Libra—is a case in point.

Neptune is feminine and rules Pisces.

PLUTO

Tiny, cold Pluto takes 248 years to orbit the Sun. Since its discovery in 1930, astrologers have had the opportunity to observe Pluto only in Cancer, Leo, Virgo, Libra, Scorpio, and starting in 1995, Sagittarius. Most astrology handbooks announce that Pluto has great, mysterious, unfathomable power. This, to me, is abject foolishness. How can we know what Pluto's realm of influence is until we observe it through an orbit? Then we may find that characteristics hitherto associated with, say, Jupiter are really Plutonian. In the meantime, instead of speculating that Pluto represents mysterious forces, I will say that Pluto is a mysterious force.

Pluto is often called the co-ruler of Scorpio, but it won't be by me until about two hundred years from now.

★   ★   ★

Before we hasten onward to the signs of the Zodiac, I must discuss the issue of "rulership." Each of the preceding planetary entries ended, as you will have observed, with a note about which sign or signs the planet in question rules. When a planet, through the vagaries of fortune, is positioned in the horoscope in a sign it rules, it is said to be dignified. A dignified planet is strengthened and is more likely to express its forces in a positive manner. Each sign has an opposing sign (more of this later), and when a planet appears in the sign opposing that which it rules, it is in detriment. In that position, its expression will be weakened or challenged. In addition, each planet has a sign and degree (remember, a planet may occupy any one of the thirty degrees that constitutes a sign's place on the ecliptic) of exaltation—a point at which the forces of the planet work exceptionally well. The point opposite that of a planet's exaltation is known as that planet's sign and degree of fall, and it means essentially the same thing that detriment does.

The following chart of dignity, exaltation, detriment, and fall should be memorized. Though dignity and detriment may be deduced, there is no easy way to calculate the degrees of exaltation and fall.

DIGNITY AND EXALTATION

planet	dignified in	detrimented in	exalted in	in fall in
Sun	Leo	Aquarius	Aries (19°)	Libra (19°)
Moon	Cancer	Capricorn	Taurus (3°)	Scorpio (3°)
Mercury	Gemini and Virgo	Sagittarius and Pisces	Aquarius (15°)	Leo (15°)
Venus	Taurus and Libra	Scorpio and Aries	Pisces (27°)	Virgo (27°)
Mars	Aries and Scorpio	Taurus and Libra	Capricorn (28°)	Cancer (28°)
Jupiter	Sagittarius	Gemini	Cancer (15°)	Capricorn (15°)
Saturn	Capricorn	Cancer	Libra (21°)	Aries (21°)
Uranus	Aquarius	Leo	Scorpio (7°)	Taurus (7°)
Neptune	Pisces	Virgo	Cancer (18°)	Capricorn (18°)
Pluto	Impossible to say.			

Signs of the Zodiac

The signs are classified in a number of different ways, the most important of which are the elements, the qualities, and the polarities (further divisions include mute signs, signs of long ascension, ingress signs—these are gravy, in my opinion). The following groupings and identifications will provide refinement and depth to your reading of a birth chart.

THE ELEMENTS

FIRE SIGNS: Aries, Leo, Sagittarius
Fiery types are dynamic and energetic—sometimes even explosive. Although these qualities make them natural leaders and innovators, their Achilles' heel is impatience.

EARTH SIGNS: Taurus, Virgo, Capricorn
These are more practical, down-to-earth types. Cautious, reliable, and hard-working, earth signs may lack verve, but they get all their chores done.

AIR SIGNS: Gemini, Libra, Aquarius
Thought, light as air, is the particular realm of the air signs. These are the active intellects and communicators of the Zodiac, but they must guard against impracticality.

WATER SIGNS: Cancer, Scorpio, Pisces
Water is the element of the emotions. People with water signs prevalent in their birth charts will be sensitive and imaginative.

THE QUALITIES

CARDINAL SIGNS: Aries, Cancer, Libra, Capricorn
Cardinal signs tend to alter and control their environment.

FIXED SIGNS: Taurus, Leo, Scorpio, Aquarius
Fixed signs tend to be immovable and self-sufficient. They are not particularly affected by their environment.

MUTABLE SIGNS: Gemini, Virgo, Sagittarius, Pisces
As the name implies, mutable signs are flexible and adaptable; they bend, but do not succumb, to environmental pressures.

Revolution of America

Ebenezer Sibly, one of the odd gentleman-occultists of eighteenth-century England, compiled a vast tome in defense of astrology, which included horoscopes of newsworthy events, such as this charming illustration of the birth chart of America. America is apparently a Cancer with her Moon in Aquarius (such old-fashioned square horoscopes are read in the same way as today's circular charts, beginning on the far left with the first house). From Ebenezer Sibly's New and Complete Illustration of the Occult Sciences, *1784.*

THE POLARITIES

Each sign has an opposing sign. This does not mean that the opposing signs loathe each other, but that they are, in a way, complementary. Each of the pair approaches the same issue from a different direction.

Aries/Libra   *Aries promotes the self; Libra promotes relationships.*

Taurus/Scorpio   *Taurus seeks physical fulfillment; Scorpio seeks emotional fulfillment.*

Gemini/Sagittarius *Gemini wants information; Sagittarius wants knowledge.*

Cancer/Capricorn *Cancer builds an emotional world; Capricorn builds a physical world.*

Leo/Aquarius   *Leo wants everyone to love him; Aquarius wants to love everyone.*

Virgo/Pisces   *Virgo obliterates the self through work; Pisces obliterates the self through love.*

THE GENDERS

In addition to these categorizations, each sign is either masculine or feminine. In traditional fashion, masculine signs are considered positive and active, while feminine signs are considered negative and receptive (try not to be annoyed by the irritating stereotypes implicit in these characterizations). These designations should not be confused with maleness and femaleness; that is, a woman with a preponderance of masculine signs in her chart will be extroverted and energetic, not mannish.

Aries: *masculine*   Libra: *masculine*

Taurus: *feminine*   Scorpio: *feminine*

Gemini: *masculine*   Sagittarius: *masculine*

Cancer: *feminine*   Capricorn: *feminine*

Leo: *masculine*   Aquarius: *masculine*

Virgo: *feminine*   Pisces: *feminine*

Note that each element is exclusively gendered. Water and earth are feminine; air and fire are masculine.

Above right and following pages: In an apparent effort to induce youthful cigarette consumption, Wills's Cigarettes packaged a series of "Lucky Charms" cards with their smokes in the 1920s. Each of the signs of the Zodiac is neatly depicted with its insignia and that of its planetary ruler (unfortunately, Aquarius and Pisces bear the emblems of their former rulers, as Neptune and Uranus had yet to be discovered), as well as the precious stone and metal associated with it.

THE SIGNS

As we begin our descriptions of the signs, bear in mind that the attributes of each sign affect each planet that happens to land there. Thus, the following should not simply be read as Sun sign characterizations.

WILLS'S CIGARETTES.

ARIES - THE RAM.

ARIES

Element: Fire
Ruling Planet: Mars

March 21–April 20
Quality: Cardinal
Gender: Masculine

The zodiacal year is born with Aries, and this sign has many of the characteristics of the infant and child. Aries is fierce, assertive, willful, ego-centered, active, courageous, and enthusiastic. Aries is the essential, primal element that gives rise to all the other signs of the Zodiac and, as such, it has the qualities of the seed that is the source of life.

Ariens love a challenge. In fact, they can't resist a challenge. They rush toward it impetuously, tackle it vigorously, and usually overcome it with dispatch. As you might guess, this kind of energy makes them powerful businesspeople, ardent lovers, and good athletes. Above all things, Aries is the sign of action, but if this leads you to expect Aries to be flashy and swashbuckling, you would be mistaken, for Ariens would rather be streamlined for speed than waste their will on mere dazzle. One of their most attractive qualities is humor; Ariens love to laugh, and they are masters of irony and sarcasm.

This most fundamental of signs has strong sexual appetites and a marked propensity for experimentation and conquest. True partnership may be impeded, however, by Aries's greatest failing, which is selfishness. Ariens are not notable for their self-discipline or patience, either, which can make the compromises of marriage difficult for them.

Ariens may be the hardest workers in the Zodiac, but here, too, they must guard against getting fed up. Often they grow so impatient with the tedium of bureaucracy that they make impulsive decisions just to get things moving. The subtleties of negotiation and the incorporeality of imaginative work are lost on Aries, but for enterprise, firmness, and determination, an Aries cannot be beat. If you have an Aries for an employee, it is useful to remember that those with this Sun sign are very competitive and respond aggressively to the merest hint that someone else is doing better work than they.

Aries children are delightful—full of enthusiasm and energy. Their parents' only trouble is carting them around to their many activities. Aries teenagers are horrible—the natural foolishness of youth is exacerbated by Arien impulsiveness.

Aries rules the head, as is only appropriate for such a headstrong sign.

This unhappy fellow documents the areas of the body and their ruling signs. He appears in Les Superstitions de tous les peuples du monde, *the magnum opus of the eighteenth-century Frenchman Piccart, who seems to have been a trifle confused about how to manufacture the symbols for Virgo, Scorpio, and Capricorn.*

WILL'S CIGARETTES.

TAURUS · THE BULL.

TAURUS

April 21–May 21

Element: Earth

Quality: Fixed

Ruling Planet: Venus

Gender: Feminine

Somewhat counterintuitively, Taurus is a feminine sign, and in its stability, sensuality, and love of comfort, Taurus represents both the essential femininity of its ruling planet, Venus, and a complete contrast to Aries's fiery, active masculinity. Among the Taurean's best qualities are patience, loyalty, and productivity. The consummate earth sign, Taurus is most at peace when she is making something—that something can range from an artwork (Taureans are very responsive to beauty) to a baby (the bull is a symbol of fertility). Taureans are naturally charming, but don't be fooled—they are also among the most practical and reliable of the signs.

The bad side to all of this is—as usual—the good side taken to extremes. Their devotion to comfort and stability can lead to the well-known Taurean inflexibility and possessiveness. Whatever Taurus gets, she hangs on to with a viselike grip.

This can be a real problem in romantic relationships, where possessiveness can devolve into the even more unbecoming trait of jealousy. And a jealous Taurus is a fearsome thing, because Taurean anger is akin to a volcano: slow to develop and lethal to oppose. However, any sign ruled by Venus is going to place a premium on love, and Taurean loyalty, sensuality, and harmoniousness make the sign particularly suited to long-term relationships.

Taureans are methodical workers, and their appreciation of beauty and material comfort gives them a strong incentive to earn a lot of money. They—and their coworkers—must be on guard against Taurus's perennial flaw: stubbornness. The compromises of teamwork are torture for a Taurus, though, like carrots, they are good for the character. Some Taureans find consensus and negotiation impossible; these people should probably focus their considerable determination on becoming self-employed.

Baby Tauruses are likely to be fat, dimpled, and happy. They are not like the Aries fireballs, but, moving slowly, they cover just as much territory. Security and structure are always a concern—Taurean children like their routines and view spontaneous events with distrust. Taurean adolescents must try not to succumb to laziness, as all habits are difficult for a Taurus to shake off.

Taurus rules the neck and throat, as is appropriate for the sign of the bull. They should be careful of thyroid disorders.

GEMINI

Element: Air	May 22–June 21
Ruling Planet: Mercury	Quality: Mutable
	Gender: Masculine

Yak, yak, yak. There must be a Gemini nearby. Gemini is driven by a powerful need to communicate, which is not surprising for an air sign (air is the element of thought) ruled by Mercury (the planet of communication and travel). This need may be expressed in any number of ways, but it will come out, usually through writing or the media or just plain talking. More than anything, Geminis want to know—they love information and use it well, applying this fact to that theory with versatility and verve. Gemini continually seeks variety and change—primarily of the intellectual ilk—and, thus, is always on the move. The dark side of this blithe braininess is not very dark: at their worst, Geminians tend to be annoyingly superfical and nosy. Their victims get the feeling that Gemini's persistent questions are motivated by pure curiosity rather than empathy. Geminians must strive to think carefully and deeply about the knowledge they have acquired and to respect the emotions of others.

This is especially true in the context of romantic relationships. A Gemini can truly be happy only with his intellectual equal. The strong, silent type is definitely a no-no, because a Geminian must have someone to talk to, preferably someone with strong opinions of her own. In general, Geminians have a rather low emotional level (although a nervous Gemini can be a very intense creature), approaching love from a rational standpoint and submitting their partners to relentless scrutiny and analysis. When confronted with emotion—whether their own or others'—Geminians often respond with logic. However, with their wit and zest for life, they can be the most appealing of companions, particularly once they have learned to dwell fully in their emotions.

Gemini is obviously well-suited to a career in communication, but no matter what his profession, Gemini's verbal ability will stand him in good stead. Gemini learns quickly and is quite capable of understanding all sides of an issue. Debates and discussions are the perfume of life to a Gemini, and he will never hold grudges against those who differ from him. Professionally, Gemini must guard against becoming too absorbed in detail; he must learn to see the whole picture before he makes a decision.

Geminian babies are the ones who lie in their cribs chattering to themselves, who roll from one place to another if they cannot crawl, and who ask "Why? Why? Why?" Although these traits can be slightly maddening, Gemini children are a lot of fun and usually do well in school. The major challenge to their parents is keeping them from becoming bored, which is the Geminian idea of hell. Parents of a Gemini teenager should take comfort in the knowledge that their son or daughter is virtually incapable of keeping a secret, so if the kid is up to no good, they will soon hear about it.

Gemini, appropriately, rules the lungs. They shouldn't smoke (but who should?).

CANCER

Element: Water	June 22–July 22
Ruling Planet: The Moon	Quality: Cardinal
	Gender: Feminine

Cancer may be the most anxious sign of the Zodiac. If that seems at odds with the symbol of the crab, think of the tender flesh that the hard shell and fierce claws protect. Like its crabby emblem, Cancer has an impressive defense system covering a soft-hearted nature. As a water sign ruled by the Moon, Cancer is a bundle of feelings, intuition, and imagination. The focus of all this emotion is usually the family, for Cancerians are devoted to their loved ones and to domestic life. Unfortunately, the family ties that give Cancer the greatest satisfaction are also the source of most of Cancer's worries. Fears about their security cast a great shadow on Cancerian lives, and defensiveness and preemptive strikes consume much of their energy. The rich Cancerian imagination is all too often absorbed in constructing elaborate bulwarks against improbable disasters. The most successful Cancers are those who recognize their weakness for worrying and learn to comfort themselves with rational evaluation. The least successful allow themselves to be overcome by worry to the point of deep depression. Self-doubt is a besetting sin for this sign, as is agonizing indecision, but Cancer is actually well-equipped to make judgments and choices, having a powerful intuition and acute instincts about people. If Cancerians can learn to trust themselves, their perceptions will prove an invaluable asset.

Devoted, sensitive, and committed, Cancerians are nearly perfect partners in love. They are not inclined to stray, being more likely to cling to a love affair long after it should have died away. Cancerians are adorably sentimental; the Cancerian partner will be the one who keeps faded bouquets and remembers all the anniversaries. Occasionally, a Cancer will become so mired in nostalgia that the relationship will be unable to progress, but this is unusual. Cancer is her own worst enemy in romance. The tendency to defensiveness, born from the anxiety to preserve the relationship, can alienate the loved one. And, on a deeper level, all that worrying, deriving as it does from the belief that events and people can be controlled, may be read as self-absorption.

The commitment and resolve that Cancerians display in relationships often appear in their career as well. Cancers are loyal to their colleagues, and on the job, they make excellent use of past experience. Their sensitivity and intuition make Cancer particularly well suited to the caregiving and teaching professions. They make great therapists.

Cancerian children are terribly sensitive, and their parents may sometimes be at a loss to determine the cause for a sudden change from smiles to tears. They respond well to plenty of reassurance and an orderly schedule, which makes them feel secure. The strong Cancerian memory comes in very handy at school.

Cancers are usually excellent cooks, specializing in large, comforting meals. Cancer rules the breasts and the alimentary canal.

LEO

July 23–August 23

Element: Fire
Ruling Planet: The Sun

Quality: Fixed
Gender: Masculine

Leos are the easiest Sun signs to pick out of a crowd. They're the ones in the middle of it, organizing and energizing the rest of the group. The Leonine temperament is naturally vigorous, creative, forceful, and enthusiastic. Even if Leo doesn't end up in an acting career, the Leonine flair for the theatrical will turn everyday events into high drama. Leos are powerful, magnetic people, and they usually have style to burn. Add to that their aptitude for directing others, and you have the perfect leader.

There's only one problem: Leos are notoriously insensitive to other people. They find it impossible to comprehend that others might disagree with their opinions or oppose their plans. It seems so clear to Leo that his way is best—and indeed, it usually is, but the dictatorial manner in which he gives orders will alienate the very people who will most benefit from them. The tricky part is that Leo is motivated by earnest idealism; he truly believes that his leadership will result in the greater good, and he is often astounded to discover that his subjects would perversely choose to imperil their own welfare in order to oppose him. In short, Leo doesn't think he's great—he thinks he's right.

Warm hearts and hot heads make Leos impetuous lovers. They are generous to their partners and loyal to a fault, and in their regal way, they are masters of seduction, but here, too, they must beware of bossiness. Leos can be so domineering—all with the best intentions—that they smother their loved ones and so dynamic that they render their partners passive and impassive, which disappoints Leo mightily. At worst, Leonine egotism turns his partner into his audience, reducing the whole personality of the partner into a mirror that reflects his own glory.

The best remedy to this proclivity for power and control is an absorbing and creative job. If Leo's energy can be diverted into a constructive task, he will expend less time managing his friends' lives. The busier Leo is, the happier, which can make him a very agreeable employee, although anyone who supervises a Leo should watch his back—Leos are terribly ambitious. When Leo is the employer himself, he can be a great motivator but should guard against his Achilles' heel—pomposity and insensitivity.

Leonine children are lively, enthusiastic, and confident. Their natural bossiness can make them terrors on the playground, however, and they need to be reminded to listen to their friends. They may also help in learning to complete tasks, particularly such pedestrian tasks as memorizing the multiplication tables, which are inimical to the Leonine penchant for the grand.

As the Sun, which rules Leo, sits in the center of the solar system, the heart—the center of the body—is ruled by Leo.

VIRGO

Element: Earth
Ruling Planet: Mercury

August 24–September 22
Quality: Mutable
Gender: Feminine

Virgos can go either of two ways. They can be the spinster virgin, persnickety, perfectionist, and controlling; or they may be the budding virgin, full of potential, fertile, devoted to making her environment prosper. Both types of Virgos share a devotion to service and productiveness; both are unselfish; both are practical. The difference is whether other people can stand to be around them.

Of course, most Virgos are a combination of the two types. Even the most abundant Virgo will find herself obsessing about a spot on the carpet or a gap in the schedule. The Virgoan goal should always be to step back from the details and see the whole picture. Only then can her substantial critical and intellectual abilities be used in the service of large ideas rather than squandered in reflexive carping, which is a grave Virgoan failing. Virgos are usually quite intelligent, which can be a great surprise to their associates, who see their penchant for nit-picking and assume they can do nothing else. Virgos are also, along with Cancers, the great worriers of the Zodiac, but what they worry about (schedules, disarray) usually seems ludicrous to others, so they get little sympathy. Here, too, Virgo should try to stand back and put her anxieties in perspective.

In love, also, Virgos divide into two camps. Natural Virgoan selflessness can result in paralyzing shyness or in generous devotion to a partner. They are loath to believe that they are a suitable object of attention, which gives them a slightly removed attitude toward romance and a coolness that can damp the ardor of their partner. However, once convinced that they are loved, they are joyful and eager to please.

Virgos are an employer's dream. Hardworking, unassuming, intelligent, and detail-oriented, they can remain at tedious tasks long after most people would have run screaming from the office. Routine jobs, however, fail to take full advantage of Virgoan verbal ability. Like loquacious Gemini, Virgo is ruled by the planet of communication, Mercury, but Virgo is less likely—being shy—to communicate by talking than by writing. As Virgos tend to be highly pragmatic, they are excellent problem solvers. Virgos must learn to be aware of their strengths so they won't be exploited by their bosses.

Virgo children are nice and tidy. They usually do well in school, excelling at the meticulous tasks that Leo deplores. Their perfectionism can be a good motivator when it is well directed, or it can become an impediment to progress (who, after all, can do anything perfectly?). Parents of Virgoan children must learn to teach them to be less critical of themselves and others.

Suitably for such a worried sign, Virgo rules the nervous system and the intestines.

LIBRA

September 23–October 22

Element: Air

Quality: Cardinal

Ruling Planet: Venus

Gender: Masculine

It is appropriate that Libra is represented by the scales in balance, because balance and harmony are the great Libran gifts. No other sign works so well with people; where Leo's leadership may cause resentment, Libra guides his fellows so gracefully toward the fulfillment of his own goals that they barely know they are being led at all. Between Virgo's thesis and Scorpio's antithesis, Libra is synthesis. The only danger to this genius for resolution is capitulation—weaker Libras want peace at any price. Libra must learn to stand up for his beliefs and make decisions; passivity is never a virtue, and Librans must fight their urge to agree with everyone.

Like their fellow Venusian, Taurus, Librans are particularly responsive to beauty; however, as an air sign, this takes a more theoretical than practical turn. While Taurean good taste is expressed in her environment (perhaps a beautifully decorated home), a Libra is more likely to be a painter or sculptor or conceptual artist.

Libra is probably the best partner in the Zodiac. Everyone should have a Libran lover—too bad there aren't enough to go around. Romantic, attractive, and sympathetic, Librans must be in a relationship, for loneliness is their nemesis, and the balance that is essential to their happiness can come only from sharing their life with another. Their major drawback in love is that their horror of confrontation can engender slyness and duplicity. Librans must strive to be straightforward with their loved ones; they have to learn that avoiding the truth just makes everything worse. It is important that Libra's partner be expressive since his second great flaw is resentfulness, to which he is especially prone when feeling unappreciated. Libra should also be aware that his great desire to please is matched by his great capacity for being pleasing; that is, he can be a terrible flirt, which may imperil the central relationship that is so vital to his happiness.

Librans have a reputation for laziness, and it's true that they love luxury, but they can be stellar workers when they are in a career that makes good use of their talents. They are well suited to work in the arts, but whatever they do, they have to be around people (the isolated *artiste* is a bad model for them). Jobs that call upon their diplomacy and tact are advantageous both to Libra, who enjoys creating harmony, and to his co-workers, who will find him a relaxing and supportive colleague. Librans have a strong sense of justice and are deeply upset by unfair treatment—of themselves or others.

Librans are charming, generous, easygoing children. They are usually popular in elementary school and heartbreakers in high school. Parents must teach them to have the courage of their convictions and to guard against self-indulgence. Little Libras do not respond well to punishment, but the lesson of self-discipline is a necessary one.

Libra rules the kidneys, an organ that reflects the Libran activity of balancing.

ZODIACUS STELLATUS CUJUS LIMITIBUS PLANETARUM OMNIUM VISIBILES VIÆ COMPREHENDUNTUR. Autore Jo: Seller Serenifimi Reg: Hydrographo.

This beautiful and unusual depiction of the constellations of the Zodiac appears in the 1675 edition of John Seller's Atlas maritimus. According to this horizontally stacked image, the 30-degree swatch of ecliptic dedicated to each of the signs has only a small chance of containing the actual constellation associated with said sign. It is best not to dwell on this.

SCORPIO - THE SCORPION.

SCORPIO October 23–November 21

Element: Water   Quality: Fixed
Ruling Planet: Mars   Gender: Feminine

There's no tactful way to put it (maybe a Libra could think of a way)—Scorpio is the most difficult of the Sun signs. On the other hand, they are also the most fascinating. As a water sign, Scorpio is driven by her feelings, but these are deep and dark emotions: passion, jealousy, obsession. The scorpion, which lashes out when disturbed, is an apt symbol for this sign; a slighted Scorpio will plot bitter revenge. It doesn't matter how long it takes, either, because Scorpio has a long memory. Her unswerving devotion to her goals virtually ensures her success; so when her fierce energy is channeled positively, Scorpio can be a powerful force for good.

Scorpios are inherently radical—their solution to opposition is never negotiation, but revolution. Once they are committed to a cause, they will do anything to promote its goals, and, while their actions may be antithetical to the prevailing morality, in Scorpios' view, they have acted correctly. Scorpios are usually quite smart but are prone to secrecy and paranoia. Humor can save them from being unbearably self-centered and grandiose, and their natural wit and sense of irony should be encouraged.

They might be mean, but they certainly are sexy. Scorpions are the most magnetic and passionate lovers in the zodiac. Many are drawn to Scorpio, but few can stand the heat. Scorpios specialize in tormented relationships; they are the original Byronic lovers, leaving a trail of mangled hearts behind them. However, when Scorpio loves deeply and well, she can be the most intensely devoted of partners. It is absolutely imperative that Scorpio's mate meet her passionate nature; coolness simply will not do. Scorpios have an unfortunate tendency to choose inappropriate objects for their affections; this leads to much Sturm und Drang and, occasionally, the aforementioned vindictive episodes. Sometimes it seems that the only good match for a Scorpio is another Scorpio (this can be disastrous, though).

A Scorpio may be successful in almost any profession as long as she feels a strong emotional involvement with it. Scorpio bosses can be unnecessarily punitive with their employees, and Scorpio employees can be unnecessarily antiauthoritarian with their bosses. Here, too, humor and humility are always a help.

Scorpio children can be extremely demanding, but if their parents teach them strategies for self-comforting and promote verbal communication (rather than fisticuffs), their little Scorpions will be much happier and easier to get along with. Most Scorpio children will have several intense interests, and rather than being all-around good students, they will excel in some areas and dismiss others.

Scorpio rules the genitals (big surprise).

SAGITTARIUS   November 22–December 20
Element: Fire   Quality: Mutable
Ruling Planet: Jupiter   Gender: Masculine

The symbol of Sagittarius is the centaur—half-man, half-horse, with bow and arrow poised—which is an apt condensation of the Sagittarian character: mind and instinct racing forward in the chase for an elusive prize. Sagittarians love a challenge, and their fiery enthusiasm will precipitate a whirlwind of activity, but what is most interesting about them is that their goals are usually ethereal rather than material. In this, we see the influence of their ruling planet, Jupiter, the guardian of growth, but also of abstract and philosophical ideals. Sagittarius is on inspired quest, not a business trip.

Notwithstanding their search for higher meaning, Sagittarians love a good time. In fact, they like to combine the two, which is why Sagittarians made great hippies. They are the most optimistic sign in the Zodiac, the most ebullient and exciting. They move through the world in leaps and bounds, and, indeed, journeys, both mental and physical, are the keynote of Sagittarius's life. The downside to this exuberance is that it can easily become foolishness and irresponsibility—activity for its own sake rather than for a higher purpose. Sagittarians must learn self-control and discipline to achieve their best selves, and though it is a struggle, they will be better off if they can respect details; a Sagittarian weakness is the dismissal of the tedious as unimportant.

Sagittarian vibrancy and humor make the sign an extremely attractive one; they are perennially popular. But prospective partners must realize that Sagittarians have to have the freedom to roam and explore. It's a bad idea to try to pin them down, and they have no patience for jealous or possessive lovers. It's not that Sagittarius is averse to commitment; he just has a fairly unconventional definition of the term. Sagittarius himself should guard against (most) frivolous sexual escapades—they dissipate the spiritual and philosophical integrity that the sign must maintain for real happiness.

Intellectually, Sagittarians are quick. They assimilate information well and use it with panache, but in their careers, they are often felled by their intolerance of repetition and detail. Few professions offer variety, excitement, and higher moral purpose at the same time. Not everyone can be an emergency room doctor, and Sagittarians will be happier when they learn to take care and be thorough. Sagittarians are horrible with money; finance is, to them, another meaningless detail. They are thus often impoverished.

Like their grown-up version, Sagittarius children are freedom-loving and popular. As a result, parents will often find that their Sagittarius has been the ringleader in some sort of rebellion or imaginative exploit. Though it's wise to teach little centaurs some self-restraint and a sense of responsibility, their parents should beware of excessive strictness—never back a Sagittarian into a corner.

Sagittarius rules the hips and thighs, so necessary for forward movement.

CAPRICORN   December 21–January 19
Element: Earth   Quality: Cardinal
Ruling Planet: Saturn   Gender: Feminine

Nothing could present a stronger contrast to Sagittarius than Capricorn. Where Sagittarius is an optimist, Capricorn is a pessimist; where Sagittarius is spiritual, Capricorn is material; where Sagittarius takes foolish risks, Capricorn prudently plans. Accordingly, where Sagittarius ends up in the poorhouse, Capricorn ends up in the White House.

Capricorns are driven by ambition, but their conservatism can engender a lack of confidence that impedes the attainment of goals—"I can't take that kind of risk." If they conquer this tendency to inhibit themselves, they can move mountains. Their strong will is matched by their self-discipline, planning, and hard work—a combination that can result in amazing achievement.

Capricorn is not a particularly warm or responsive sign, but it is of paramount importance that a Capricorn Sun be read in the context of the rest of the birth chart—the placement of Venus and the Moon often provide a sensuality and capacity for emotion that the sign of Capricorn seems to lack. Patience and pragmatism are not fashionable virtues, but they are virtues nonetheless, and when these qualities are combined with Capricornian humor, which is dry and self-deprecating, you have the salt of the earth, the quintessential "reasonable man," who rests at the core of all forms of justice and who seems to be an endangered species in our present era.

Prudent Capricorn chooses her mate carefully. Once the decision has been made, she will launch her campaign with a series of well-executed maneuvers and diplomatic negotiation. This may not seem romantic, but it is often quite effective (though occasionally the prospective partner gets attached to someone else during the long planning phase). It's no use trying to get a Capricorn to become spontaneous, but she will be happier if she learns to accept the priority of emotions, both her own and others'.

Obviously, Capricorn is the most professionally oriented of all the signs. These are the paradigmatic business titans—hard-headed, ambitious, financially apt. They are willing to work in isolation—often they prefer it—as long as they can take charge of matters and are remunerated well. Even the less-confident Capricorn will be endowed with a large hunk of ambition, but she will lack the competitive edge that bedevils the more self-assured brand of Capricorn. When Capricorn is the boss, which she often is, she must strive to develop sympathy and respect for employees who are unlike her.

Capricorn children do very well in school, having a fondness for the structure and discipline of the classroom. However, they are all too likely to become despondent if they fail at anything, so their parents should encourage them to develop self-acceptance. Born mature, Capricorns need to be taught how to have fun and relax.

The knee is ruled by Capricorn.

AQUARIUS,
THE
WATER-BEARER.

AQUARIUS

January 20–February 18

Element: Air

Quality: Fixed

Ruling Planet: Uranus

Gender: Masculine

The symbol of Aquarius is the water carrier, but it is crucial to remember that the element of this sign is air, because of all the signs, Aquarius needs air the most, both in the zodiacal meaning of the term, signifying intellectual stimulation, and in the more quotidian sense of just plain space. Aquarius is the radical freethinker of the Zodiac, and as such, he is likely to be a loner. Luckily, that's fine with him: while Aquarians care deeply for humanity, they don't care much for individual people. Aquarians are concerned with ideas—original, revolutionary ideas—and the way things *should* be, rather than the way things are. Sometimes eccentric, but always interesting and likable, Aquarians are positive thinkers and kindly—if somewhat detached—characters.

One of Aquarius's many quirks is an unshakable belief in his own way of doing things (he is, after all, a fixed sign). The result is that the most radical of signs can also be, unfortunately, dogmatic and unbending. Aquarians should be aware of this tendency and learn to accept others' ideas.

Aquarians have a very difficult time developing strong romantic relationships. Their need for independence combined with their demanding idealism make them slow to commit and absolutely appalled when anyone else is. The real problem, though, is the invisible wall of air that surrounds them and prevents them from intimacy. This detachment makes them a most discouraging love interest to more ardent signs, but when appropriately matched—with a nice Sagittarius, perhaps—Aquarius will be firmly committed. Another consideration is that, like Capricorn, the placement of Venus in the birth chart can alter Aquarius's position on romance considerably.

Careerwise, Aquarians are born to be freelancers. They are usually incapable of submitting to the routines and structures of working in a large office, where their dismissive attitude toward punctuality and teamwork may be read as disrespect. This sign's idealism may endow its bearer with great vision and powers of leadership, but Aquarians can't stand the endless committees and compromises in the preparation for the revolution, so they should team up with an organizer who will carry out their radical plans.

Not surprisingly, Aquarian children march to their own drummer. They will have intense interests that they will pursue to the exclusion of all else, and it's no use trying to get them involved in group projects such as camping or team sports. Their parents should encourage their natural creativity while emphasizing the importance of finishing tasks. Rigid discipline and order will alienate a little Aquarian, exacerbating his inclination toward cool detachment. Plenty of free time and a room of his own is a better solution.

Aquarius rules the circulation and the shins.

PISCES

February 19–March 20

Element: Water

Quality: Mutable

Ruling Planet: Neptune

Gender: Feminine

Unlike the other two water signs, Pisces has no protective shell, and, accordingly, it is the most vulnerable of all the signs. Dreamy, sensitive, compassionate, and selfless, Pisceans are altogether too good for the world, which accounts for their tendency to withdraw whenever the going gets rough. Pisceans will always choose defense over offense, and all too often they race down the path of least resistance, concealing their real opinions in order to agree with others. This is just another name for deceptiveness, and gentle Pisces must learn to be honest rather than agreeable. Difficult as it is to face opposition, a life spent avoiding disapproval is a misspent life. This is particularly true for Pisces because her vivid imagination and profound sense of poetry should be devoted to creative endeavors rather than squandered on evasion and escapism.

If Pisces can combat her weakness, which is weakness, she can be the center of a devoted circle of admirers, for she combines perceptiveness with ability, intuition with kindness. And since her deepest wish is to love and be loved, it is worth her while to learn to resist and to be straightforward.

It is a fine thing to be the beloved of a Pisces, because Pisceans are firmly convinced that their partners are the most enchanting creatures in the world. Their selflessness, charm, and sympathy make them ideal lovers and their natural obligingness makes them well suited for marriage. However, their mates must keep an eye out for that pleasant deceptiveness that Pisces specializes in. Though well intentioned—"I didn't want to hurt your feelings"—Pisceans are prone to lying. Dreamy and romantic rather than passionately sexual, Pisces are best approached delicately.

Piscean idealism has no place in corporate culture, and poor Pisces usually feels like a fish out of water when she tries to behave in a businesslike fashion. An abysmal lack of organizational skill doesn't help either. Pisceans do best when they turn their compassion into a career; they are exceptional caregivers and healers. Less benignly but with equal success, their talent for deception and manipulation makes them admirable performers and charlatans.

Piscean children are both sensitive and easygoing, which makes the job of raising them fairly easy. Or at least it *seems* easy; Pisces children will play fast and loose with the truth in order to be pleasing, so it is up to their parents to insist on scrupulous honesty. Parents should also be sure to encourage the creative spirit in their little Pisces, who needs to develop the confidence to persevere in her projects.

The fishes rule the feet, which seems odd, since fish don't have feet.

THE TWELVE HOUSES

The birth chart, which depicts the heavens at the moment of the querent's birth, shows the planets as they appear against the band of the ecliptic. The twelve houses are a further division of the band. Think of it this way: the planets represent forces; the signs show us the manner in which these forces will be acted out; and the houses show in which arena of life the forces will manifest themselves.

The subject of house division—the system by which the ecliptic is divided into houses—is a contentious one among astrologers. In the interests of getting on with it, I will simply say that the system I employ (and discuss below) is the Quadrant system, though the Equal House system has many distinguished proponents. The following four lines constitute the scaffolding of house division:

1. *THE ASCENDANT:* The degree of the sign rising over the horizon at the minute of birth is the ascendant, which also serves as the cusp of the first house. The ascendant together with its sign and the ruling planet of that sign are equal in importance to the Sun sign in determining the querent's personality and ability to adapt to life's circumstances.

2. *THE DESCENDANT:* Directly opposite to the ascendant on the cusp of the seventh house, the descendant is the degree of the ecliptic that is setting on the horizon at the minute of birth. It represents the querent's attitude in one-to-one relationships.

3. *THE MIDHEAVEN:* Also known as the MC (*medium coeli*), the Midheaven is, in the Quadrant system of house division, on the cusp of the tenth house. It

An early twentieth-century astrological manual. The astrologer is employing the Quadrant system of house division, but the most remarkable aspect of her work is the giant, crankable tablet upon which she has arrayed the horoscope.

rules the need and potential for status within a community—in a profession, say—and shows how the querent presents himself in groups.

4. *THE IC:* Appearing on the cusp of the fourth house, the IC (*imum coeli*) reveals the interior personality and the background of the querent.

Each of the houses is associated with a sign and a planet, though it is a rare birth chart in which the houses appear in the signs that correspond to them.

THE FIRST HOUSE (Aries) has general rulership over the disposition, appearance, and characteristics of the querent. How people seem is closely related to the sign and planets (if any) appearing in the first house.

THE SECOND HOUSE (Taurus) reveals the individual's attitude towards money and possessions and, sometimes, towards partners, who may be regarded as possessions. This house may indicate how much the querent values herself.

THE THIRD HOUSE (Gemini) is concerned with communication—its quantity and manner. It is also the house of short journeys, which are regarded as a type of communication, and of siblings.

THE FOURTH HOUSE (Cancer) rules the home, both the childhood home and the querent's mature domestic life. It reveals the attitude toward the parents, especially the mother.

THE FIFTH HOUSE (Leo) is the fun house, representing creativity, pleasure, romance, and children, particularly the first child. It is the house of love affairs but not relationships.

THE SIXTH HOUSE (Virgo) rules health as well as work. However, this is not work in the sense of career but in the sense of capacity for work and service. In a general way, it reveals the querent's vitality and viability.

THE SEVENTH HOUSE (Libra) is the house of partnerships—close emotional relationships as well as business associations and social interactions. It reveals the subject's ability to bond.

THE EIGHTH HOUSE (Scorpio) is the Eros and Thanatos house. It rules death, that which endures after death (including inheritances), and sex, the essential act of regeneration that mimics death. In other words, the cycle of life is represented here.

THE NINTH HOUSE (Sagittarius) rules higher thought—philosophy, religion, law (as in justice)—and major journeys. The Ninth House is associated with grand human endeavor.

THE TENTH HOUSE (Capricorn) is the house of career. It represents the querent's abilities and attitudes toward work, as well as toward authority.

THE ELEVENTH HOUSE (Aquarius) rules the querent's desire for community. All forms of social life not relating to career, such as long-term friendships, involvement in politics, and membership in clubs, are represented by the Eleventh House.

THE TWELFTH HOUSE (Pisces) is sometimes called the house of troubles. The unconscious, dreams, idealism, mysteries, and secrets are its inhabitants. All the deep, dark thoughts that have no place in the bustling world are in the domain of the twelfth house.

Genesis Chap. 1. Ver. 14   Prov. 3 Verse 1   Pfalms 19 Ver. 2   Job 38 Ver. 31

*This purports to be the horoscope of the Creation, and, as is fitting for the pristine universe, each
sign is perched on the cusp of the house it rules. From Ebenezer Sibly's* New and Complete Illustration
of the Occult Sciences, *1784.*

THE ASPECTS

The last piece of the puzzle is calculating the aspects. An aspect is the distance between any two elements of the horoscope. Usually this refers to the relationship between two planets, but the ascendant, descendant, MC, and IC can also be aspected. As you can see in Figure 3 on page 48, the birth chart has the planets splayed around the circle that depicts the ecliptic; thus, on the 360-degree band represented by the horoscope, the distances between the planets may be counted in degrees. The relationship between any two planets is described in terms of the number of degrees that separates them; that is, planets in opposition are 180 degrees apart, planets in square are 90 degrees apart. Since every chart is different, the number of patterns that can be formed by the planets is nearly infinite, but within each pattern, the same kinds of aspects form. Thus, the fact that your querent has Mercury 16 degrees in Cancer in the twelfth house and Saturn 16 degrees in Capricorn in the sixth is unique (almost, anyway), but the fact that his horoscope contains an opposition aspect is very common indeed.

There are major and minor aspects, and there are positive and negative aspects. Each aspect has its own symbol, which is important to memorize, along with the distance (the number of degrees) the aspect represents and its strength and type:

Aspect	Symbol	Strength	Type	Distance	Orb
Conjunction	☌	major	positive or negative	0°	8°
Opposition	☍	major	negative	180°	8°
Trine	△	major	positive	120°	8°
Square	□	major	negative	90°	8°
Sextile	✳	major	positive	60°	6°
Semi-square	∟	minor	negative	45°	2°
Quincunx	⚻	minor	negative	150°	2°
Semi-sextile	⚺	minor	positive	30°	2°

Every aspect has a particular orb, which appears in the last column. Orb has nothing whatever to do with glowing spheroid objects; it is, instead, the term used by astrologers for the number of degrees of deviation from the required distance within which an aspect still holds. For example, planets will be in square even if they are only separated by 86 degrees. Think of it as margin. As you'll notice, the major aspects have a larger allowable variance than the minor aspects. The issue of orb is moot if you are using a software program, which handily calculates the aspects for you, taking orbs into account, and emits an easy-to-read grid of aspects. If, for some reason, you're feeling medieval and you want to calculate aspects yourself, you need to remember to consider the orb when you're counting degrees between planets.

CONJUNCTION is the most powerful aspect, combining the forces of two planets into one, which can be beneficial or disastrous, depending on the planets.

OPPOSITION is the most important negative aspect. It frustrates and inhibits the powers of the two planets involved, but such friction can strengthen the character.

TRINE is a powerful positive aspect, strengthening the planets concerned and allowing them to work together easily.

SQUARE indicates a disharmonious relationship between planets. It is less powerful than an opposition.

SEMI-SQUARE and *QUINCUNX* are minor negative aspects; do not rely too heavily on their implications in an analysis.

SEMI-SEXTILE is a minor positive aspect; again, not too much should be made of it.

An unaspected planet is a rarer occurrence than you would think, but if you do come across one in a birth chart, it is an important signal, for it generally implies that the force represented by the planet remains unintegrated in your querent's personality. This kind of gap usually causes a great deal of anxiety, and your querent may have overcompensated for his lacuna. For instance, an unaspected Sun indicates a weak sense of self, which may be hidden under a mask of egotism or self-aggrandizement.

After you have tabulated the individual aspects, it is time to step back and look for aspect patterns. There are numerous formulations, each of which has its own meaning. The most important are:

THE T-SQUARE Two planets in opposition are both in square to a third. This concatenation of negative aspects results in the expected high level of tension and difficulty, but it also generates strength and resilience.

THE GRAND CROSS Four planets in square and two of the four in opposition form the extremely rare Grand Cross. This is, in essence, a quadrupled T-Square, and, for interpretive purposes, its effect is exactly that of the T-Square times four: lots of struggle, lots of opposition, lots of force and character.

THE GRAND TRINE Three planets connected by trines compose a Grand Trine. In most cases, Grand Trines occur within one element and predict the subject's style and natural talent in the manner represented by that element.

YOD (also known as the Finger of Fate) A Yod is made up of two planets in opposition, one in quincunx to a third and fourth, which are semi-sextile to the second. This strange formation indicates trouble and stress, but the planet at the pinnacle points the way to the solution.

Queen Elizabeth I, whose birth chart is shown here, was a Virgo in the sex and death house (the eighth) with Sagittarius rising and her moon in Taurus—a combination that produced a wily, controlling, pragmatic, and charismatic character who learned well from her mother. From Ebenezer Sibly's New and Complete Illustration of the Occult Sciences, 1784.

INTERPRETING THE HOROSCOPE

So, you have your subject's birth chart laid out before you. There are the planets, the signs, the houses, the Ascendant, the MC, and the aspects. What do you do now? To give the most thorough reading, you should analyze the indicators in the following order:

1. Major tendencies:
    A. Balance of elements (earth, air, fire, water): is there a preponderance of one or two?
    B. Aspect pattern: is there a major aspect pattern or an unaspected planet?
    C. Balance of qualities (cardinal, fixed, mutable): is there an emphasis or exclusion of one of the qualities?
2. The Sun sign, its house and aspects.
3. The ascendant and the rising sign (the sign in which the ascendant lies), as well as the sign and house of the ascendant ruler, which is the planet that rules the rising sign. The ascendant ruler, also known as the chart ruler, is a very important element in the horoscope.
4. The Sun ruler, that is, the planet ruling the sign containing the Sun, and its sign, house, and aspects.
5. The Moon's sign, house, and aspects.
6. The remaining planets in order from Mercury to Pluto and their signs, houses, and aspects.
7. The Moon ruler, that is, the planet ruling the sign in which the Moon resides, and its sign, house, and aspect.

For a good reading, you will have to address the following issues (always realizing that the importance of individual areas will vary greatly from querent to querent). The following list tells you where to look for your interpretation.

1. General character: element emphasis; the ascendant; planets in the first house; the Sun; the Moon; the chart ruler; a major aspect pattern.
2. Relationships: the descendant; planets in the seventh house (close partnerships and marriage); the seventh house ruler (i.e., the planet ruling the sign on the cusp of the seventh house); planets in the fifth house (romance); the fifth house ruler; planets in Libra; the position of Mars (masculine ideal) or position of Venus (feminine ideal); the position of the moon.
3. Career: the MC; planets in the tenth house (career); tenth house ruler; planets in the sixth house (service); sixth house ruler; position of Saturn (discipline and self-control); position of Mars (practicality).
4. Emotional character: the position of the Moon; planets in the water signs; the position of Venus (especially for women).

5. Family relationships: planets in the fourth house (the home and childhood); fourth house ruler; planets in fifth house (children); fifth house ruler; planets in the third house (siblings); third house ruler; the position of the Moon (mother); the position of Saturn, where Saturn is associated with the father.

6. Money: planets in the second house (possessions); second house ruler; planets in the eighth house (inheritance, cycles of getting and spending); eighth house ruler; position of Saturn (ambition).

7. Intelligence and education: position of Mercury; planets in the third house (communication, school, interests); third house ruler; position of Jupiter; planets in the ninth house (philosophy and higher education); ninth house ruler; position of Neptune (imagination); disposition of the twelfth house (intuition).

8. Creativity and artistic talents: planets in the fifth house (creativity); fifth house ruler; positions of Mercury, Neptune, and Venus; position of Mars.

9. Health: planets in the sixth house (health); sixth house ruler; negative significators in the eighth or twelfth houses.

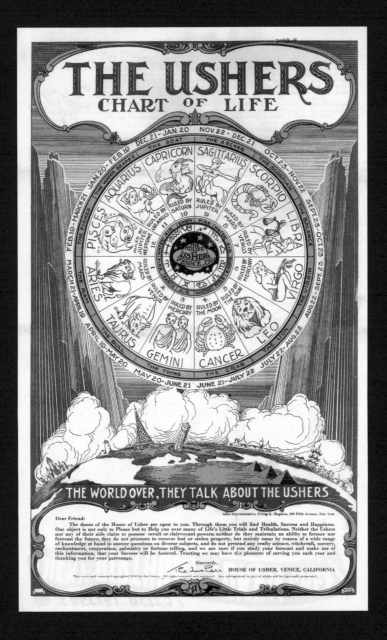

The Ushers Chart of Life was the last word in mail-order astrology in the 1940s. Direct from the House of Usher in Venice, California, this 1942 chart for Gemini gravely announces that it is "quite likely the prospective marriage partner will be met at some sort of entertainment, especially in connection with church, club, or other social interest."

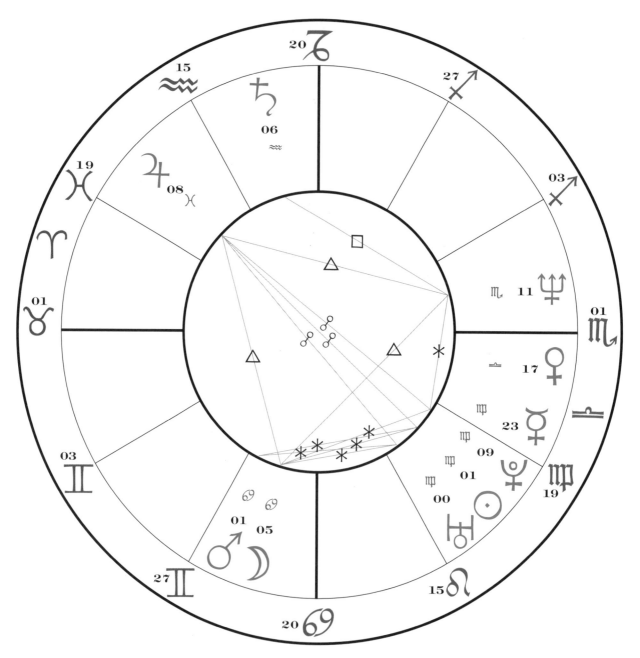

FIGURE 3.

The following short reading will give you a notion of how to approach a birth chart. I will begin by listing and briefly explicating the components of the sample chart in Figure 3 and then integrate this information into a character analysis. The querent is a woman in her mid-thirties whom I will call Sarah.

The first thing to do is take a good long look at the chart itself. With one very important exception, it displays a fairly normal distribution of aspects and elements. An uncommonly high proportion of its planets are dignified, which is nice for the querent, but, in essence, this is your basic, garden-variety birth chart—though you would never be so crass as to announce that during a reading. Nobody wants to hear that she is only normal.

1. *Major tendencies.* Clearly, we have a glut of two elements: earth and water (four planets apiece). There are only two planets in air signs and no fire signs at all. Earth signs are practical and hardworking; water signs are emotional and imaginative. However, their combined forces can be rather muddy, resulting in, for example, a sensitive yet inexpressive character. As to qualities, Sarah has five planets in mutable signs, three cardinals, and two fixed, which essentially results in a sweep for mutability, producing a character who is very responsive to her environment.

The aspects are where the real story lies. The most notable is the Grand Trine that connects the Moon, Jupiter, and Neptune in the water signs. This betokens a sensitive nature, deeply though not morbidly emotional. The idealism of Jupiter is supported by the devotion and caring of the Moon and spiritualized by mystical Neptune. This is a very strong aspect that lessens the immanence and pragmatism of the earth signs in Sarah's chart, allowing her the possibility of artistic, political, or religious inclinations. Jupiter's three oppositions are equally noticeable, though the opposition to the Sun is the only really salient aspect for a personality sketch. I will discuss this aspect, Saturn square Neptune, and the plethora of sextiles when I get to the planets they affect.

The most important component of this chart is the most difficult to see: Mercury is unaspected. This throws the whole chart for a loop. Mercury is not some vague, impersonal planet like Pluto; it expresses the querent's manner of thinking and communicating, which makes it integral to the character. In addition, since Sarah's Sun is in Virgo, Mercury is the Sun ruler, which gives it a lot of influence in the chart. Now, we know that an unaspected planet reveals a focal point in the character, the locus of a great expenditure of energy. It generally represents a lacuna or a quality that the querent cannot incorporate into her character. Initially, you might read the unaspected Mercury as the sign of a rather limited intelligence. However, that interpretation is counterindicated by the placement of the planet, which is very positive indeed. Mercury is dignified in Virgo and indirectly dignified in the sixth house (because the sixth house is ruled by Virgo), which puts it in the best possible position to express its powers. It is therefore unlikely that there is anything organically wrong with Sarah's intellect. The better interpretation, it seems to me, lies in a direct translation of what we see in the birth chart: Mercury stands alone, isolated from the rest of the personality, producing the coldness, the aloofness, of the unmitigatedly cerebral. The coexistence of the unaspected Mercury and a Grand Trine in water produces a terribly divided character, full of emotional response, yet unable to express a bit of it (In Figure 3, Venus, too, appears to be unaspected, but it is actually semi-square to the Sun and to Uranus).

2. *The Sun sign.* Sarah is a Virgo, but only just. She is two degrees away from being a Leo. This Leonine influence, coupled with the fact that Sarah's Sun occupies Leo's house (the fifth), provides some of the fiery element that would otherwise be missing from her chart. The Sun is also conjunct Uranus, which, given its position in the fifth house, connotes a creative and original personality. Unfortunately, the Sun is also in opposition to Jupiter (as are Uranus and Pluto), which generates grandiosity and a self-indulgent nature. The Sun is sextile both the Moon and Mars, the former fostering self-confidence and the latter promoting enthusiasm and élan vital. In short, every aspect of the Sun counters, for good or evil, the plodding, pragmatic nature of its sign.

3. *The Ascendant.* In an exceptionally artistic parallel, Sarah's ascendant is also an earth sign poised two degrees away from fire. Taurus is aesthetically oriented, and here, its ruler—and thus, the chart ruler—Venus, lolls happily in Libra, where she is dignified. This permits an easy expression of Venusian appeal, although the theater for her charms is centered on her work life, denoted by the sixth house. Taurus ascendant with the Sun in Virgo and such a beneficent Venus is likely to produce a practical, hard-working lover of beauty (perhaps a career in the arts), who is absolutely adamant about having her way in the home (perhaps a career in interior decoration).

4. *The Sun ruler.* The ruler of the sign containing the Sun is the unaspected Mercury I have discussed above.

5. *The Moon.* The Moon is dignified in Cancer, intensifying the emotions and accentuating family feeling. Its placement in the house of communication generates a strong imagination and the ability to convey emotional states, though, given Mercury, probably not her own. The Moon's conjunction with Mars produces aggressive feelings, such as passion, jealousy, and the desire for revenge.

6. *The remaining planets.* We have pretty well covered Mercury. Venus, as we suggested, is happy in Libra, and her residence in the sixth house promotes gratification from work. Venus is semi-square to the Sun, which can generate some minor conflict about feminine identity. Mars in fall in Cancer creates an unfortunate tendency to confound physical needs with emotional ones. Likewise, its position in the third house makes our querent prone to rash mistakes of judgment. Jupiter in Pisces promotes an emotional commitment to ideas; however, the negative implications of this are probably ameliorated by the Grand Trine. Its position in the eleventh house points to good fortune through friends and community. Saturn, that old malefic, is indirectly dignified by its position in the tenth house (because that house is ruled by Capricorn, which is ruled by Saturn), which implies that Sarah has both a great deal of ambition and a

great deal of ability. Saturn's position in Aquarius implies impartiality and detachment, beneficial qualities in professional life. However, Saturn is also in square to Neptune, a very inauspicious aspect indeed, connoting that worst of failings—self-deceit. Neptune in the seventh house in the sign of Scorpio portends delusional relationships. Neptunian idealism in the house of marriage is bad enough, but the malevolent aspect with Saturn practically guarantees an unhappy marriage. Uranus conjunct Sun produces creativity, as I have discussed. Given Pluto's grand scope, its placement has little personal meaning in a birth chart.

7. *The Moon ruler.* In this chart, the Moon ruler is the Moon itself, owing to the Moon's position in Cancer. See the previous discussion of the Moon.

One final component of the chart is the dispersal of planets in the houses. Sarah's house of communication, creativity, and work are heavily populated, and she has one major planetary influence apiece in her career and community houses. We can deduce that Sarah is work-oriented and that her best opportunities for satisfaction lie in a career that makes use of her creative talents and communication skills. The more transcendental houses—Eighth, Ninth, and Twelfth—are unpopulated, which underscores Sarah's pragmatic nature.

Sarah's strong earth signs determine her most noticeable qualities: she is practical, hardworking, reliable, and constructive. The predominance of the mutable quality in her chart results in a character that adapts to and works with her environment. Sarah is undoubtedly seen as exceptionally competent, the kind of person who follows through and takes care of things. It's clear that she is highly motivated and quite ambitious, though she may not appear to be so (Venus in the sixth house may give the appearance of an easygoing attitude towards work). Much of her sense of self—and much of others' sense of her—comes from her ability to work hard. Thankfully, this tendency to a life of unspeakable drudgery is countered by the Grand Trine in water, which betokens a depth of emotion and psychological acuity that provides resonance and sympathy to Sarah's character. She is likely to be passionately devoted to certain ideals, and may even convert others to her way of thinking, because of the powerful planets in her third house. Moon conjunct Mars is not typically considered an auspicious aspect, but in this case, the intense emotions will add flavor to a generally Earthy character.

Sarah's mysterious Mercury will probably be a great sorrow to her. Her inability to communicate her thoughts or connect her intellectual life to her outward self will generate a sense of detachment. She will probably seem aloof to others, who may complain that they don't know what she is thinking. If she is as intelligent as the position of Mercury implies, she may be quite intimidating, which will add to her loneliness.

This coolness is alleviated by the position of her Sun in the house of creativity, fun, romance, and play. Her Sun's proximity to Leo will add some dash and verve. The happily placed Venus gives Sarah a certain amount of charm, and this, together with the enthusiasm and self-confidence of the Sun's sextiles to the Moon and Mars, produces an outgoing and attractive, if somewhat impenetrable, public persona. Given her Sun's opposition to Jupiter, Sarah may appear to be overbearing and insensitive to others, but the prevalence of her water signs tells us otherwise.

The unaspected Mercury, in addition to creating a nearly unbridgeable gap between Sarah's public self and her private self, will have a negative effect on Sarah's primary relationships. She will seem unavailable and secretive, which will dampen romance. Unfortunately, Sarah's descendant is in Scorpio, which promotes passionate but unstable—even hostile—partnerships. The seventh house is occupied only by dreamy Neptune square to Saturn, which again does not portend a healthy relationship. The only consolation is the placement of Leo on the cusp of the fifth house (romance) and the easy position of Venus, both factors that promote appeal; Sarah may have to satisfy herself with a series of superficial relationships, though, in truth, Virgos rarely go for that kind of thing. Sarah's ideal partner, represented by Mars in Cancer, is a sensitive, nurturing presence.

Sarah's devotion to work for its own sake is so strong as to form a personality trait. Her MC is in Capricorn, another earth sign that promotes career objectives. Saturn in Aquarius promises some sort of cerebral occupation, but regardless of focus, its placement in the tenth house promotes success.

In sum, Sarah is destined for a life of hard work, which she will find deeply gratifying. Her best hope for happiness is to work on integrating her intelligence with her deep feelings in order to give them voice. Though she may never find the perfect partner, a heightened ability to convey her passionate emotions will result in a more satisfying life.

Raphael's Prophetic Messenger Almanack *was an annual compendium of predictions—usually dire— published in Victorian London. Each issue began with an illustration of the catastrophes to come, the "Hieroglyphic for the Eventful Year." Shown here is the array of emergencies and disasters that awaited those unfortunate enough to live in 1840. According to Raphael, who, by the way, is the man in the graduation cap near the top of the image, the year would bring explosions, the collapse of religion, shipwreck, war, a royal death, clerical flagellation, a reasonably serene parliament, and riot. Interestingly, Raphael explained the hieroglyphic in the volume following the one in which it was published. That is, this picture was interpreted in the almanac for 1841, where the collapse of the Church was downgraded to the collapse of a church, in Surrey, due to faulty construction.*

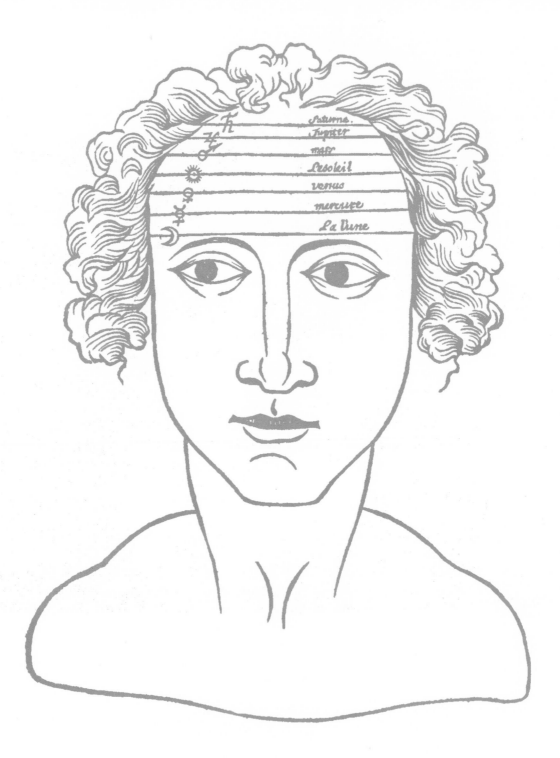

This and all other metoposcopic diagrams are from Cardan's Metoposcopia, *published in 1658.*

METOPOSCOPY

Jerome Cardan was a great mathematician of the sixteenth century, but unlike the mathematicians of the present day, he was no prisoner of the proven. So great was his devotion to astrology that he starved himself to death in order to fulfill his horoscope's prediction that he would die at the age of seventy-five.

Cardan's belief in the influence of the stars on individuals was common for his era (though his mortal dedication to his principles was not). More extreme was his literal interpretation of that influence: he believed that heavenly bodies left marks on human bodies—specifically, on the forehead. Accordingly, he drew up a system of character analysis based on forehead wrinkles. This is metoposcopy, the science of the frontal lines.

Cardan's system was based on the correlation of a strip of forehead space with each of the planets; luckily, in his day there were only seven planets. Thus, the influence of the Moon was to be seen in the band of head directly above the eyebrows. This is followed, in order up the head toward the hair, by the bands of Mercury, Venus, the Sun, Mars, Jupiter, and Saturn. Obviously, only the most wizened among us could claim lines from all the planets. The two or three lines that most of us sport, once scrutinized carefully to determine the band to which they belong, reveal the planets that most influence our characters. (If you can't figure out where your lines fall, planetarily speaking, get a ruler and divide your forehead into seven equal strata with a felt-tip pen.)

According to Cardan, the longer and straighter your wrinkles, the more noble your character. Waves or breaks in your wrinkles are indicative of various faults and flaws, but the real villains have vertical lines plummeting down their brows. More than one vertical line or, worst of all, a crossed line (i.e., an **x**-shaped wrinkle) are the signs of the most hideous criminals.

Taking our examples from the more than eight hundred illustrations that appear in Cardan's masterpiece, *Metoposcopia,* which was published in 1658, we learn that a low straight line in the region devoted to Mercury (Figure 4) reveals a man who has engaged in much land travel (sea-travel lines are bumpier). Figure 5, who looks like St. Peter, is actually, metoposcopically speaking, a debauchee; the dip from Jupiter to Venus is what undoes him. Figure 6 does well to smirk; according to Cardan, she has the fore-head of a low-class courtesan (the high-class courtesan appears to have an ampersand between her eyes).

For swift character analysis, metoposcopy has no rival. It is fast, clean, and you don't need your subject's permission to do it. However, since metoposcopic expertise requires that you memorize Cardan's eight hundred illustrations, it is not surprising that the science of the frontal lines never caught on.

FIGURE 4.

FIGURE 5.

FIGURE 6.

John Martin, Belshazzar's Feast, 1820. One of the great oracular interventions of all time occurred during a magnificent party hosted by Belshazzar, the newly crowned king of Babylon. Just as the thousand guests were lifting their cups to toast the king and various heathen deities, "There appeared the fingers of a man's hand, writing upon the wall of the king's palace. . . . Then the king's face changed, and his thoughts troubled him so that the joints of his legs were loose and his knees knocked together." Horrified, Belshazzar ordered his minions to bring in the Chaldeans, the astrologers, the soothsayers—anyone who could interpret the strange words. Scouring the palace, they retrieved Daniel—the black-clad central figure in the painting—who did not shrink from giving Belshazzar the bad news: he was a goner. The crowd gasped, the ladies fainted, the wise men clasped their brows, and the aides-de-camp decamped. And that very night, the oracle was proved, for Belshazzar was killed and Darius the Persian conquered the throne.

ORACLES

The best method of divination is also the diciest: consultation of an oracle. No system of card reading or hand interpretation can exceed the authority of the oracle's direct link to the supernatural. But, likewise, nothing can be so easily faked, since its basis is mere assertion. Despite this liability to charlatanism, claims of oracular power have been met by eager believers for thousands of years. Some of the world's earliest civilizations were more or less run by the mandates of sibyls and illuminati. The Greeks, as usual, did it up best: the oracles at Delphi, Dordona, Didyma, and Claros flourished for hundreds of years. Notwithstanding what seems to have been a deliberate policy of sowing confusion, their proclamations were scrupulously obeyed.

The consultation process followed a rigid format, particularly at Delphi, which, like an exclusive restaurant, required reservations, since it was open only one day each month (the oracle took a three-month vacation in winter, too). The oracle could be consulted by either individuals or states, though the cost for states was ten times higher than that for individuals, presumably because stately questions taxed the gods' patience more. Each month on the big day, three sibyls—putative virgins who acted as mediums for the gods—went into trances (induced by inhaling incense, according to some sources) from sunrise to sunset. Once fully possessed by the divine spirits, the sibyl would emit the answer to the inquiry at hand, but the attending priest, the maitre d' of the oracle, was the one who conveyed her statement to the waiting querent, often translating the answer into pithy verse. The priests exerted the real power at Delphi, since the sibyls could not be approached directly.

Above: An oracular postcard from 1910.

Delphi was the most ominous oracle, but Dordona was the most democratic. Less expensive than Delphi, it received more quotidian queries, which were written down on thin strips of lead and rolled up for secrecy. The priests of Dordona, who ritually did not wash their feet, interpreted the pronouncement of the oracle, which apparently lived inside an oak tree. Unfortunately, this interesting site has altogether disappeared.

Claros, the last of the great Greek oracles, had the most dramatic presentation. In the deep of night, the querents were led single-file though a maze of passages underneath a great temple to Apollo. Finally, they reached a cavernous hall, where they remained while the sibyl continued on to the sacred fountain that inspired her trance.

The Greek oracles continued to prosper into the third century A.D., though as the balance of power shifted Romeward, so did the balance of prophesy. The homegrown brand of fortune-telling in the Roman Empire was augury, divination by omens (e.g., if an eagle drops dead at your feet, you're going to be emperor), but oracles were also popular. Among the avalanche of papyri left by the documentarian Romans is a list of questions posed to a provincial oracle: "Should I remain where I am going?" "Am I to become a Senator?" "Have I been poisoned?"

The rise of Christianity put an end to the classical oracular tradition, or, rather, the church transferred the authority to its own. The great desert fathers of Late Antiquity and the mystics of the Middle Ages filled the oracular shoes admirably. Hildegard of Bingen, a twelfth-century nun, is a case in point. Immured from the age of eleven in a small nunnery on the Rhine, she became famous for her visions and ensuing edicts. According to the pictures she bid her faithful scribe to draw, the spirit came down on her head in tongues of flame and she wrote the words it told her. She was consulted by peasants and lords for miles around—she was, in some ways, a pilgrimage destination—and she freely dispensed opinions and advice that were, she said, not hers but God's. Nervous at this special access to the divine, Saint Bernard of Clairvaux told her to stop it, and she did.

A variant on table tilting is table turning, in which the spirits, after proper cajoling, turn a table a certain number of times in order to answer questions. The seance pictured here is Swiss and appears in an 1853 volume entitled Mystères de la science.

The Enlightenment put a damper on the oracles of Europe, but the Romantic Era fanned the flames. Seances held by mediums became fashionable in mid-nineteenth-century Europe, and England, particularly, was gripped by a frenzy of trances, spirit visits, and table tilting. This latter—a predecessor of the modern Ouija board—was the parlor game of choice in the Victorian era. A somber group would gather round a small table in a darkened room. Each person laid a single finger on a tabletop while one posed a question. After a few moments, the table would heave up one leg and crash back down again. The quantity of "tilts" revealed the answer—one knock for yes, two for maybe, three for no. Stuffy Queen Victoria herself once played at table tilting.

Like the tilting table, the Ouija board's workings are inexplicable, but work it does. To consult Ouija, you and a partner lay your fingers on a small, heart-shaped stool that rests on a board containing the words *"Yes," "No,"* the alphabet, and numbers. After you have asked a question, the pointed end of the stool will move from spot to spot, spelling out your answer, which can be quite alarming in its prescience.

Almost every oracle has been accused of fraud (or bad faith), but they persist. Perhaps this is a testament to humankind's gullibility, or perhaps it is a sign of the eagerness of the inhabitants of the other world to help us.

Christ in a halo of numbers, from Jakob Böhme's Mysterium magnum.

NUMEROLOGY

Number mysticism is as pervasive as it is ancient. Pretty much every civilization you can think of devoted a good deal of its primordial intellectual energy to contemplating numbers and devising numerical systems. Our own form of numbering, those glyphs we call "Arabic" numbers, are actually Indian (their origins betray themselves by the fact that the numbers are written from left to right even when they appear in Arabic texts, which are written from right to left). Indian mathematicians were the first to wrestle the concept of zero to the ground, a feat that facilitated all sorts of useful things like the decimal system and the significance of the position of numbers. Zero was, therefore, eagerly embraced by Islamic scholars, first, and by the slow-witted Western Europeans some five hundred years later, in 1143.

Bear in mind, however, that the Arabic numbers and numbering systems are simply a method for arranging and conveying numbers. It's not as though nobody could count until 1143. When the ancient Greeks saw six rocks, they said "Look, there are six rocks." Which brings us right to Pythagoras, who was an ancient Greek (sixth century B.C.) and an aficionado of the number six, which he considered the perfect number. Pythagoras was the founder of mystical numerology as well as of geometry; he and his followers believed that all things—ideas, emotions, material entities—are related to the first nine numbers. The numerical relations among things was, according to Pythagoras, the motive force of the universe. This is, in essence, the basis for numerology, for if all things are fueled by their numerical relationships, then exegesis of

Above: The Gold Dust Mystic Fortune Teller, who seems to have combined the best features of numerology and crystal ball-gazing, advised readers about their "number vibrations" as well as their cleaning problems, which were resolvable only with Gold Dust Cleaning Powder.

PYTHAGORAS

Pythagoras, looking worried and cross-eyed in the 1701 edition of Thomas Stanley's History of Philosophy.

Though his name now lingers primarily in the curses of geometry students, Pythagoras himself was more of a mystic than a mathematician. To call him a Renaissance man would be an understatement as well as an anachronism, but his range of ideas and occupations was mind-boggling even to his contemporaries. Born around 580 B.C., Pythagoras won the heavyweight boxing championship in the Forty-eighth Olympiad. Brawn established, he then undertook a quest for knowledge throughout the known world. Since none of Pythagoras's own writings exists, the fruits of his travels vary with the teller. Some followers have him studying with the Brahmins in India and the Druids in Britain, which, though unlikely, would account on one hand for his theory of reincarnation and on the other for some of his purifying rituals. However, it is pretty well established that he developed his ideas about geometry and astronomy in Egypt and his ideas about astrology and numerology in Persia. Returning from his travels, he acquired a band of disciples, whom he organized into a school in Croton, Italy. There, he developed and taught his essential doctrine, that of the harmonics that relate all things. Harmonic relationships may, of course, be stated as numerical ones, which is the source of Pythagoras's famous dictum "Number Is All." Though much pooh-poohed by later scientists, Pythagoras's theory of harmonics bears a striking resemblance to twentieth-century wave theory.

Pythagorean doctrine is not only an explanation for the material world; its moral skeleton is hung on the notion that the creation of the world was achieved by the division of the divine unity into multiplicity. Thus, each and every thing and being in the world contains within it a divine spark. Not only is this the source of the relationships among all things—that is, the source of the harmonics—but it is this spark that man must keep alight by good behavior and an upright life.

Unfortunately, Pythagoras attempted to establish a government founded upon his principles, and, like most attempts to realize the ideal, it ended in disaster. The discipline and asceticism of a spiritual community look a lot like oppression in a city government, and Pythagoras and his followers were soon overthrown and, probably, massacred.

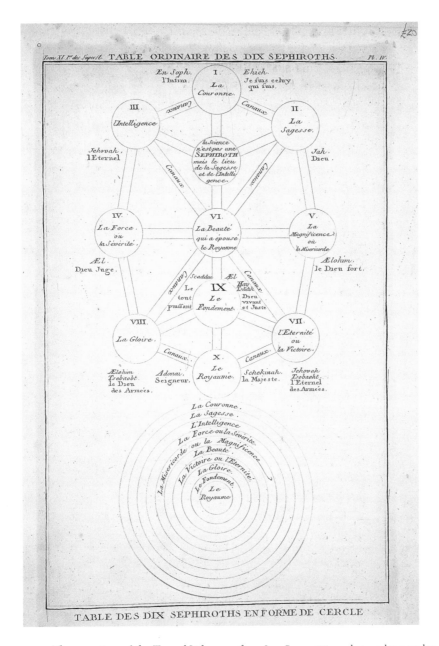

FIGURE 7. *These versions of the Tree of Life come from* Les Superstitions de tous les peuples du monde, *by the peripatetic Frenchman Piccart. His arrangement of the Sefirotic Tree includes an identification of the various forms of the divine associated with each* sefirot, *culminating in* Je suis celuy qui suis, *"I am that am," which we call—or don't call —Yaweh. The circular depiction of the* sefirah, *below, was popular with the Christian Kabbalists, who found in it a comforting similarity to Christian depictions of the cosmos.*

those relationships will reveal the divine organization of the world and bestow upon the cognoscenti an understanding of its direction. Numerology seeks to discover the secret passageways that connect all things. It is less concerned with predicting the future than with understanding the present.

Number mysticism persisted in a variety of forms—some of them more mystical than others—well into the eighteenth century. The Roman emperors were addicted to it, as were the early Christian fathers. St. Augustine devoted a lot of time to decoding the divine plan through numbers. He was one of the founders—and legitimators—of the practice of interpreting the Bible numerologically.

Medieval Christian scholars were particularly fond of this kind of "transcendental arithmetic." By the time of St. Thomas Aquinas, whole dictionaries of biblical numbers had been compiled, and the significance of three (the trinity) and twelve (the apostles) had been solidified into Christian dogma.

The most interesting numerological development of the Middle Ages was not exclusively numerological. The Kabbalah, a profoundly complex Jewish spiritual philosophy, sought to elucidate the divine structure of the universe. Kabbalistic mysticism differentiates between the unknowable, divine It, whose laws and reasons will never be understood, and the God who may be revealed by appropriate study of His creation. The central text of the Kabbalah, the *Sefer yetsirah,* or Book of Creation, proposed a diagram of the divine ordering principles of the universe, which were, essentially, emanations of the godhead. This diagram, known as the Tree of Life, shows ten manifestations of God, called the *sefirot,* in the form of circular stations connected by a pattern of energy shaped like a lightning bolt moving from sky to earth. As you can see in Figure 7, the *sefirot* are also aligned vertically into what Kabbalists call the pillars: in the center is the Pillar of Equilibrium; on the left, the Pillar of Mercy (composed of active forces); and on the right, the Pillar of Severity or Judgment (composed of passive forces). At the top or beginning of the tree is *Keter,* the crown. This is the highest sefirah and the closest to the Divine; the light of God moves from it in its lightning-bolt

Right: An illustrated edition of the works of the seventeenth-century shoemaker, Kabbalist, and mystic Jakob Böhme included this rendition of the Tree of Life, which he termed the Tree of the Cosmos. The topmost sphere, Adonai, *emanates the two middle spheres,* Nature *and* Eternal. *They in turn exude, via the* Shrack, *or lightning bolt, in the center, our own sphere, that of the Solar World, where we see the familiar celestial figures of the Zodiac and the planet. According to Böhme, the universe is engaged in a progression toward the divine comprised of seven stages and impelled by a dialectic that mirrors that of the alchemical process. Böhme's vision of spiritualized matter made him unpopular with the Lutheran church, which liked its spirit unincorporated, and he was censored during his lifetime, although* samizdat *editions of his many works were read avidly. Though Böhme was clearly influenced by the Kabbalah, his most famous books were received as veiled alchemical instructions and studied closely, the more so as Böhme acknowledged that he was an adept. About the transformation of base metal into gold, he wrote, "It doth not cost any money but what is spent upon the time and the maintenance, else it might be prepared with four shillings. The work is easy, the act simple. A boy of sixteen years might make it, but the wisdom therein is great, and it is the greatest mystery."*

formation, to *Hokkmah*, wisdom, and thence to *Binah*, understanding. From there it travels to *Hesed*, mercy; then *Gevurah*, judgment; then to *Tiferet*, beauty; and moving on to *Nezah*, eternity, and, in human terms, passion. From there, the energy flows into *Hod*, glory or mastery; below and next is *Yesod*, foundation, or connection and perception. Finally, the divine will connects to the earth at *Malkhut*, the kingdom, which signifies the existence of God in all things. Each of the *sefirah* manifests an attribute of God, but each has a human aspect as well. The Tree of Life may, in fact, be overlaid on any human endeavor or construct to show the relationships within it.

In addition to the *sefirot* themselves, the twenty-two paths between them constitute a further revelation of God's plan. Together, they describe a path toward the divine, to which, by intense study, the Kabbalist may ascend.

Where, you may ask, is the numerology in all this? Actually, numbers are integral to the Kabbalistic theosophy, for the divine universe is composed of thirty-two elements, all represented in the Tree of Life. Each of the *sefirah* has its number—from 1 to 10—as does each of the paths between them—from 11 to 32. These numbers are not mere tags but important constituents of the dynamic of the sefirot. Thus, for instance, the number four is eternally endowed with the quality of Hesed, mercy or compassion. (Indeed, much of the modern characterizations of the numbers are derived from such Kabbalistic interpretations.) The numbers associated with the *sefirot* are as much a subject of contemplation as the qualities themselves and, indeed, are regarded as a vehicle for understanding.

The Kabbalistic tradition of spiritualizing numbers was reinforced by an even more ancient numerological method called *gematria*. In applying *gematria*, each letter of an alphabet is associated with a number, and any two words that have the same total numerical value are thought to have a relationship. *Gematria* is practiced in most cultures, but Hebrew is particularly well adapted to the system because its letters and

GEMATRIA

There are many ways to apply *gematria*; among the most common is the technique of relating words on the basis of their equivalent numerical values (that is, their letters have identical sums). For example, *Yayin* (wine) and *Sod* (secret) have the same number value, seventy. This reveals the truth of the saying "When wine goes in, secrets go out." In another, more sober instance, the ladder (*Sulan*) in Jacob's dream has the same value as *Sinai*, which means that the Torah, revealed on Mt. Sinai, is the ladder that goes from earth to heaven.

A second form of *gematria* involves calculating the sum of the squares of the numerical value of letters within a word. Two words that share the same sum are, inevitably, related. For example, the Tetragrammaton *YHWH* yields a total of 186, as does the word *makom* (place). The revealed meaning is that God is everyplace.

numbers share the same symbols. For Kabbalists, *gematria* provided yet another means to discerning the occult connections between all things. In the fifteenth and sixteenth centuries, Christians got wind of the Kabbalah and set about adapting it for their own purposes. Through the use of *gematria* and *notarikon* (another occult numerological system), they reassigned the meanings of certain Kabbalistic texts to affirm the divinity of Jesus.

This Christianized Kabbalah became all the rage in renaissance Florence, where the philosopher Giovanni Pico della Mirandola started the ball rolling by deriving, via a semi-numerological process, the name of Jesus from the Tetragrammaton, the sacred four-letter name of God. In seventeenth-century England, the weird and wonderful Robert Fludd, a devoted Kabbalist, devised a fairly inexplicable system of numerology based on the shapes of numbers, the Pythagorean idea of number pantheism, and his own bizarre view of the structure of the universe, which involved monkeys. In the eighteenth century, the chilly wind of rationalism toppled the numerological philosophies so carefully constructed in the preceding millennia. However, the great nineteenth-century magicians and spiritualists considered numerology to be a crucial foundation of the universal occult system for which they were perpetually searching. The French magician Eliphas Levi, for example, constructed a grand synthesis of occult knowledge combining numerology with tarot, astrology, and Kabbalah.

Despite the depredations and additions of history, predictive numerology has remained fairly true to its Pythagorean roots. The philosophy is straightforward: every person is formed and guided by the numerical relationships that are embedded within him or her. These relationships find avenues of expression in names and dates, which can be understood when they are reduced, by simple calculations, into single numbers. Anything composed of letters or numbers may be translated into a number of numerological significance. However, some letters and numbers are more relevant than others. The usual candidates for numerological

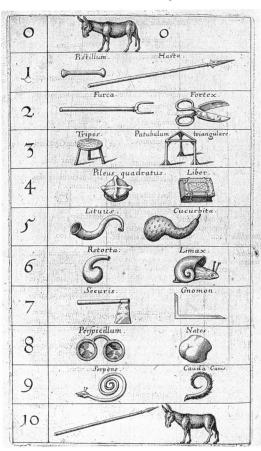

Robert Fludd, creator of some of the strangest representations of theological concepts the world has ever seen, proclaimed himself a Pythagorean. However, as this chart from Fludd's masterpiece, Utriusqe cosmi maioris et minoris historia, *shows, he believed that the forms of objects were derived from the forms of numbers, which is more Pythagorean than Pythagoras.*

1	2	3	4	5	6	7	8	9
A	B	C	D	E	F	G	H	I
J	K	L	M	N	O	P	Q	R
S	T	U	V	W	X	Y	Z	

investigation are your birthday and your name. The former, when translated numero-logically, produces your birth number, which reveals the core of your personality, your natural abilities and attitudes. Your birth number shows what you are, rather than what you do. The number derived from your name, on the other hand, will tell your future. This is your number of destiny, the manifestation of the character intrinsic to your birth number.

The numerological technique is quite simple. All dates or names must be reduced to single numbers. For dates, we achieve this by adding strings of numbers together. For example, say your birthday is December 5, 1954. This may be restated as 12-5-1954, and then the numbers are simply added together as they appear: $1 + 2 + 5 + 1 + 9 + 5 + 4$. This totals 27, but, as you undoubtedly remember, we must achieve a single digit, so 27 itself must be calculated as $2 + 7 = 9$. Hence, your birth number is 9.

To derive the number of destiny from your name, you must convert letters to numbers. Use the conversion table (above) to achieve this. (For Spanish names, a double-l should be converted to six.) It is imperative that you calculate your full, given name. Even if you hate it, the name you were given at birth is your numerologically significant name. No avoiding your middle name, either; you have to count the whole thing. If you were adopted, do your best to find your birth certificate and use the name that appears there. Last names acquired by marriage do not qualify. As with your birth number, the numbers derived from your name must be added together and reduced to a single digit.

This undoubtedly seems very simple. And it is! But—just to keep you on your toes—there are a few numbers that have special properties and are therefore not to be reduced to a single digit. These, called the master numbers, are eleven and twenty-two (some numerologists designate thirty-three as a master number, too, but I do not). The master numbers always indicate an orientation toward the spiritual, a profound and advanced consciousness. Unfortunately, master numbers also denote a predisposition for a very stress-filled mode of living, which can be exhausting for the master numberee as well as for his or her intimates.

Now that the calculations are complete, we must proceed to the characteristics of the numbers themselves.

Pythagoras held that One contained vast primordial power; it was everything rolled into one, the source of all the rest of the numbers (and hence, to him, of the universe), as well as the essential Unity. A monolithic, all-embracing force, One was active, elemental, the predecessor of the world. This is actually a tidy character sketch of birth number One. Ones are leaders; they are bold, enthusiastic, driven to succeed, and desperately impatient. They want things—and people—to work according to their plans. One can be a superachiever, provided that he is not opposed, in which case he tends to fritter away his energies in pitched battles over meaningless symbols of power. At his best, One is a daring and constructive thinker, an energetic worker, a witty conversationalist, and an ardent lover. At his worst, One is unimaginative, bossy, and resentful. One must be aware that his *bête noire* is self-confidence; he seems so sure of himself that friends simply never realize how fragile his sense of well-being is. Birth number One should, therefore, protect himself and cultivate self-reliance.

If One is your number of destiny, your leadership skills will be called upon in some pronounced way in your life. Your energy and activity will make you an inspiring boss or innovator, and you will achieve your goals in triumph. However, you must not forget your colleagues or co-workers—you tend to have little respect for those you consider your inferiors. Your justifiable pride in your accomplishments must not be tarnished by a narrow-minded inability to recognize the value of those who think differently from you. You will probably choose a profession on the cutting edge, since new ideas and creativity are precious to you. It is often wise for destiny One to be self-employed. In romantic affairs you will probably be the dominant partner, but it would be best to find a mate whose energy level matches yours. Although you despise being alone, you may end up that way because you often find intimacy cloying.

Historically, Two is trouble. Cornelius Agrippa von Nettesheim, a sometime numerologist and noted geomancer of the sixteenth century, described Two as "the number of man, who is called 'another.'" Two, spiritually speaking, represents a fall into materiality and divisiveness from the spiritual unity expressed by One. It is, for reasons that are obvious, the number of sex and was, accordingly, regarded with distaste by clerical philosophers.

Modern numerologists are more tolerant. Two is the Moon to One's Sun, they argue, and therefore, the embodiment of partnership. And indeed, birth number Two excels in relationships. Where One is headstrong and individualistic, Two is conciliatory and sensitive to others. Endowed with a strong, intuitive psychological understanding, Two is emotionally adept and intellectually reflective. Friendly, reliable, and peace-loving, Two has tendency to take care of other people that will result in many strong friendships. However, Two's generosity is often accompanied by timidity and—sometimes—wishy-washiness. A powerful inner critic doesn't help much either, and Two finds herself overburdened and overworked far too often. Two will have to learn self-assertion, but it will be an extremely useful lesson.

As a number of destiny, Two ensures that your tact, cooperation, and strong artistic sense will be called into play in your life. Your intuition may reach slightly creepy proportions—it's no fun being able to read other people's minds—and you will definitely work closely with others. Twos are usually well organized and analytical, and provided that stress levels are kept under control, they can be wonderful managers. Professionally, the only thing Twos have to fear is fear itself; panic and self-doubt can virtually paralyze a Two.

If Two is your number of destiny, it's clear that romantic partnership is of critical importance in your life. Twos make lovely, sympathetic mates, but here, too, you must steel yourself to assertiveness. Don't let your partner walk all over you; force yourself to communicate negative feelings as well as positive ones. Keep honest and you will avoid a resentment buildup. If you have a preponderance of Twos in your name (six or more), you may be bisexual.

From Aristotle onward, the concept of Three has been interchangeable with the concept of Many. It signifies multiplicity and fertility, the fullness of life. In the Western world, Three is a mystical number, representing spiritual synthesis after the Thesis of One (God) and the Antithesis of Two (Man). The folklore of Three is manifold: three wishes, three curses, and three blind mice all serve to remind us that Three is a magical force to be reckoned with.

The central characteristic of birth number Three is dynamic expression. Threes are whirlwinds of energy; they have a finger in every pie and a foot in every door. They love change, new ideas, and a swarm of people surrounding them. They are the most cheerful of all the birth numbers, radiating good humor and enthusiasm and joining in group activities at the drop of a hat. Though Three loves a crowd, he loves even more to be the center of the crowd. And certainly, birth number Three is attractive enough to have a large coterie of admirers. However, the dynamic energy and easygoing charm of Three are often accompanied by disorganization and impatience. Three's characteristic love of the easy life can obstruct his ability to finish tasks; in his effort to avoid the mundane, he may even resort to evasion and dishonesty. This applies to personal relationships as well: Three prefers the commencement pyrotechnics to the more quotidian sweetness of a long-term relationship.

The picture is sunnier when Three is the number of destiny, for there, the creativity and enthusiasm of three surmount the slippery and volatile aspects that reveal themselves when Three is the birth number. Here, too, the synthesizing aspect of Three comes into play: destiny Three combines existing concepts to form new ones, which is a valuable talent in any career. Impatience will be a professional liability, but destiny Three tends to be one of the luckiest numbers, pulling success out of disaster time and time again (Threes make alarmingly good gamblers). One instance of Three's luck is natural good health. Despite his extravagant lifestyle and predilection for rich food, Three remains vigorous and fit, much to the annoyance of Four, who thinks Threes should pay for their indulgences.

To Pythagoras and pretty much every philosopher of numbers who followed him, Four represented natural order. The four elements are but one expression of nature's inclination for tetrads. Perfect balance in material form is symbolized by Four.

Order is, accordingly, the great hallmark of birth number Four, the most practical, serious, and determined of all numbers. Four is hardworking and conservative, eschewing flights of fancy for facts. Four has no truck with wild schemes and daring innovation, but birth number Four is exactly the kind of person needed to make concepts concrete, to nail down the details, and to follow through on the plan. In fact, rhythm and routine are the very heartbeat of Four, which signifies not dullness but an inherent understanding of and sympathy for the natural world. Four's earthiness is best expressed in her constructive character; all that common sense and ability to work are ultimately quite creative and nurturing. (This aspect is reinforced if the Four is a woman.) The downside of all of this is, of course, narrow-mindedness, lack of imagination, and rigidity. Four will be better off if she does not demand that everyone be exactly like her. Likewise, a little humor is a good thing and should be cultivated.

As a number of destiny, Four indicates a tireless worker. Four prefers hands-on jobs that include lots of details, deadlines, and discipline. Four's pragmatism and determination ensure that any task undertaken will be competently concluded, but Four's talents are best applied to How? tasks rather than Why? tasks. Those with destiny Four need to be careful not to let their valuable determination degenerate into mere stubbornness.

In romantic matters, destiny Four makes an exceptionally loyal and devoted spouse. Regardless of gender, a Four is always very domestic. Order, comfort, and serenity in the home are necessary to Four's peace of mind, and because Four tends to want to make the arrangements herself, her partner usually gets to enjoy this domestic paradise without lifting a finger. These same loved ones must realize, however, that security is of paramount importance to Four; they must guard against giving Four any cause for anxiety, or they will bear the brunt of her anger. In love, as in most aspects of life, destiny Four should work on flexibility.

Historically, Five has been the number of marriage, as it combines the female Two with the male Three. Natural philosophers also observed that five was the most common structuring number in plants (e.g., five petals on a flower), which has given Five a reputation for earthiness and fertility. The combination of these two traditions has endowed Five with a bawdy, erotic flavor, which has seeped into its numerological significance.

Birth number Five is a robust, risk-taking, raucous character, full of fun and excitement. Unlike Three, who is motivated mostly by the desire to keep busy and know everything, Five plunges into adventures just for the fun of it. Passionate, exciting, gregarious, and incurably romantic, Fives have a million friends and only slightly fewer lovers, as well as a plethora of jobs, hobbies, locations, and bright ideas. Restless, curious, energetic, and enthusiastic, birth number Five is a kick to have around as long as you don't mind the mess. Unfortunately, birth number Five is often distracted from his goals by a new interest, which he leaps to pursue before he has concluded his last project. Alternately, and much more dangerously, Five becomes obsessed with a person or project and cannot break away from it even when he knows he should (Fives are prone to addiction).

As a number of destiny, Five ensures an adventurous life. The roller coaster of ups and downs is too alarming for most people, but destiny Five, with his love of variety, likes the wild ride. Professionally, Five is deeply competitive and is not above using his sexual charms to advance his career, but his own restlessness may jeopardize his job security. Destiny Five often gets the reputation for being a flirt or a seducer. Even when he's in the best of relationships, Five is rarely monogamous and never much of a devotee of the cozy domestic life.

The Pythagoreans regarded Six as the perfect number because its divisors (1, 2, and 3), when added together, produce Six itself. Though modern arithmeticians have found, at last count, twenty-three such perfect numbers, to the Pythagoreans, Six stood alone in perfection.

Reasonably enough, the quest for perfection is characteristic of birth number Six. But Six doesn't want perfection for the usual aggrandizing reasons; idealistic Six seeks to make the world a better, more harmonious place for everyone. Six supports, helps, and serves. She is nurturing, careful, competent, and loving. The most generous of the birth numbers, Six often devotes her life to helping others. Where Five gets a bang out of adventure, Six's greatest satisfaction comes from being needed and loved. Obviously, this sacrificial role has a negative aspect—several, in fact. First, it tips all too easily into a penchant for martyrdom, which *is* self-aggrandizing. Second, the Ones, Threes, Fives, and Eights to whom Six gives so much are likely to be unappreciative, even cavalier, about Six's devotion, which disappoints Six mightily. Most of the world simply isn't perfectible, and Sixes are often sad. Third and finally, Six will benefit from pacing herself; discretion—

and even a little bit of selfishness—is the better part of valor and may keep Six from exhaustion and despair.

Every boss in the world wants a destiny Six as an employee. Hardworking, creative, loyal, and serene, these are the people who keep everything and everyone working smoothly. Not only is destiny Six industrious, she is also an innovator. Good ideas come to her, and then she turns them into functioning systems. Six is a natural teacher and is especially well adapted to work in the caring professions. Though generally sympathetic and tolerant, Six occasionally overdoes the schemes for the improvement of others or grows too rigid in her regulations and conventions. As a romantic partner, Six is loving and loyal; she loves children and makes a wonderful parent.

Seven is always a mystical number, not only in the Western European tradition but in civilizations as diverse as contemporary China, ancient Babylon, pre-Columbian America, and medieval Persia. In virtually every tradition, Seven signifies the mysteries of the spirit. The Pythagoreans held that Seven was the number of crisis, but whether the interpretation is positive or negative, Seven has ever been a number of great power.

It makes sense then, that those born under the influence of Seven are spiritual and intellectual seekers. They are reflective, thoughtful, serious, and cerebral. Deeply curious, birth number Seven questions and analyzes everything he encounters; he is capable of understanding complex and arcane ideas, and he loves intellectual challenges of all

. . . of the famous:

Fred Astaire	6
Groucho Marx	3
Kate Winslet	1
Jacques Tati	1
e.e. cummings	1
Oscar Wilde	8
Lee Harvey Oswald	5
Sarah Bernhardt	4
Bill Gates	4
Martin Scorsese	3
Jimi Hendrix	4
Maria Callas	2
Diego Rivera	7
Ludwig van Beethoven	7
Josef Stalin	4
Tiger Woods	1
Virginia Woolf	9
Abraham Lincoln	5
Michael Jordan	7
Jackie Chan	3
Adolf Hitler	5
William Shakespeare	7
Ho Chi Minh	6
Sigmund Freud	4
John Paul II	8
Prince William	2
Franz Kafka	3
Frederico Fellini	6
Jacqueline Kennedy Onassis	2
Martha Stewart	8
Al Capone	9
Madonna	2
Mary Shelley	8
Sid Caesar	4
Linda Hamilton	2

kinds. These are the philosophers, the scholars, and the scientists who push the world forward with their discoveries. The difficulty for Seven lies in relationships. Though elegant, birth number Seven is cool and aloof. His tendency to dwell in the realms of thought makes him seem somber or out of touch. Seven is rarely aware of the impression he gives; in fact, he has a hard time using his analytical ability to understand himself or other people. Shy Seven needs lots of peace and quiet, but he should make an effort to have some sort of social life, because he does gain pleasure from conversation and debate with his intellectual peers.

Destiny Seven is a bit easier to get along with, particularly when combined with a Five or Six birth number. Destiny Seven affects the choice and manner of working and loving but may leave the personality relatively untouched by Sevenish coolness. His sharp intellect, energetic curiosity, and ability to concentrate make destiny Seven an important contributor in his field, and his high personal standards and self-esteem ensure independence, honesty, and scrupulous attention to detail. Destiny Seven's failing tends to be arrogance: fully aware of his superiority, he may succumb to the error of treating other people dismissively. Another negative trait is grandiosity, derived from the same overestimation of his own abilities. This can lead destiny Seven to surround himself with an air of secrecy that is most annoying.

Destiny Seven is not to the type for affairs or philandering, and in long-term relationships, he must find a partner who excites him intellectually as well as sexually. In general, Seven is not the most sexually oriented of numbers, and we often find that the entire impulse has been converted into a spiritual one. Unsurprisingly, as parents Sevens are somewhat remote, and they are often more interested in their child's intellectual development than in his or her emotional life.

Albrecht Durer, Melencolia I, 1514. In this odd scene, a gloom-stricken and earthbound angel glares at a polyhedron, while an equally mournful cherub slumps beside her. About them are scattered the implements of geometry, a subject that could drive any thinking angel to melancholy. The true theme of the work is the despair caused by the limits of human understanding. In the prevailing medical philosophy of the day, such despair—otherwise known as melancholy—was attributed to the influence of Saturn. The antidote can be seen in the curious square that appears almost directly over the angel's head. This is a magic square, a potent numerological talisman. Each of the numbers in the square may appear only once, yet the verticals, horizontals, and long diagonals must add up to the same number. The square pictured here is the square of Jupiter; all the rows add up to thirty-four, and it provides its bearer with the force and energy to combat Saturnine malaise.

Less loaded with lore than Seven, Eight was the subject of much mathematical scrutiny in antiquity, as it yields several lovely algebraic formulas. The early Greeks, for example, were quite taken with the discovery that when squared, every odd number above one produces a multiple of eight plus one (e.g., 7 squared equals 49 equals $[6 \times 8] + 1$). Mathematical interest aside, Eight was designated as the number of regeneration and transcendence. After the spheres of the seven planets, ancient philosophers postulated an eighth sphere of the gods. Later, Christ's appearance to Thomas on the eighth day imbued the number with the spirit of renewal.

Numerologically, birth number Eight is an altogether more worldly creature than the heritage of the number would suggest. Eight is a number of power; she is decisive, masterful, organized, and highly directed. A born leader, she assesses people quickly—and usually correctly—and acts swiftly. As a result of all these traits, birth number Eight is almost inevitably successful in anything she undertakes. But however much Eight appears to be working for her own advancement, she is, instead, almost always seeking to restore or regain balance and reason with her labor. Her motives are really much more moral than they appear, and with her appalling stores of energy and fierce determination, birth number Eight will force the world (or her world, anyway) to become a better place. Despite Eight's will of steel and assertive character, she is generally admired by all and loved by plenty because of her warmth and humor. In the best-case scenario, Eight is an honest laborer for justice, but an Eight gone to extremes can become power-mad.

If Eight is your number of destiny, the situation is touchier. Destiny Eight is an intense character. Though she is still decisive and authoritative, she is less sure of herself and her goals than birth number Eight. The tension between opposites will play a larger role in her life: material versus spiritual goals, success versus failure, destruction versus creation—these dyads will be a source of concern and confusion for destiny Eight. This is not to say that destiny Eight will dither about; no, Eight will always make major decisions with dispatch and elan. But she may look back on some of these snap decisions with regret, for as she moves through life, and her spiritual mission becomes clearer to her, the goals of her youth will seem less and less compelling.

In love, as in all things, destiny Eight is a leader. Forceful, ardent, and romantic, Eight will undoubtedly be the instigator of her relationships. Eight's bluntness can sometimes be a liability, and her intolerance of weakness, chaos, or foolishness makes her a rather doughty companion, but Eight's powerful character and lively mind make her ultimately lovable.

Nine is representative of universality. All numbers, according to the Greeks, are contained in Nine, and it is therefore imbued with all their qualities. Christian exegetes had mixed feelings about Nine: for some, it was the number of sorrow, for others, it was the number of the magnified Trinity.

Birth number Nine is considered by numerologists to be the most fully evolved of all the numbers (though there are a few holdouts for Twenty-two), and Nines usually live up to the designation. Unlike birth number Seven, who is also endowed with uncommon perceptiveness and intellectual acuity, birth number Nine has remarkable charisma and emotional intuition. Others will be drawn to Nine, and for that reason, his wisdom can truly make a difference. Though Nine usually seems slightly detached—not cold, but somewhat distant—as a result of his involvement with spiritual and moral goals, he is nonetheless truly sympathetic and humanitarian. Not ambitious for his own sake, Nine is an idealist and a tireless worker for the fulfillment of his dreams. Generous, tolerant, and altruistic, birth number Nine may lack common sense, but he never lacks heart. Pinning him down to a schedule or a system is probably an exercise in frustration, for despite his best intentions, Nine is chronically disorganized. This is indicative of his greatest trouble: the inability to see the trees for the forest. Adept at dealing with major issues, Nine tends to ignore the minor ones until they threaten to overtake his life.

Destiny Nine lives an equally intense existence. His imagination, morality, and artistic sense make him a creative force in whatever profession he chooses, but destiny Nine most often dedicates his life to humanitarian causes, artistic movements, political action, or spiritual development. He is always an instigator of change. However, Nine needs to be wary about what he devotes himself to; a tendency to gullibility is his downfall. Equally problematic is a disposition toward depression; though Nine probably has a greater effect on his world than most people, he often feels as though he has not accomplished enough. Setbacks alarm him unduly, and he may slide into despondency at the drop of a hat.

Destiny Nine's passion and commitment make him a fine candidate for long-term relationships. Nine does well with difficult people, but even the most easygoing partner may be driven mad by Nine's dreaminess and disorganization. Nines should never pair up with Sixes or Fours.

MASTER NUMBERS

It is wise to remember that the master numbers are misnamed. Their recipients are especially perceptive and talented, but they are also especially fraught. Their lives are full of vigorous battles, ending sometimes in triumph, sometimes in defeat. They are the embodiment of the saying "From him to whom much has been given, much will be exacted."

Birth number Eleven is the great artist of the numbers. Compelled by a vibrant aesthetic sense and an overwhelming need to express herself, Eleven throws herself into her work. A wild imagination fuels her creativity, and with her powerful intuition, Eleven can become an aesthetic trendsetter. Discriminating and acute within her field, Eleven must learn to respect the expertise of others and the value of different ways of life. On a more alarming level, Elevens account for most of the world's population of fanatics. Those intense powers of concentration are a liability as well as an ability, and Eleven should try to lighten up and broaden her horizons on occasion.

As a number of destiny, Eleven can go either way. Her devotion to her calling may be rewarding, or it may be utterly frustrating. This does not refer to money. Material gain is not something destiny Eleven cares about: success is being understood; failure is the inability to make others see her vision. Obviously, destiny Eleven is no good at all in professions that require attention to mundane detail, but she shines in careers that make use of her creativity and intuition.

Destiny Eleven has a very dramatic love life; her passionate character demands lots of attention, and her artistic sense demands lots of expression. As a result, her affairs are vivid and various. Eleven is a particularly feminine number; male Elevens will be expressive and romantic and much prized by their partners.

Birth number Twenty-two has just as many ideals as Eleven, but he is no idealist. Like the Four that would be its reduced number, Twenty-two is eminently competent, practical, and hardworking. The combination of vision and skill is a powerful one, and Twenty-two is destined (or doomed) to achieve a good deal in his lifetime. Achievement will be the theme of his life, for he keeps moving forward to conquer new lands, never stopping to acknowledge what he has wrought or, God forbid, put his feet up for minute. Twenty-two does not labor for himself, either; his quick intelligence, superior logical ability, and psychological acuity are matched by a highly developed moral sense that guarantees that he will devote himself to the greater good. Generosity of spirit is the great virtue of Twenty-two, but it has a price. Twenty-two is particularly liable to exhaustion and depression; the former, obviously, from overwork; the latter from the realization that the world is a fairly loathsome place.

Twenty-two must remember that taking care of himself is not an indulgence.

This high-level of achievement holds true for Twenty-two as a number of destiny as well. Organized, highly skilled, and smart (though not intellectual), destiny Twenty-two makes an excellent manager in a variety of professions. If destiny Twenty-two has a mission (perhaps through a birth number of Seven or Nine) about which he is truly passionate, he can be an inspired leader. Great devotion to ideals is incipient in destiny Twenty-two, though he lacks the inborn spiritual sense of birth number Twenty-two, which makes his life a little easier. Without a higher purpose, destiny Twenty-two may become narrow-minded, a stickler for detail, which is a real waste, so he should attempt to find a good cause early in life in order to stay vital.

A committed and respectful partner, destiny Twenty-two may have some problems with intimacy, arising primarily because he is hesitant to "burden" others with his problems. A secure relationship is very important to destiny Twenty-two.

A FEW OTHER CALCULATIONS

The birth number and the number of destiny are not the only significant numbers that your name and birth date can yield. Among the other possibilities are the personal year and month and your challenge number.

For those who found numerological counting too taxing, the Mystic Crystal offered an easy solution. Unfortunately, the key to the meaning of the ensuing Fate Numbers has disappeared in the sands of time.

It's all very well to plumb the depths of your character, but for good old-fashioned fortune-telling, the personal year is much more salient. To learn your destiny in the coming year (or any other year, for that matter), simply add up the month and day of your birth (as you would in calculating your birth number) and then add to the digits of the year in question. This will reduce to a number that will embody the qualities of the year for you. Compare the characteristics of your birth number with those of the coming year and you'll find your instructions. For example, a birth number Seven should probably hunker down in a personal year Four. The practical, rigid aspects of Four will be constraining to the spiritual, free-thinking Seven. However, a personal year Four

The "Mystical Wheel of Pythagoras" is from Raphael's Witch, a nineteenth-century ancestor of the drugstore astrology guide. Not exactly a numerological tool, the Mystical Wheel of Pythagoras was more like an oracle: a list of questions was associated with a list of numbers, which in turn provided the answer. Apparently, Raphael was able to conjure up angels, gnomes, Vesuvius, and "The Enchantress of the Waters" with his divinatory powers.

may also be seen as an opportunity for Seven to get more efficient and down-to-earth.

To learn about a specific month in a personal year, simply add the number of the month to the personal year number and reduce it to a single digit. If, for example, your personal year is Nine (birth number Seven + year 2000), and you want to know what will befall you in October, 2000, you must add 9 + 1 + 0 equals 10 equals a One personal month. The relationship between the personal year number and the personal month number is the one to watch here (i.e., your birth number is not terribly important with regard to personal months). For instance, a Two personal month in the midst of a Seven personal year is a time to cultivate your intuition, learn from others, and wait patiently, but it is absolutely not the time to pick a fight with someone.

CHALLENGE NUMBER

Though they are generally crystal clear to others, our greatest failings or weaknesses are often a mystery to us. Your challenge number, derived from your whole name, shows the characteristics that are most likely to cause you trouble or exasperate those you love. Simply count the letters of your name and reduce the total to a single number.

One: The assertiveness and bravado of One are taken to extremes of bossiness, bombast, and belligerence.

Two: The relational skills and sensitivity of Two degenerate into toadying, indecision, and slyness.

Three: The vigor and creativity of Three slide into self-aggrandizement and dissipation. Challenge number Three may indicate an inability to finish projects.

Four: Practicality and competence give way to self-righteousness and disparagement of others.

Five: Dynamic, daring Five becomes excessive and unstable as a challenge number. Those with challenge Five may be predisposed to addiction.

Six: The helpfulness and devotion to service that Six displays turns into nosiness and gossiping when Six is a challenge number. Occasionally, challenge Six is expressed as an inability to make commitments or handle responsibility.

Seven: Seven's focus on the mental and spiritual planes assumes an unhealthy rigidity as a challenge number. Overly cerebral and cold, those with challenge number Seven have social problems.

Eight: While birth number Eight is powerful and clear-headed, challenge number Eight is manipulative and power-hungry.

Nine: Even challenge Nines are well-intentioned. They are just too impractical and consumed with their ideals to get anything accomplished.

Some numerologists permit master challenge numbers:

Eleven: The visionary Eleven becomes impersonal and bitter as a challenge number.

Twenty-two: High achiever Twenty-two becomes a compulsive worker and drudge as a challenge number.

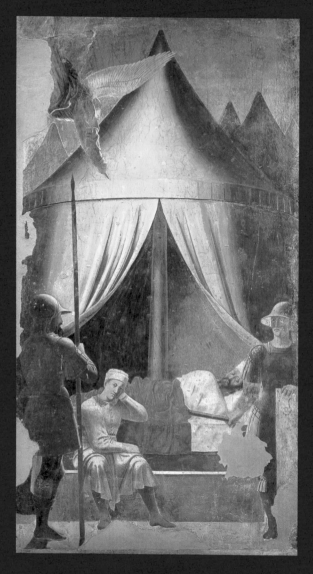

Perhaps the most famous prophetic dream in history was that bestowed upon Constantine in 312 as he prepared to invade Rome and claim the throne of Emperor Maxentius. The night before the great battle, an angel appeared in Constantine's dreams bearing the Chi-Rho monogram of Christ. "By this conquer," directed the angel. Accordingly, Constantine's men went into combat with the emblem on their shields, and Maxentius obligingly made the dumbest military move of his life (never fight with your back to a river). Thunderstruck, Constantine called his advisers together and inquired which god was represented by the sign. Finding that it was the symbol of Christ, Constantine promptly converted, and with him, Europe. Piero's depiction of the event is, incidentally, the first rendering of a night scene in the history of Western art. Piero della Francesca, The Dream of Constantine, *from* The Legend of the True Cross, *fifteenth century.*

ONEIROMANCY
or Dream Interpretation

God created sleep to this end only, that we should attain the
insights we cannot attain when our soul is joined to the body . . .
Rabbi Elijah of Vilna

The prophetic dream is a staple of human history. Ancient civilizations as diverse as those of Egypt, Assyria, and Greece held the view that dreams offer divine guidance and recognized that the gods had cloaked their messages in perplexing images and events that required a professional translator. The oneiromancer, or dream reader, was therefore a highly esteemed variety of fortune-teller in most early cultures. The Greeks, always forward-thinking, combined the functions of a medical doctor and an oneiromancer in their temples to Asclepius, the god of medicine. There, the sickly would come to bathe and to pray, but chiefly to sleep and so receive a house call from Asclepius in the form of a dream. The god might prescribe a remedy or he might actually treat the ailment himself, sometimes going so far as to remove the afflicted body part and replace it with a new one in the night. This dream medicine was widely practiced and profoundly believed; it seems to have been the rare patient who failed to dream of Asclepius as required.

The Bible abounds with prophetic dreams, which usually provide some worthy dream interpreter with the opportunity for spiritual (and professional) recognition. Pharaoh, for instance, is stymied by his dream of seven nice plump cows devoured by seven skinny cows and seven succulent ears of corn consumed by seven withered ears. Joseph, modestly giving the credit to God, says the dream foretells seven years of plenty followed by seven years of famine. Joseph recommends that Pharaoh quickly hire an overseer to store grain against the seven lean years; Pharaoh wisely appoints Joseph to this task, and everyone lives happily ever after (sort of).

Dream interpreters enjoyed a privileged position in the Western world for about three and half thousand years. Despite some vagaries of fashion, dreams were regarded fairly steadily as messages whose codes only a dream interpreter could break. Imagine the tantalizing position of the populace—they knew that each dream was a piece of personal advice from God, but it was advice given in another language. Because actual human oneiromancers were an expensive proposition, dream manuals became more and more popular as more and more people learned to read. The first of these manuals was the famous sixteenth-century work entitled *La Physiognomie des songes et visions fantastiques des personnes*, which offered highly efficient interpretations of a variety of dreams: "To dream you are a tree means illness." "To dream you eat cheese means profit." Etcetera.

Though the educated few had for centuries questioned such mechanistic one-to-one correlations between dream and event, the premise—that dreams foretold the future—had a considerable purchase on the Western imagination; up until the nineteenth century, there was no other particularly convincing explanation for the strange visitations we all experience at night. Throughout the 1800s, there were grumblings and mumblings about the physical and mental sources of dreams, but it was Sigmund Freud's publication of the *Interpretation of Dreams* in 1900 that let the cat out of the bag with finality. His discoveries were both deflating and thrilling: the bad news was that dreams, with their peculiar mixture of the familiar and the irrational, were the products of our own unconscious mind, rather than divine messages. The good news was that dreams, once interpreted, could unlock the mysteries of our psyches.

To Freud, dreams were "the royal road to the unconscious." With the goal of lingering in the road, excavating dream symbols for clues to self-understanding, we can use Freud's map of the mind to find our way. This map is divided into two countries: that of the conscious and that of the unconscious. The realm of the conscious is ruled by the ego and that evil chief of police, the superego. It is here that most of our activities are performed as ordered by our ideas and hopes about ourselves. The unconscious, on the other hand, is a realm of chaos. Here, primordial instincts—desires, fears, rage—struggle for expression and gratification. These two realms are locked in eternal battle. Usually, the unconscious—and its unrepentant ruler, the id—is vanquished by the conscious, which is why we don't run around killing each other all the time. However, the unconscious is indefatigable as well as wily, so, like an alligator in the sewer, it erupts at night, while our poor beleaguered consciousness is resting. This is what our dreams are: the fantasies of our id. And their function is to release and resolve the energies of the unconscious mind so that they don't explode out of our heads during waking hours. Why, then, do we have some dreams that seem so normal? How can my id be gratified by a dream in which I iron a shirt? This is precisely where interpretation begins: such is the disgusting and despicable nature of our unconscious instincts that to dream of them directly would wake us up, along with the ego and the superego. Slyly, the unconscious cloaks its true motives under a heavy disguise, and this is the source of the difference between manifest and latent dream content. The former is the often illogical or at least nonsequiturial story of the dream, and the latter is what lurks just beneath the surface and requires the intelligent archaeologist to find the symbolic value in the crazy plot, characters, and structure of that story.

The troubled dreamer floats in an unhappy sea of fears; the usual monsters are joined by a creeping triumvirate of ladies' gloves. Max Klinger, Ein Handschuh (A Glove), *1881.*

Obviously, the unconscious is faced with a difficult task. It must use dreams to present its information to the conscious mind, but it must render that information innocuous enough to evade the censor of the dreamer, who will wake up—and thereby return the unconscious to its dungeon—if the dreams are too alarming. Like every other beast, the unconscious is committed to its own survival, and like every other beast, it has developed a number of tricks in order to make that survival more likely. One of the forms of protective coloring that it has adopted is condensation, in which a number of elements are fused into one symbol. Usually the elements are linked by their similar emotional positions in the dreamer's life; for example, when your mother and your first-grade teacher are combined in the same dream character, you are probably dealing with the issues of authority embodied by both of them. Another technique of the unconscious mind is displacement, in which one thing is represented by another. This device works by association, often visual or phonetic association, rather than logical connections. To take a particularly shopworn and Freudian example, an unsheathed sword dangling about in a dream is a displaced image for a penis. What is surprising about displacement is how often the same elements symbolize the same thing to different dreamers. This universality may be the source of the earlier dream handbooks, and it will be the source of our directory of dream symbols that follows.

In the language of dreams, simultaneity, contiguity, transformation, and unity are the grammar. The craziness and utter illogic of dreams are simply further methods by which the unconscious shields itself from the censor. Disparate dream elements are connected; they just aren't connected in the temporal way that we understand best. In the world of dreams, links between ideas are indicated by the devices of simultaneity,

RETURN TO THE FUTURE:

J. W. DUNNE'S DREAM THEORY

Like a woolly mammoth in Central Park, British physicist J. W. Dunne advanced a theory of precognitive dreams in 1927. However, Dunne was no throwback; his belief that dreams foretold the future was based not on magical thinking but on a complicated notion of time (something to do with a serial universe). Precognitive dreams were to Dunne merely a proof of his time theory, but he nonetheless offered detailed instructions for finding the future in dreams. The chief problem, he noted with admirable stolidness, was remembering dreams at all. The second problem was the propensity of weak minds to focus on the major event of the dream and neglect the details. Third, he warned sternly, people wanted their precognition to be exciting, and it was rarely so. Forging onward, Dunne explains that the dreamer must, immediately upon waking, before he opens his eyes, write down the rapidly vanishing dream. Even if this amounts to just one element, he wrote, "fix your attention on a single incident and to try to remember its details." This, he posited, will lead to further memories of the larger dream. The more you amplify a dream, the more likely you are to note a dream image that will appear in your future waking life. Dunne asserted that if you keep such a record of your dreams for several weeks, you are bound to find yourself experiencing something of which you had previously only dreamed. He offered several examples from his own experience—all terrifically dull—and a few from those of his friends, including his cousin, who dreamt of a German lady with an unattractive hairdo and then encountered just such a German lady with just such a hairdo.

In 1932, Theodore Besterman, an investigator for the Society for Psychical Research, published *An Inquiry into Precognitive Dreams,* a study of Dunne's dream theory. Taking as his rats twenty-two Oxford undergraduates, Besterman compiled statistics on their precognitive dreams. "Partly owing to the incidence of examinations," the twenty-two students produced a total of only 143 dreams. Ten of the students denied any precognitive dreams whatever. The remaining twelve, who were responsible for 113 dreams, claimed 32 precognitive dreams. Despite this wealth of precognition, Besterman found the evidence inconclusive, and Dunne's theory retreated to the halls of the obscure. I, however, have found Dunne's claims justified; various dream details have turned up in "real" life after their dream appearance. Since the most spectacular was a green bench that played a meager role in an especially exciting sex dream and then, drably enough, turned up in a bakery, I have decided that there is no percentage in precognition and recommend that the first few moments of awakening be spent in more highly developed contemplation.

when things are presented together; contiguity, when things are presented in sequence; transformation, when one thing turns into another; and unity, when one thing resembles or evokes the response of another. Unity is the vaguest of the techniques but by far the most pervasive; it includes such standard expressions as "I was in my house, but it wasn't really my house, it was the office I work in."

Freud's goal, identical to that of oneiromancers throughout the ages, was to translate the dream into the language of the dreamer. We would all be a lot better off—more integrated, more sane—if the whispers of the unconscious mind could be heard by the consciousness, Freud contended. An unconscious without an audience is a thwarted unconscious, and a thwarted unconscious is more likely to rise up in strange ways against its warden, the conscious mind.

But how, you might well ask, can Freud or anyone else translate a dream? The images themselves, and even more, their values, seem so entirely personal as to make an interpretation impossible. It is true that the significance of some dream elements varies wildly with each dreamer; a dream of one's uncle, for instance, has a value that depends entirely on the relationship with the uncle. However, there are certain dream events and elements that have a consistent meaning across the range of dreamers. Although particular experience may endow an element with a meaning that supersedes its usual significance, it is a rare dreamer who has created an entirely individual set of symbols. According to the eminent Swiss psychologist Carl Gustav Jung, some themes and motifs appear in nearly every culture; these archetypes, as he called them, occur in symbol systems, myths, and dreams throughout the world, bearing similar meanings and values. This consistency—of incidence and import—led Jung to posit a collective unconscious, which you may picture as a large pool of inherited mind that contains these recurring ideas and themes. Just as our instincts for survival are transmitted genetically, so is our collection of archetypes an inborn phenomenon.

The significance of archetypes in relation to dreams is clear: they almost always mean the same thing, no matter who dreams them. But, just as clearly, we don't dream in archetypes all the time. Sometimes we just dream about cleaning the house. Let us, therefore, divide dreams into three types. Type A dreams are the least significant and the most common. They concern daily life and details and seem to be born of the conscious mind rather than the unconscious. The images and events of these dreams are usually quite clear but evoke little response from the dreamer. These dreams are difficult to interpret because the material is quite specific to the dreamer, but luckily, few people care to have these dreams read.

Like the Type A dream, the Type B dream contains material particular to dreamer, but it is drawn from the richer realms of the unconscious, with its suppressed memories and emotions, latent fears and desires. Although the characters and settings of these dreams will be specific to the dreamer's experience, these dreams' themes—anxiety, lust, and revenge—are nearly universal. Type B dreams are really the most interesting to interpret, for it is here that the unconscious does its fanciest footwork to evade

ARCHETYPES

Upon scrutiny, a being in a dream may prove to have an archetypal character. The following are some of the usual suspects:

THE ANIMA/ANIMUS: The Anima is the feminine aspect of a male dreamer, the embodiment of his intuition and caretaking abilities. Likewise, the Animus represents the masculine aspect of the female dreamer, her vigor and perseverance. Thus, a woman's dream of an admirably adventurous man may be about her own bravery.

THE MOTHER: This is not a comforting mother, but the embodiment of implacable nature. Male terror in the face of the mystery of fertility gives rise to the character of the devouring mother.

THE SHADOW: This dark figure holds all the aspects of your personality that your consciousness can't tolerate. The Shadow may appear in your dreams as another self or as a separate being who causes trouble.

THE TRICKSTER: Instinctual, uninhibited, and immature, the Trickster's function is to defy the rules and obtain gratification at the expense of others.

THE WISE ELDER: Disguised in dreams as a witch, magician, priest, teacher, or other authority figure, the wise old woman or man is a guide to the realization of your goals.

censorship, and, correspondingly, it is here that we find the real revelations about the hidden urges and forces in our characters.

The Type C dream, which Jung called "the grand dream," is rare—some people never have one. These dreams consist almost exclusively of material drawn from the collective unconscious and have little to do with the dreamer's daily life. They are, rather, warnings or messages about where the dreamer is in the larger journey. In a certain way, grand dreams are prophetic dreams, but instead of revealing the future, they reveal the past. One way to recognize a grand dream is by the appearance in it of archetypal figures such as the Anima, the Animus, the Shadow, and the Trickster, which are discussed above.

Obviously, Type B and C dreams lend themselves to interpretation much more docilely than do Type A dreams, but every would-be oneiromancer must be aware of the limitations of his art. True dream interpretation requires an in-depth knowledge of the dreamer's life; you cannot hope to merely apply the given meaning to the dream element at hand and arrive at a real interpretation. After hearing your subject recount his or her dream, your first question must be "What do you think it means?" You must pay close attention to the dreamer's description of the emotional tone of the dream,

राजसूयधनप्राप्तिः तथामित्रसमागमं दाराग्रहार्थसंत्व
कपीतेनविनिर्दिशेत्

This exquisite eighteenth-century watercolor comes from an Indian book of dreams illustrated by an anonymous Rajput artist.

the significance of the characters, and the sources of the setting. These elements are inevitably particular to your dreamer, but within every dream there are components with specieswide meanings, just as there are genres of dream that almost everyone has. The Dream Guide, which follows, will list the common expressions of the major dream themes as well as symbols related to those themes.

THE DREAM GUIDE

The dreams included in this guide are the kind that almost everyone has at one point or another. Whether or not we recognize what they are trying to tell us is another matter, and this is the purpose of the guide. The anxiety, desire, and anger that are expressed in dreams are all too often dismissed rather than integrated into our character, and, as we all well know, an ignored emotion simply grows stronger and meaner. This guide will give you a listing of dream representations of the emotional states; when using it, bear in mind, first, that there are zillions of other ways in which the emotions make their appearances in dreams, and, second, that the id—the source of all these dream denizens—is not a benign force. If there seems to be an excess of unpleasant news emanating from your dreams, this is because the elemental human character is nasty—brutal, bad-tempered, and selfish. Prettiness and pleasantries are inventions of the conscious mind.

ANXIETY

The School Dream: It's the first day of school, and you can't find your classroom. Fruitlessly, you search through empty halls, knowing that everyone else is already seated at their desks. Alternately, it is the end of the term, and you have suddenly realized that you forgot about one of your classes: now you have to take the final exam without knowing anything.

The Center Cannot Hold: You are responsible for a collection of things, usually small living things such as such as babies or kittens that wander off in all directions, try as you might to keep them together.

The Dream of Nakedness: Your clothes begin to slip off your body in some public place, though you clutch after them. Similarly, you may appear in front of some authoritative group with crucial garments missing.

FEAR

Distinct from anxiety, which is related to the failure to do what we believe we should be able to do, true fear presents us with threats that we know will overpower us.

Paralysis: You are being assaulted by a terrifying presence and yet you cannot scream. Likewise, you are being pursued by a vile being, but your legs are like sausages, thick and slow, and they crumple beneath you.

The Tightening Tunnel: You are walking through an enclosed space that shrinks as

A thirty-year old woman had this dream:

So, my sister and I are walking along the banks of a clear stream. We begin high up on the bank, where the light brown ground is sand made of fine pebbles. It's slippery; several times we stumble, but without falling outright. Overhead, the stream is bordered on both sides by a lovely stand of tall, open-branched trees. As we move down closer to the stream, the pebbles underfoot grow larger, until at the edge of the stream they're about one inch wide. They are a beautiful gray; the stream is crystal clear. Beneath the water, the rocks are as big as a hand. My sister wades in, but I stay on shore. The rocks in the stream tickle my feet and are too difficult to walk on. Later, she and I stand beside the stream. She holds a small, pale, spotted snake, very beautiful. She's pleased with it, but I suddenly see venom dripping from the fangs. I say to her, "Just do as I say. Put the snake on the ground and step slowly to the side, like this." She does, and just as it hits the ground, it strikes—but she is already out of the way. The snake slithers away, hissing.

The whole thing is about fear—probably justified—of delving into the unconscious, with particular emphasis on the family and childhood, since you are with your sister. See, the trees are beautiful, up is beautiful, the surface of the water is beautiful; everything that is not in the water is beautiful (remember, water is the unconscious). You are happy walking along the fine sand, looking at all this sparkle, *but* the way becomes slippery and impossible to negotiate as you get closer to the deep memories. In fact, you say that the rocks "tickle," which is unlikely and probably denotes a tendency toward euphemism and wordplay as a defense against emotional chaos. You choose—and remember, it's a choice—to stay upon the shore, but you watch your sister go in, that is, pursue the discomfort you could not tolerate yourself. In some way, she is doing it for you, because what does she bring back to you but the symbol of killer information itself (this specific snake is the old snake wisdom rather than a nasty penis snake), which she doesn't even realize is poisonous. You basically tell her to accept without questioning your instruction to abandon the information she has obtained from her unconscious; you urge her to join you in safety, and she does. But bear in mind that since she's the snake handler, she has the power to knock you unconscious, even though she chooses not to do it. She's the message bearer, and you are frightened of what she is capable of unleashing. And rightly so, I expect.

A forty-year-old man told this dream:

I'm eating this sandwich and I'm really enjoying it, but even as I'm chewing, I'm thinking to myself: it will be okay as long as I don't look at it. And I don't, for a long time, but I'm getting more and more nervous about what kind of sandwich it is. Finally, I can't help it and I look in between the bread: it's spiders. I feel really sick.

It sure sounds as though you're contemplating a romantic relationship, or perhaps you've just begun one. Spiders are almost exclusively symbolic of women, particularly to male dreamers, who inevitably (and somewhat tediously) associate the spider's web with the smothering coils of domesticity in which they see themselves writhing while the female approaches to suck the very life blood from them. Clearly, you have been hungry for love—such a tasty sandwich betrays a certain appetite—but you would like to think of your current dalliance as casual, romantic fast food. Your nerves, however, know better; you find that you must inspect your relationship more closely. And what you see terrifies you. You are unprepared for real commitment.

This illustration from a nineteenth-century nature book entitled World of Wonders *aptly displays the subject's feeling about women, as embodied by spiders. He is, of course, the bird.*

you progress, forcing you first to crouch, then to crawl, and then to heave yourself along on your belly. You cannot go back, and yet you know that you will soon suffocate (some experts believe this dream to be a relic of the birth experience).

The Free Fall: You are upon a great height (usually a structure such as an office building or bridge) and you remind yourself to be careful, that you could fall. Despite all your precautions, you lose control and begin hurtling toward Earth. Right before you wake up, you realize with sickening clarity that you're about to hit the ground.

Proliferation: In this particularly nasty dream scenario, you're going about your business when you suddenly notice that the people (or animals) that surround you look strange. Upon closer inspection, it's clear that parts of their bodies are duplicating. Since your body remains normal, you realize that the others will soon turn on you (the unconscious is a devout paranoid).

The Cassandra Dream: You, and you alone, are aware of an impending disaster— perhaps you can even see the approaching wall of water or the great roll of earth—and as you frantically attempt to tell others, they ignore you, or they can't seem to hear you, or they don't believe you.

A pregnant woman had the following dream:

I'm at a ruined church—it looks like York Cathedral or something—where an enormous funeral is taking place. In fact, it seems like multiple funerals are taking place: there are several groups of mourners, all dressed in beautiful party clothes. Far in the distance, I see a woman I know, but I can only identify her by her beautiful, curly red hair, which glints in the sun. Quickly it begins to seem that everywhere I look, her hair appears, which is kind of scary. I want to escape from her hair, and I find myself hiding in one of the church's burned-out chimneys.

We are dealing with some very powerful fears about pregnancy and body image here. As we know, all buildings are stand-ins for relationships. Since you are not particularly religious, the church is probably a symbol for your marriage, as that is the only ceremony of your life that happened in a church. That the church is ruined and that funerals are taking place there indicate your perception that your marriage is dead. Now why should this be so? Your dream obligingly provides the answer in the glinting red hair that pervades the scene: sexuality. Since it is not your hair, but another's, we may deduce that you feel that others—not you—are sexually powerful. You find this scary and you want to hide, not just within the ruins of your marriage but in a burned-out chimney, which is a figure for female genitalia. Interestingly, by doing this, you're putting yourself in the position of your baby, showing that in some way you wish to be reborn by giving birth.

LUST AND DESIRE

The Hair, Cut: Oddly enough, hair is a potent symbol of sexual power. To dream of having your hair cut signifies a wish to submit to the sexual desires of another (beware of automatically assuming that the focus of this desire is the dream barber). Cutting someone else's hair signals a wish to obtain power over another in sexual matters.

The Impossible Partner: If you dream of an erotic encounter with a completely inappropriate partner, it can mean one of three things. The first is that the dream partner is a canard, a stand-in for someone ever so much more threatening whom you truly desire. Second, if you are heterosexual, and your dream encounter is homosexual (or vice versa), the dream is the vehicle for expressing your minor chord sexuality, which is repressed by the conscious mind. Third, some dream experts believe that everyone who appears in your dreams is a version of yourself, so your dream partner may simply signify your assessment of your own sexual charms.

Sex Symbols: On occasion your unconscious daintily prefers to avoid overt sexuality in its dream factory. As an alternative, it employs a variety of ringers. You are actually dreaming of sex when you dream of horseback riding; most flowers (particularly

orchids); purses (closed or open or worrisome); gloves and stockings; swords (duh); snakes (although snakes are also a classic symbol of wisdom); cudgels, sticks, and clubs (duh, again); caves; and money.

SELF-DOUBT

These dreams tend to occur when you have made a faux pas or a feeble decision. Often, they signal anxiety about others' assessment of you, as well as self-disgust.

The Spinning Car: You are driving a car that suddenly begins to career out of control. You search madly for the brake pedals but can find only the accelerator. The landscape is a blur, but you do see faces looking at you with horror. Another common affliction is trying to drive from the backseat or trunk of the car.

The Border Guard: You are required to show your driver's license or passport to a uniformed officer. No problem, you think, taking it from your wallet. Just before you hand it over, you see that the photo is of someone else, and, accordingly, you panic. (Clearly, this pertains to feelings of being a fraud.)

Slippery Slope: You are facing a broad landscape that slips gently away from you. You begin to slip, then to roll, then to hurtle down the slope, which turns into a steep incline. Sometimes you're rolling inside an object, such as a tire, that blinds you to your direction.

FEAR OF AGE AND DEATH

The id hates mortality and yet is obsessed with it.

Crumbling: As you look at your own face (possibly in a mirror and possibly by virtue of that magic of dreams), you see cracks forming in your teeth. Soon they are crumbling like chalk and dropping from their sockets. You try to hold one in and it turns to powder in your hands (a variation on this theme is to feel your teeth turn soft and stringy, like cheese).

Strange Hair: Though hair specifically refers to sexual power, it is also a sign of potency in general. A dream in which your hair begins to fall out in great clumps is one thing. Less usual but more alarming is the dream in which hair (or worse yet, a single hair) grows someplace it shouldn't, say, out of the top of your nose. Both types of hair dreams reflect fear of betrayal by the body.

Foreign Bodies: To dream that something inorganic has been placed in your body or is growing inside you is a common means of expressing anxiety about sickness, though in a woman it can symbolize a terror of pregnancy. More directly, to have something organic ripped from you reflects a terror of childbirth.

Left: With her plump and pearly purse dangling fruitlike against her thigh, a young lady recoils from the gropes and leers (and lolling naked men) that assail her in a nightmare. When contemplating this image, it is productive to remember Freud's notion that all dreams are wish fulfillment. Theodor M. von Holst, A Nightmare.

Animals	
Birds	*hope and spirituality*
Cats	*feminine mystery*
Fish	*intuition*
Horses	*the father*
Octopus	*male fear of women*
Board games	*the journey through life, progress*
Candle	*spirit*
Chest or toy box	*childhood*
Chocolate	*self-indulgence and ensuing guilt*
Cities, on a hill	*heaven, the home of the gods, the goal*
Cities, ruined	*neglected obligations*
Cities, walled	*protectiveness*
Clocks, watches	*the heart, love*
Coffins	*remorse*
Colors	
Black	*mystery, winter, and death*
Blue	*spiritual or mental aspects, transcendence*
Green	*forces of nature and the cycles of life*
Orange	*change*
Purple	*dignity, authority, and wisdom*
Red	*passion and sensuality*
Yellow	*new vigor, rebirth*
Copy machine	*anxiety that your possessions are being stolen*
Corpse	*immediate misfortune, particularly in business*
Cyclops	*conspiracy*
Dancing	*sexual activity*
Defecating	*desire for creative expression*
Doors and windows	*feminine sexuality*
Emeralds	*fertility*
Fruit	*creativity, artistic efflorescence*
Ghosts	*unacknowledged truths that will require the dreamer's attention*
Gold	*the inner self*

A collection of Russian octopi from a nineteenth-century natural encyclopedia: the top octopus has a distinctly feminine look.

Lawn mowers	*a tedious social obligation*
Letters, unexpected	*a forthcoming surprise*
Letters, unopened	*virginity*
Meat	*instinctual energy*
Milk	*kindness, nurturing*
Money, hoarded	*anal retention or bowel obstruction*
Museums	*the past*
Musical instruments	*all musical instruments except organs signify joie de vivre*
Organs	*exhaustion and dismay*
Police	*inhibitions and self-censorship*
Portrait	*the need to preserve the relationship with the one pictured*
Rainbows	*good news to come, forgiveness*
Rake	*delegated duties will not be completed*
Rooms, attics	*ideals and spiritual beliefs*
Rooms, basements	*unconscious*
Rooms, living rooms	*conscious*
Rubies	*passion*
Sapphires	*truth*
Shells	*the divine female*
Silver	*intellect*
Spoons	*the ability to take care of oneself*
Stars	*fate, inexorability of time*
Suitcases, too heavy	*crippling memories*
Suitcases, too many	*preoccupation with death*
Sun	*masculinity, the father*
Toilets, exposed while on	*fear of public humiliation*
Toilets, exposing someone else	*jealousy of the exposed one's creativity*
Trains	*guidelines and support structure*
Travel, by balloon	*fantasies of escape*
Travel, by bus	*following the crowd, lack of individualism*
Travel, eastward	*vigor*
Travel, westward	*old age, impending death*
Tweezers	*anxiety about the opinions of others*
Urinating	*realization of limitations*
Vase, broken	*imperfect love*
Waiter	*a representation of the dreamer's ability to help others*

SELF-KNOWLEDGE

It is rare for the unconscious to give you any advice, but every so often, it will provide a helping hand. Usually this comes in the form of an exhortation to focus on what is truly important.

To dream of a giant squid swamping your boat (particularly if the squid is shaped like this one) symbolizes a fear of your latent sexual desires.

Water World: Water always signifies the realm of the unconscious and the instinctual. Water is the symbol of what you know without knowing that you know it. Therefore, a dream of viewing a sparkling body of water from a distance encourages you to plumb your emotional depths. To dream of water lapping threateningly at your toes is a warning that your unconscious mind will not permit you to ignore it for long. To dream of drinking or bathing in cool, clear water is a sign that you have achieved a balance between your conscious and unconscious mind. A dream in which water beasts such as fishes or turtles touch you or talk to you is a directive to listen to your intuition.

Bridge over the River I: Bridges imply transitions, and their position over water signifies that the transitions are from one state of mind to another. Thus, a dream of crossing a bridge that twists and lurches in the wind indicates the fear of change, whereas a benign bridge dream shows a healthy acceptance of developments.

Your Younger Self: Pay close attention to the appearance of children in your dreams, for they signify clarity and renewal. If a group of children asks you to join them, you are being advised to simplify your life. If you encounter your younger self, your childhood may hold the key to a dilemma. A baby may signify rebirth.

KNOWLEDGE OF OTHERS

Of course, the characters who appear in dreams are specific to the dreamer, but unrecognized aspects of your relationships take a variety of dream forms.

The Double Room: It is common for relationships to be figured by a building. The more solid the edifice the more permanent the tie. Thus, to dream you are in a hotel indicates ephemeral connections. If you dream that you have left something (particularly if that something is a purse, wallet, or shoe) in your room and must go back to get it, it means you are looking back on an old love with nostalgia and regret. If you dream that you are in a familiar room that has become wretchedly dirty or has been repainted in vile colors, look to your primary relationship, for something is amiss. Being trapped in your room, or finding that the windows have been sealed, is too obvious to discuss.

Sun and Moon: The Moon is a maternal figure, the Sun is a paternal one. Dreams that are set at nighttime may refer to your relationship to your mother. Spiders and cats also can symbolize the mother.

Screens: To dream that you know that certain important people are present, but they are swathed in fabric or thickly screened implies that you feel that you are not getting the attention you deserve in a relationship.

ANGER

Dreams of violence are much more common than we like to admit. Since the dreamer is usually the perpetrator, it feels shameful to discuss these dreams; however, they are attempts by your unconscious to acknowledge your anger at the dream recipient of the violence.

Fire: If you dream that you set fire to something or someone, do not be unduly alarmed. Fire is a purifying force in the world of dreams, so your unconscious is telling you that this element of your life needs a rigorous scouring.

Murder: Aside from the clear-cut dream of killing somebody you actually hate in your conscious life, the murder victim in most dream homicides is the dreamer him- or herself. In our dreams, we project our most shameful quality onto someone else and then kill that person in some excruciating fashion. Don't worry. You're not a sadist. You're a masochist.

Larceny: To dream of stealing another's possessions is exactly what you think it is—a sign of jealousy.

Blood: Contrary to real-life blood, dream blood is more intimately related to fear of mothers and motherhood than to violence.

Obviously, this Dream Guide is the merest dust mote of possibilities in the gargantuan Milky Way of dream symbols. Those in pursuit of a deeper knowledge of the subject should read Freud's *Interpretation of Dreams.* Those who want to check a particular symbol should read *The Secret Language of Dreams,* by David Fontana.

This arresting image appears on the cover of a popular phreno-autobiography of the nineteenth century. The author describes great and defective heads he has known.

PHRENOLOGY

Among the nineteenth century's perversions of the Enlightenment, phrenology is a particularly dark note. Though it now seems entirely ludicrous, phrenology was once a widely practiced method of character analysis, touted by reputable scientists and supported by public figures such as Queen Victoria and Charles Dickens.

The premise of phrenology is that different sections of the brain have different functions. So far, so good—contemporary physiologists also believe this to be true. However, according to phrenologists, these functions are the sole determinants of character; that is, circumstances play no part in development. Instead, they merely reflect the mandates of the character. Thus, if you are poor, it is because your character destines you to be poor, and your character destines you to be poor because you have an underdeveloped organ of acquisitiveness. This is how phrenologists made their money: by inspecting the shape of the head, they could determine the quality and size of the sections of the brain responsible for various traits.

It all began with Franz Joseph Gall, a fashionable Viennese doctor. It was his idea that behavior and personality could be traced to the organic composition of the brain, and it was he who made the quantum—and ridiculous—leap of imagination that allowed him to assume that the shape of the skull denoted the shape of the brain (it was distinctly more difficult to get your hands on a brain than a head attached to a living body). In the course of Gall's career, he located thirty-three different "organs" of the brain, each responsible for a different trait. His disciple, J. K. Spurzheim, who was, if anything, even less devoted to scientific methodology than Gall, found another four. Typically, the organs were located by finding a subject with a pronounced characteristic and measuring his head. For example, Gall determined the placement of the "organ of self-esteem" by inspecting the head of a beggar who said he had been brought low by excessive pride. Both Gall and Spurzheim were censored and then run out of town—

primarily because their theory that a person's physical composition creates his char-acter contradicts all religious belief—but were later accepted and even welcomed in France and England. Spurzheim, less austere than Gall, allowed as how the organs themselves could perhaps be altered by exemplary living, which made phrenology com-patible with liberal ideals and therefore palatable to a wider audience than ever before. By the 1830s, phrenology was hailed as an infallible judge of character.

The science was particularly popular in America, due mostly to the proselytizing of Spurzheim's followers, who ranged from serious scholars of medicine to sideshow quacks. The Fowler Brothers, who should probably be placed in the center of that con-tinuum, were the most vociferous popularizers of phrenological theory. Between them, they wrote dozens of pamphlets and books on the topic, including *Matrimony; or Phrenology and Physiology Applied to the Selection of Congenial Companions for Life* and *Temperance and Tight Lacing: Founded on Phrenology and Physiology, showing the Injurious Effects of Stimulants and the Evils inflicted on the Human Constitution by com-pressing the Organs of Animal Life.* In their manual, *The Illustrated Self-Instructor in Phrenology,* the Fowlers thoughtfully provided their readers with a map of the human head in which the thirty-seven organs were located and displayed in tiny dioramas. As you can see in Figure 8, the human character begins at the back of the neck with Amativeness (sexual or connubial love) and proceeds all the way around the front of the head to Inductive Reasoning. The thirty-seven organs are as follows:

1. Amativeness, sexual and connubial love
2. Philoprogenitiveness, parental love
3. Adhesiveness, friendship, sociability
4. Inhabitiveness, love of home
5. Continuity, doing one thing at a time, connectedness of thought and feeling
6. Combativeness, resistance, defensiveness
7. Destructiveness, severity, disposition to break, crush, and tear down
8. Alimentiveness, appetite, hunger
9. Acquisitiveness, accumulation
10. Secretiveness, self-government, reserve
11. Cautiousness, prudence, provision
12. Approbativeness, ambition, desire to please
13. Self-esteem, self-respect, dignity
14. Firmness, decision, perseverance
15. Conscientiousness, justice, equity

Old Series, Vol. 65
Oct., 1877.

New Series, Vol. 16.
NUMBER 4.

KNOW THYSELF

THE PHRENOLOGICAL JOURNAL
AND SCIENCE OF HEALTH

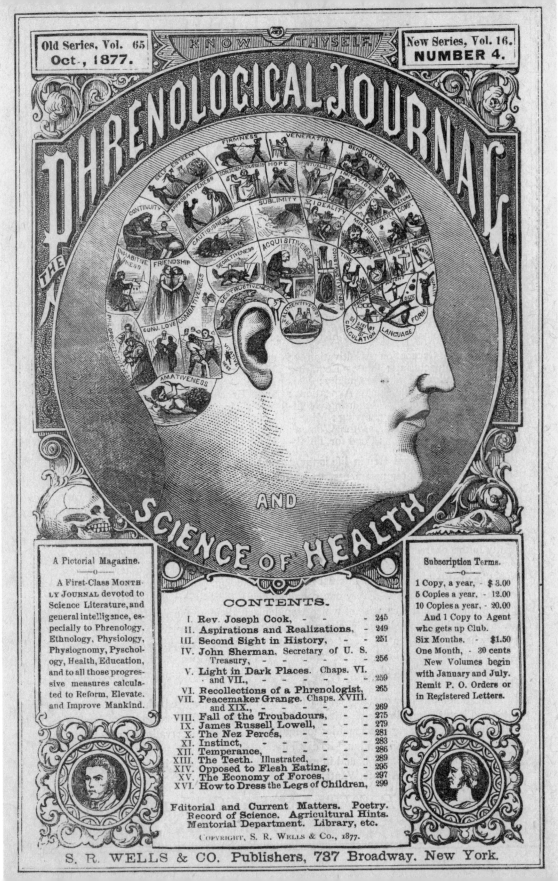

A Pictorial Magazine.

A First-Class Monthly Journal devoted to Science Literature, and general intelligence, especially to Phrenology, Ethnology, Physiology, Physiognomy, Psychology, Health, Education, and to all those progressive measures calculated to Reform, Elevate, and Improve Mankind.

Subscription Terms.

1 Copy, a year, - $3.00
5 Copies a year, - 12.00
10 Copies a year, - 20.00
And 1 Copy to Agent who gets up Club.
Six Months, - $1.50
One Month, - 30 cents
New Volumes begin with January and July.
Remit P. O. Orders or in Registered Letters.

CONTENTS.

Editorial and Current Matters. Poetry. Record of Science. Agricultural Hints. Mentorial Department. Library, etc.

S. R. WELLS & CO. Publishers, 737 Broadway, New York.

16. Hope, expectation, enterprise
17. Spirituality, intuition and faith, the light within
18. Veneration, devotion, respect
19. Benevolence, kindness, goodness
20. Constructiveness, mechanical ingenuity
21. Ideality, good taste, refinement, gentility
22. Imitation, ability to copy and pattern, to learn from models
23. Mirthfulness, jocoseness, wit
24. Individuality, cognizance of individual objects
25. Form, recollection of shape
26. Size, ability to measure by the eye
27. Weight, intuitive perception and application of the laws of gravity
28. Color, perception of color
29. Order, predilection for method and system
30. Calculation, ability to perform mental arithmetic
31. Locality, recollection of place
32. Eventuality, memory of facts and events
33. Time, cognizance of duration
34. Tune, music, musicality
35. Language, expression in words
36. Causality, perception of cause and effect
37. Comparison, inductive reasoning

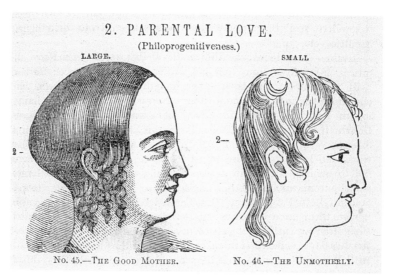

2. PARENTAL LOVE.
(Philoprogenitiveness.)

LARGE.   SMALL.

NO. 45.—THE GOOD MOTHER.   NO. 46.—THE UNMOTHERLY.

FIGURE 9.

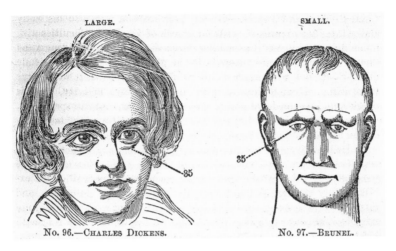

LARGE.   SMALL.

No. 96.—CHARLES DICKENS.   No. 97.—BRUNEL.

FIGURE 10.

Lest we should be uncertain, the Fowlers go on to illustrate each quality with two exemplary heads. Philoprogenitiveness, for instance, is embodied in the poor ladies of Figure 9. The woman with the bizarrely shaped head on the left is, according to the Fowlers, a devoted mother. That tumorous-looking lump at the back of her head is a Large organ of Philoprogenitiveness, which reveals that its possessor "loves its own children devotedly; values them above all price; cheerfully endures toil and watching for their sake; forebears with their faults . . ." On the other hand, the depleted lady on the right has a small organ of Philoprogenitiveness, which damns her to caring "little for its own children and still less for those of others; and with Combativeness and Destructiveness large, is liable to treat them unkindly and harshly, and is utterly unqualified to have charge of them."

It is interesting to note that the organ of language occurs in bags under the eyes. Figure 10 illustrates the faculty for language with a portrait of Charles Dickens (expressing a large organ but not a very large one, which would indicate garrulity and gossiping) and one of a manifest clod, who can "hardly remember or use words at all, or even remember their meaning."

Phrenology would be very amusing to contemplate if it had not been so successful. It codified and, in so doing, authorized the primitive and infantile aversion that we all have toward the different and the ugly. Moreover, the notion that character is biological—and therefore inescapable and unchangeable—has been the basis for racism of the most repulsive kind. Among the more insidious forms of propaganda that the Nazis promulgated against the Jew was the argument of biological inferiority based on phrenology. In this regard, phrenology—or, rather, the parade of white, Anglo-Saxon males who propounded it—has a lot to answer for.

Figure 22.

DV GOVVERNEMENT DV FEV.

This sweet and rather childlike depiction of the attainment of the Philosopher's Stone appears in a 1608 edition of Salomon Trismosin's Splendor solis. Though the image is considerably less ornate than the famous illuminated version in the British Museum, its point is the same: at the end of the process, the Earth and the Sun are made one.

ALCHEMY

Alchemy is an odd bird in the divinatory flock. It is not, by rights, a divination system at all, and yet, it is impossible—or at least disheartening—to discuss divination without taking an a short flight into alchemy, the science and philosophy of turning base metal into gold. Some of the world's greatest diviners were also alchemists, and it may well have been their participation in alchemy's Great Work that endowed these sometimes quite ordinary people with their moments of extraordinary clarity. Furthermore, the fascination that alchemy exerted over the practitioners of a wide range of occult sciences ensured that the symbols of alchemy crept into a number of divinatory systems, such as Tarot. I have to admit, though, that the Great Work is somewhat difficult to re-create in your living room (though not impossible), and those readers who simply want to find out what's going to happen to them should probably read another chapter (try Numerology).

The official history of alchemy—if anything about alchemy can be said to be official—begins with the eighth-century Arab scholar named Geber or Jabir, whose ideas spread through western Europe like wildfire. By the sixteenth century, alchemy's practitioners and proselytizers were cutting an intellectual swath more or less equivalent to that of our herd of deconstructionists. As we have seen so many times in the course of this book, the eighteenth century brought with it a suspension of belief. A few adepts carried on the Work in the Victorian era, but, surprisingly enough, it was in the twentieth century that an alchemical renaissance occurred, and, even as I write, alchemists (primarily in France) are struggling to achieve the mysterious product their forefathers called by so many names: The Elixir, The Red Stone, The Red Powder, The Tincture, The Philosopher's Stone.

But what, you may well ask, *is* the Great Work? This is a good question. Outwardly, the goal of the alchemists was to transform ordinary metals—lead, for instance—into

Closely associated with the history of alchemy is the mysterious Fraternity of the Rosy Cross, also known as the Rosicrucian Order and, in a current incarnation, as the Ancient and Mystical Order Rosae Crucis.

It all began in 1614, when the first of three obscure pamphlets appeared. Entitled *Fama Fraternitatis*, it described the travels of a young man, Christian Rosenkreutz, and his eight companions as they sought and acquired great esoteric and scientific wisdom. According to the pamphlet, Rosenkreutz died in 1484 at the age of 106, replete with esoteric knowledge from around the world. Vowing to keep the Order secret for a hundred years, his disciples passed occult wis-

This allegorical illustration of the "College of the Fraternity" is virtually an encyclopedia of Rosicrucian symbols. The rose and the cross are featured prominently, of course, and the male figure ascending to heaven in the coils of a serpent may well be Christian Rosenkreutz himself. From Theophilus Schweighardt's Speculum Sophicum Rhodo-Stauroticum, *1618.*

dom down from one generation of initiates to the next. The narrative ends with the announcement of the rediscovery of Rosenkreutz's crypt, in which his body lay in a state of perfect preservation. The second pamphlet continues the story in the same hermetic manner, and though it exhorts its readers to join the Order, it gives no instructions on how this is to be achieved. The third pamphlet, *The Chemical Wedding*, is a description of the alchemical process clothed in the flimsiest of allegorical drapes. Indeed, all of the tracts could be read as camouflaged alchemy manuals, and notwithstanding their impenetrability, their great popularity was at least partly due to the impression they gave that the secrets of the ages were knowable and known. For they were tremendously popular; the three pamphlets—particularly the last—caused a furor across northern Europe, especially in Germany, the putative home of Rosenkreutz, where there was endless speculation about who was or wasn't part of the brotherhood. Though the pamphlets were anonymous and nobody ever claimed to be a member of the Order, belief in the existence and occult power of the Rosicrucians persisted. Their apologists explained that they revealed themselves only to the deserving, and even after the theologian Johann Valentin Andreae admitted that he had written *The Chemical Wedding* as a joke, the rumors of Rosicrucianism refused to die.

Thus it simmered for about three hundred years, until, in 1904, one Harvey Spencer Lewis resurrected the rosy cross as the Ancient and Mystic Order Rosae Crucis, complete with a brand-new pedigree. According to Lewis, Rosicrucianism originated in ancient Egypt as a mystic cult under the direction of the world's first monotheist, Amenhotep IV. The wisdom of his sages was passed down in strictest secrecy within the brotherhood, and the long periods of silence were explained by the divine decree that 108 years of activity should be followed by 108 years of hunkering down.

In preparation for the Order's rebirth into a cycle of activity, the members were to advertise the event to the public. Thus, the three pamphlets of 1614, 1615, and 1616, which were, said Lewis, no more than the beginning of a normal cycle blown completely out of proportion by the advent of the printing press. Lewis's Order Rosae Crucis, based in San Jose, California, since 1927, has a complicated hierarchy but a simple goal: the attainment of Cosmic Consciousness through study and ritual.

In addition to such legitimate descendants of the *fama fraternitatis,* elements of Rosicrucianism appear in a number of esoteric doctrines. As the granddaddy of mystic cults, the Order was much mined for symbols and rituals by the up-and-coming mystic movements of the late nineteenth and early twentieth centuries. The Theosophists made good use of Rosicrucianism, as did the Hermetic Order of the Golden Dawn, and the Ordo Templi Orientis.

pure gold. If this seems distressingly capitalistic, don't fret, because alchemical gold, in addition to being real, spendable gold, is a metaphor for a life transformed, for Creation itself. The Great Work in which all alchemists are engaged is, on one level, the laborious search for the Philosopher's Stone that will achieve the physical transmutation of one substance into another, and, on another level, a process of self-transformation and transcendence. The alchemical objective was to harness the forces of nature in order to replicate the act of creation, and behind that objective was the true goal, the Holy Grail of alchemy, for in that moment of creation—as gold was formed—the alchemist would achieve oneness with the Divine. It was this potent reward, rather than money, that motivated the true alchemists.

The big issue, though, was how to do it. A series of elements, cunningly called by names that give no clue of their actual composition, is submitted to a series of transformational processes, and, after many metaphorically described events took place, *something* is formed. This something is not gold. It is, rather, the material that turns lead into gold. Commonly referred to as a red powder (though this is probably a canard), this, the Elixer, was the most valuable of all substances.

Clearly, I have no idea how this powder was achieved. If I knew, I probably wouldn't tell, but I don't know, and in this, I have good company. Among alchemy's thousands of practitioners through the centuries, the roster of adepts— alchemists who have achieved the Philosopher's Stone—includes perhaps thirty names. However, it is true that anyone wise enough to achieve the Philosopher's Stone was probably wise enough to make himself scarce, for the more public adepts were apt to meet unfortunate ends.

* * *

The artifacts are profuse—library shelves groan under their many alchemical treatises and tomes, and the books themselves bristle with illustrations of the Great Work. But alchemical texts constitute a revolution against western tradition, in which the book's earnest purpose (at least until the twentieth century) has always been to illuminate, to reflect reality, to serve the

In this singularly literal engraving, which appears in Steffan Michelspacher's 1616 Cabala, Spiegel der Kunst und Natur, the steps of the alchemical process are represented by—steps, neatly labeled. These lead the royal marriage chamber, symbolizing the conjunction of elements that results in the Phoenix—gold—that rises from the roof. Mercury, dancing on the pinnacle of the mountain, alludes to Philosopher's Mercury, the prime ingredient in the Elixir. The blindfolded man and his rabbit-chasing companion in the bottom portion of the image are a symbolic warning against relying on the senses. In the pursuit of the Great Work, exhorts the image, we should be intuitive, like rabbits.

reader as pleasingly as possible. The art of alchemy has other motives altogether; information is deliberately obscured, sequence shuffled, references multivalent. The peculiar brilliance of many alchemical texts lies in their use of the idea of process; the act of understanding—or misunderstanding—the book is a mirror of the Great Work itself. The reader must transmute what she reads just as the first matter is transmuted. The radical reflexiveness of alchemical literature is not only bizarrely anachronistic, it is also bizarrely antigeographical—it is as though a little seed of Zen wisdom sprouted like a daisy in central Europe. In the tradition of the Zen koan whose impenetrability and illogic drive the monk to the moment of madness in which all is clear, the major works of alchemy seem to yield their true meaning only when the reader has given up on literal meaning. However, for those of us who cleave to the western tradition of literary pedagogy, childish though it may be, alchemical texts can be frustrating.

As is standard in the divinatory arts, the language of alchemy is predicated on certain correspondences between celestial and earthly entities. Thus,

Moon	=	Silver	=	Crystal	=	White	=	Dog
Mercury	=	Mercury	=	Agate	=	Gray	=	Swallow
Venus	=	Copper	=	Emerald	=	Green	=	Dove
Sun	=	Gold	=	Diamond Lodestone	=	Yellow	=	Lion
Mars	=	Iron	=	Ruby	=	Red	=	Horse
Jupiter	=	Tin	=	Sapphire	=	Blue	=	Eagle
Saturn	=	Lead	=	Onyx	=	Black	=	Crocodile

In an image, any one of these things may represent any one of its equivalents. To pick an excruciatingly simple example, the Sun that appears in the final illumination of the *Splendor solis* is a stand-in for the golden result of the operations. Most interpretations are not that easy; much more frequently, illustrations are dauntingly devious means of camouflaging the material they are supposed to reveal. Inculcating the correct mentality for the Great Work was certainly one objective in creating such richly obscure works, but creating confusion must have been another. This is evident in the great alchemical tradition of placing instructions and illustrations for the first stage of the process smack in the middle of the second or third stage. This hardly seems fair, but fairness was not uppermost in the alchemical mind.

Despite the policy of obfuscation, the duration of the task, and the singularly low returns, alchemy has exerted an enduring fascination over the centuries. In our own day, the stated objective—that of turning base metal into gold—can easily be achieved in a nuclear laboratory by slinging molecules into lead until gold is composed. That process is, however, more expensive than gold, and, more important, it lacks the spiritual elements that render the quest for lucre an allegory of personal transmutation and make a chemical procedure into a Great Work.

The future is obviously shocking in this nineteenth-century engraving featuring a paradigmatic Gypsy.

TASSEOMANCY

Matrons, who toss the cup, and see
The grounds of fate in grounds of tea
Alexander Pope

People have been drinking tea for about five thousand years, and it's likely they have been reading tea leaves that long as well. Tea-leaf reading, also known as tasseomancy or tasseography, began with the ancient Chinese, who read the residue in the bottoms of their cups for patterns, signs, and omens. As tea found its way to the Western world, the art of tea-leaf reading took root in Europe. In the mid-seventeenth century, tea drinking was still mainly an aristocratic affair, but as trade and, hence, availability increased, so too did the popularity of this exotic brew, with all its ritual, social, and purported curative possibilities. Soon, the lower classes, who had been burning their extremities for centuries in such outmoded divinatory practices as molybdomancy (reading the future from molten lead in water) and ceromancy (ditto from melted candle wax), saw the error of their ways and turned to reading liquid leftovers ranging from wine to coffee. Tea was quickly adopted as the revelatory beverage of choice (why waste perfectly good wine?). By the mid-nineteenth century, the Gypsy soothsayer, calling door-to-door to read leaves, was a social fixture. According to one "Highland Seer," author of what is probably the oldest book in English on the practice of tea-leaf reading, generations of Scottish spae-wives (from the old Norse *spa*, meaning prophesy) used their skill and intuition to examine the dregs of their morning tea for signs of things to come.

Tradition has established a generally accepted canon of symbols and their implications, but reading leaves is among the more imaginative and intuitive of the divinatory arts, and discovering the patterns and deeper meanings in the bottom of a cup is much

Above: Despite the message on this 1907 postcard, if your tea leaves coagulate to form a perfect four-leaf clover, your luck has undoubtedly been exhausted by the event.

like seeing shapes revealed in cloud formations. Occult lore finds a correlation between the bowl shape of the cup and the celestial dome of the heavens, and between the leaves and the stars; some companies market tea cups with the signs of the Zodiac printed in the bowl, to facilitate just such a reading. This is an unnecessary complication, for tea-leaf reading is really just a homey variation of geomancy, the reading of seemingly random marks and patterns on earth or ink on paper. Among the most accessible of divination systems, tasseomancy requires nothing more than a simple cup, a bit of tea, and a quiet, receptive mood.

PREPARATION

Loose tea is necessary for reading, because the stems and varying leaf sizes offer a wider range of shapes to interpret than the grounds from a teabag. A good reading usually involves from a pinch to a half-teaspoonful of leaves; too much and the leaves will clump together, too little and the leaves will drip weakly down the sides of the cup. Cream and sugar are to be avoided, as they tend to render the leaves gooey and illegible.

As for the cup, the closer its resemblance to a bowl, the better. Mugs won't work because their sides are perpendicular—the leaves won't stick. The cup's handle is used as a reference point in the reading, so an actual bowl won't do, either. Avoid cups with patterns or decorations printed on the inside, as the print will interfere with your reading of the patterns of the leaves.

Each tasseomancer orchestrates the reading ritual a bit differently, but typically, the procedure is as follows. The tasseomancer will ask the querent to stir the dried tea, a tradition akin to shuffling a deck of cards, and then spoon a measure of tea into a heated pot (two teaspoonfuls) or prewarmed china cup (half a teaspoonful). Boiling water is added, and the querent concentrates on the future in general or on a specific question he or she would like answered while stirring the brew. If a pot is being used, the querent swirls the tea after it steeps and then pours it into the cup; the tasseomancer may spoon in more leaves if not enough are dispensed. When the tea has cooled, the querent sips the tea, again focusing on his or her question, until about a

Ladies reading coffee grounds, 1855.

Reading coffee grounds came into vogue at about the same time as reading tea leaves, and the two methods yield essentially the same results. It's best to use a mixture of fine and coarser grinds of coffee to ensure a better variation of shapes. Add two tablespoons of coarse- and one teaspoon fine-ground coffee to a prewarmed, dry cup as you would to prepare a cup of tea. Add boiling water, cover, and let steep for a minute or so. Drink or, more likely, pour off all but a tablespoonful, swirl, turn the cup over on its saucer to drain, turn it right side up, and you're in business. The difference in reading coffee grounds is that the reading is conducted primarily with the grounds on the saucer, or better, a plate.

Eighteenth-century Italian soothsayers claimed to have originated the practice of coffee-ground reading, and they believed its results to be influenced by demons. It was therefore critical that certain words be spoken at specific times during the procedure. Before adding the boiling water: *"Aqua boraxit venias carajos."* While stirring the water and grounds: *"Fixitur et patricam explinabit tornae."* After pouring off the coffee-water and while draining the dregs onto a plate: *"Hax verticaline, pax Fantas marobum, max destinatus, veida porol."* Though these look like ancient Latin incantations, their relationship to Latin is utterly cosmetic. So don't worry about your pronunciation. (Worry about getting coffee grounds all over the table.)

tablespoonful of liquid is left at the bottom of the cup. This contact with the cup is crucial to the personalization and accuracy of the reading. Tasseomancy, like tarot and other inductive systems of divination, may seem to depend on indications of chance (the scatter of leaves, the cut of the deck, etcetera), but it really has its basis in the disbelief of chance: contact with the cup is assumed to influence the patterns of the leaves. If the querent absolutely loathes tea, it may be poured off rather than drunk, but I don't recommend it, and in such a case, the subject must hold the cup in his or her hand for a significant period before the reading can commence. The querent then swirls the tea and remaining liquid around the inside of the cup three times, to distribute the leaves, and then, in the same motion, turns the cup face-down onto a saucer. After giving the liquid a moment to drain, the querent must turn the cup rightside up. The tasseomancer will consider the leaves remaining in the cup, but also the pattern of leaves on the saucer, as part of the complete reading.

READING THE LEAVES

As in the preparation of the cup, the procedure for interpreting the leaves varies with the disposition of the reader, but there are certain consistencies that may be considered as guidelines for a traditional reading.

There are chronological and nonchronological readings (the choice is usually determined by whether the question at hand contains a time element), but both begin from the cup's handle, which represents the querent in the here and now. Chronological readings trace time beginning with the right side of the handle and proceeding clockwise around the cup to the handle's left side, which in traditional readings describes the span of one year, with the side directly across from the handle indicating six months into the future. However, the cup may designate a shorter or longer period—the important thing is for the querent and tasseomancer to agree upon the time span before the reading begins. Leaves near the brim of the cup symbolize events that will take place closer to the beginning of the month, and leaves toward the bottom show events that will occur at the end of the month. Patterns at the bottom of the cup and any patterns left on the saucer influence the whole of the fortune or question being considered.

In a nonchronological reading, which is most suitable for love and money questions, the position of the leaves in the cup determines their effect. A symbol at the rim of the cup has a positive connotation, while the same pattern near the cup's bottom

Le Petit Journal

ADMINISTRATION · 61, RUE LAFAYETTE, 61 · 15 CENT. · SUPPLÉMENT ILLUSTRÉ · 15 CENT. · ABONNEMENTS

Les manuscrits ne sont pas rendus · 29me Année · Numéro 1.421 · France et colonies · Étranger

DIMANCHE 17 MARS 1918

Avant de partir pour la guerre en Europe, Sammy interroge la "tasse de thé" de la vieille sorcière peau-rouge.

The caption to this 1918 French magazine reads "Before leaving for the war in Europe, Sammy consults the tea leaves with an old redskin sorceress."

PATTERNS AND THEIR MEANINGS

Airplane	*travel*
Bed	*peace*
Beehive	*invitation, activity*
Bird	*good luck; on a branch, a bird indicates a journey*
Bottle	*excess, flirtation*
Butterfly	*society, sociability, change*
Cat	*treachery, deception*
Circle	*marriage, partnership, union*
Clown	*happiness, pretending to be happy*
Cross	*crossroads, personal sacrifice*
Cross within a circle	*confinement*
Cup	*criticism*
Dagger	*loss, danger, enmity*
Dog	*faithfulness, devotion*
Door	*possibility*
Envelope or letter	*news*
Fish	*gain, usually material, sometimes spiritual*
Flowers	*simple happiness*
Forest	*unclear thinking*
Fruit	*good fortune, children*
Frying pan	*accusation, trouble*
Gun	*conflict, danger*
Hammer	*hard work*
Hat	*opportunity*
Heart	*love, affection*
Horseshoe	*luck*
Lamp	*guidance*
Moon	*increase or decrease*
Musical instruments	*good company*
Rabbit	*carefree*
Scissors	*argument, angry words*
Shoe	*increased effort*
Snake	*treachery (coiled), wisdom (uncoiled)*
Square	*solidity; protection, the need for protection*
Squirrel	*thrift*
Star	*success, genius, spiritual enlightenment*
Tree	*family*
Triangle	*emotional involvement—jealousy if pointing down, ambition if pointing up; luck*
Umbrella	*protection*
Window	*vision, psychic ability*

will be negative. For example, leaves that form a hatlike pattern betoken new opportunities; at the top of the cup, these will be opportunities for success. At the bottom, they are canards, leading the querent into dangerous new territory. Leaves that appear opposite the cup's handle indicate the influence of strangers.

Once the tea leaves have come to rest, the tasseomancer should inspect the cup from different angles. This is no time to hurry: patience is a virtue. The images in the leaves may not reveal themselves with flash-card clarity: Is that a spider (a symbol of good fortune) or a wreath (a symbol of sorrow) at the bottom of the cup? A careful, imaginative attention and receptivity are a reader's most valuable job skills. An inconclusive or unremarkable cup, in which you discern no patterns or shapes of note, means that nothing very important will happen in the course of time covered by the reading and is a valid finding in itself.

The clearer and larger the symbols or patterns, the stronger and more significant their implications. Proximity of shapes suggests their relation; shapes within a quarter-inch are always considered together. A scattering of the leaves indicates a more diffuse personality, while clustering suggests intensity and conflict. Few leaves in the cup denotes clarity and direct action, while many, well-dispersed leaves suggests confusion or extravagance. Some shapes have special meanings, but many are exactly as they appear: a heart situated near an airplane may suggest that the querent will go somewhere he or she has been longing to go. Here are some of the more common leaf cluster formations and their general indications. A brief glossary of common symbols appears on page 120.

Three small leaves close to one leaf: *A man.*
Two leaves close to a small leaf: *A woman.*
Small leaves in a triangular shape: *A child or children.*
Chain of leaves: *A journey. The more serpentine the chain,*
    the more circuitous the travel.
Initials or letters: *Initials of people having some relationship*
    or contact with the querent.
Numbers: *Always interpreted literally as the number represented.*
Straight lines: *Tranquillity; planning.*
Wavy lines: *Uncertainty; aggravation.*
Dots: *Small spots in a cluster indicate money.*

This exemplary Norse warrior is covered with runes. They appear on his belt, his quiver strap, and his shield. From the great nineteenth-century bible of rune scholarship, The Old-Northern Runic Monuments of Scandanavia and England, *by George Stephens.*

RUNES

Two thousand years ago, the lands we now call Germany and Scandinavia were blanketed in dark forests and populated by fierce warrior tribes, whom the Romans referred to loftily as "savages." Among the few relics of the mysterious culture of these northerners are the runes, strange symbols carved into stones, worked into metal vessels, or written in ancient manuscripts. From a few elusive texts, we have learned some of the history of the runes: that they were regarded as gifts from the Nordic gods and that every rune was thought to be laden with magical power. Each of the twenty-four runic symbols was carved into a small piece of wood or stone, which the tribal priests cast to resolve disputes, call upon the gods, or predict the future.

In the past several decades, more and more people have returned to this ancient method of divination. Books of instruction and little pouches of rune tiles abound, but though the undeniable prophetic power of the runes makes them very enticing, they should be approached with caution. These are the relics of a culture born of long, black nights and the inexorable freezing cold of the northern winter. Unlike the divinatory systems that emerged in the sunny climates of Chaldea, Egypt, Greece, and the Roman Empire, the runes are a response to a profound and perennial fear of annihilation. Runic magic is, accordingly, powerful and harsh. This is not a light system, and it should not be approached frivolously.

Although runes resemble letters, the rune sequence should not be mistaken for an alphabet. While the letters of a word are the components of a sign, each rune is a complete sign in itself. The majority of the runes originally symbolized natural forces and events, as is only reasonable in a culture shaped by weather and the search for refuge. Later, the runes were layered with more complex meanings, which are the basis of our modern runecraft. There are several different runic systems, each containing a different number of runes, but the most widely used in contemporary rune casting is the oldest of the Germanic *futharks*, which contains twenty-four runes. *Futhark* is an acronym composed of the sounds that begin the words signified by the first six runes. As you would guess, most *futharks* begin with the same runes (else how could they be *futharks*?), but some include a larger number of runes. The Anglo-Saxon *futhark*, for example, contains twenty-nine runes. A few present-day rune mavens have rearranged the sequence of the runes in order to claim a progression from the concrete to the spiritual, which, they seem to think, enhances the value of rune casting. This, in my opinion, is gratuitous interference. Who can tell what the significance of the rune order might be? We must not assume that the traditional sequence is meaningless simply because we see no meaning there.

THE MEANING OF THE RUNES

Each of the runes has a literal meaning and a prophetic meaning. For example, you will not be much enlightened by receiving ᛒ in your cast if you interpret it literally: birch tree. In a deeper sense, though, ᛒ indicates growth and fertility, which are undoubtedly more meaningful to the average participant of the twentieth century. In addition to this prophetic meaning, sixteen of the twenty-four runes may be reversed (appearing either upside-down or backward) by the action of casting; in such a case, a rune's significance is reversed, or to put it more clearly, the forces represented by the rune are blocked and frustrated. As we proceed through the *futhark,* I will supply the literal meaning (briefly) and explicate the prophetic meaning of each rune, as well as discussing its reversed meaning where applicable. Following this festival of interpretation, I will discuss several methods of rune casting.

ᚠ *(feoh)*: This rune's original meaning—cattle or livestock—denotes the agricultural society of the rune creators. More generally, it implies wealth and possessions (notice the word *fee* lurking within *feoh*). However, in a rune spread, the appearance of ᚠ should not be read as a sudden inheritance, because together with the idea of wealth is the idea of generosity, of giving wealth away, of creating credit. ᚠ urges you to consider giving away that which you have in abundance. Divestment may be the best investment. A positive rune, ᚠ implies that you are, or soon will be, in a position to be generous.

ᚠ reversed points out a selfishness—a tightness, really—that should be attended to.

ᚢ *(ur)*: The infamous wild ox that once stormed throughout the northern fields and forests is represented by ᚢ. Known as the *aurochs,* this fierce beast figured heavily in the Germanic imagination as a symbol of power and pure strength (although, in truth, the *aurochs* was hunted to extinction by the middle of the seventeenth century). Its divinatory significance is not far from its definition: ᚢ implies strength but also the need for strength.

Those who can bear the most get the most to bear, and you should take comfort in the knowledge that nothing that is to come will overwhelm you. You have the stamina and determination to work through difficulties, and you will ultimately achieve your ends. ᚢ is a weighty rune; it implies an elemental, animalistic power that cannot be ignored and should not be expended on minor goals.

Reversed, ᚢ reveals a weakness, usually disguised as a show of bravado. You must demand more of yourself—more honesty and more perseverance.

ᚦ *(thorn)*: This is a rune of misfortune, both literally and prophetically. Like the thorn it represents, ᚦ is all about defense. Its appearance in a spread urges you to close up shop, to crawl under the house, to retract, to retreat. Inaction is the best course at this time; ᚦ is static, resistant, nonaggressive, but effective against attack. This is not the time to fight; it is the time to hide. The rune itself is often worn as an amulet to protect against danger (for instructions on how to create such an amulet, see page 133).

ᚦ reversed turns the meaning of the rune into an exhortation: you're going too fast, you're too impatient, you're endangering yourself—stop it!

ᚨ *(as)*: At the most concrete level, ᚨ means mouth, but in a fuller sense, it implies language and the spiritual power of the Word, God's great, primary utterance by which the universe was called into existence. If you get ᚨ in a spread, its significance is more earthly than divine. This is the rune of listening as well as talking. The mandate of ᚨ is to receive communication, to allow yourself to be guided by what you learn rather than by your will (i.e., what you think you already know).

ᚨ reversed portends a failed communication. Usually, the failure lies with you—the implication being that you weren't paying attention. Instead of engaging in a bout of senseless recrimination, seize the next opportunity to listen, not as penance but as practice.

ᚱ *(rad)*: Bearing a striking resemblance to our R, ᚱ is the rune for riding, a souvenir of the ubiquitous horse riding that supported the warrior culture. It is notable that the rune stands for the activity of riding rather than the horse itself, for the significance of ᚱ is process over product. You are in the midst of a necessary process, and, though it seems arduous, even futile, it should not be abandoned. The journey is the destination.

If ᚱ is reversed, expect the sudden interruption of a process or the sudden loss of faith in its value.

ᚻ *(ken)*: The symbol for torch, and, by extension, for light, ᚻ's prophetic meaning is tied to illumination and clarity. This is a rune of activity; it gives a positive exhortation to scrutinize your activities and plans for false motives and flawed reasoning. ᚻ also represents knowledge itself; its appearance may indicate that forthcoming information is significant.

Beware ᚻ reversed—you are in the dark about something important. If crucial information continues to be withheld, you will suffer for it.

ᚷ *(gyfu)*: This beneficent rune, the symbol for gift, signifies rewards to come, the dessert after a lot of vegetables. ᚷ should not only be regarded as a sign of material gain; the form of the rune—two lines intersecting—shows us that the relationship between giver and receiver is at least as important as what is given. ᚷ urges you to allow yourself to be in debt to another, to learn to receive graciously. It is, in fact, a sign both of good luck and of willingness to accept that good luck.

ᚷ cannot be reversed, which is part of its lesson.

ᚹ *(wyn)*: This is the rune of joy, both literally and prophetically. The happiness that ᚹ portends differs from that of ᚷ in that it represents a less tangible good. You will experience the calmer, deeper joy that comes from achieving a peaceful balance. ᚹ foretells a respite from chaos, an interlude of harmony, and a period of regeneration. Note that ᚹ is not relational but comes from your own sense of self.

ᚹ reversed predicts trouble—your balance will be upset by a disruptive element. A peaceful resolution to your problem is within your grasp but for one thorny issue. ᚹ reversed encourages you to seek a solution immediately.

ᚻ *(hagal)*: This is the symbol for hail, in northerly climates the most terrifyingly destructive sign of the gods' displeasure. Abrupt endings, upheaval, and disruption are signified by the presence of ᚻ in a rune spread, but bear in mind that fresh beginnings are truly possible only if they are preceded by the total annihilation of earlier conditions. Brace yourself for a sudden change and look forward to the growth it will bring.

ᚻ reversed is considered to be a distinction without a difference. There's no sidestepping ᚻ.

ᚾ *(nyd)*: Close upon the heels of hail is need. As joy (ᚹ) is the internal form of the gift (ᚷ), so is need the internal manifestation of hail. When you receive ᚻ in your rune spread, it implies that disaster has been thrust upon you. ᚾ, on the other hand, leaves it all up to you. It foretells a period in which you must exercise severe self-discipline and restraint. This is a time of necessity, not indulgence, and you must be prepared to experience frustration and misery. Limitation is inescapable; the best lesson you can learn from it is patience.

ᛏ reversed is need disguised. Don't fool yourself—voluntary sacrifice is preferable to forceable seizure. Better to set your own parameters than to have an outside authority do so.

ᛁ *(is)*: The third element in this triad of troubles is ᛁ, the rune for ice. Icelike, ᛁ signifies immobility. Your will is frozen and you must lie still and helpless. You can achieve nothing and you can force nothing to happen. You must withdraw and be still until the ice melts. In some traditions, ᛁ also means destiny—that is, man's destiny is death—but that seems both too obvious and too grim to be useful. Even glaciers melt eventually.

ᛃ *(jera)*: Though its literal meaning is year, ᛃ bears with it the connotation of regeneration through the passage of time. In Viking culture, the new year began when winter ended, so that the concept of the year is paired with the promise of spring. After hail, need, and ice, ᛃ encourages you to have faith that the cycles of time will bring relief and renewal. ᛃ is the light at the end of the tunnel. Accordingly, you should cultivate new ideas and projects, while being aware that the old issues must follow their course. Be prepared for the future, but don't rush to conclude the past.

ᛇ *(eoh)*: The yew symbolized by ᛇ was thought, in the naturalistic religion of the northerners, to be a tree of extraordinary magical power and strength. Embodying the principles of firmness, resistance, and durability, the yew tree is also terrifically poisonous, a combination of characteristics that contributed to ᛇ's divinatory meaning: you are going to need to dig in your heels and hold your ground. This is no time to be clever; just be stubborn. Your strength lies in your ability to withstand discomfort. Determination will win the day.

ᛈ *(peorth)*: Probably the rune most resistant to translation, ᛈ has been interpreted as "dice cup," "pawn," "tune," and even "penis." Perhaps we can just generalize and say that ᛈ signifies a game of chance, and, by extrapolation, the play of forces between set rules and free will. In a rune spread, ᛈ represents the requirement that you accept—and try to understand—the machinery of fate. What we are talking about here is karma—fate you create yourself—and ᛈ urges you to consider your actions in that light. ᛈ is a call to moral self-examination. Have you done those things which you ought not have done? Have you left undone those things which you ought to have done?

Reversed, ᛈ signifies a failure of understanding. You may be thinking that you've gotten away with something. You are probably incorrect.

Y *(elhaz):* This rune is nearly a pictograph for the plant it signifies, the elksedge, which looks innocent enough growing on the edge of the bog but is, in truth, a vicious vegetation that draws blood if you try to pull it. Its presence in a rune spread tells you that you are protected by forces larger than you know. You are not required to do anything to maintain this protection; it is simply there. Scandinavian and British timbered houses often have their beams arranged in a Y pattern as a sort of divine security system.

Upside-down, Y bids you to guard your health. Walk softly and carry a big stick. You may be less secure than you think.

ᔑ *(sigel):* Imagine the reverence for the Sun in this northern Dark Age culture, where nighttime lasted as long as eighteen hours during the winter, and you will understand the meaning of ᔑ, the rune for the Sun. It stands for hope, healing, and the victory of light over darkness. This especially potent rune assures you of your ultimate triumph. ᔑ is whole and beneficent; it defies the disintegration and chaos that happen at night. If you receive ᔑ in your rune spread, you are enjoined to practice honesty and generosity—it will redound to your benefit; there's no way you can lose.

↑ *(tyr):* Tyr is an important deity of the Nordic pantheon, the ruler of the skies. Tyr is a warrior god but also a regulator of the cosmos (he's less manic than Jupiter), and for this reason, ↑ foretells success through regulation. Many people take this to mean victorious litigation, but the regulation is just as likely to be self-regulation as the regulation of others. In general, ↑ encourages working within boundaries, sticking with the plan, and playing by the rules. It does not reward maverick behavior; it rewards people who do their chores.

Accordingly, ↑ upside-down is a warning to get in line, to stop acting like a prima donna. Grandiosity will result in failure.

ᛒ *(beorc):* Whereas most of the runes represent natural forces or the necessary tools of tribal life, ᛒ stands for the delicate birch tree, which provides little other than beauty. Accordingly, ᛒ's appearance in a rune spread predicts a period of intellectual or aesthetic development. We aren't talking here of getting good grades or selling a painting; we are talking about an internal, wholly serendipitous efflorescence. The gifts of ᛒ are freely given; like the beauty of the birch tree, they toil not and neither do they spin, so forget hard work and discipline—enjoy. An abundant and generous rune, ᛒ is associated with the feminine and with the birth of a child.

Reversed, ᛒ indicates that you are trying to control the future in a counterproductive way. You are counseled to let go, to leave it alone.

M *(ehwaz)*: The link is clear between the literal meaning of M, horse, and its prophetic meaning, which is movement and progress. In a rune spread, this is a sign of change, most often a physical change, but possibly a change of attitude or heart. It bears with it the idea of loyalty and of the importance of bonds—again derived from the steadfast loyalty of the horse—making the rune as a whole an advocate of reasoned transitions, rather than change merely for the sake of excitement. In other words, keep the value of your past connections and experiences in mind, even as you decide to leave them.

Upside-down, M is trying to rouse you from a rut. Get moving! Time for a change!

ᛗ *(man)*: This is the rune for human beings, in all their power and weakness. The idea here can be understood best by recognizing man's place in the runic continuum—after the horse and before the sea. ᛗ should prompt a reflection on our relative insignificance, our frail place in the Great Chain of Being. We are the lords of all we survey and we will surely die. This rune predicts no future that we don't already know, but it reminds us not to take our lives so seriously.

If you receive ᛗ upside-down, you are being given a heightened version of the same message, which is, in essence, get over yourself.

ᚱ *(lagu)*: This, the rune for the sea, is no day at the beach. Whereas in most divinatory traditions, the sea is a symbol of intuition and emotion, the Viking people regarded the sea with awe and distrust. Not the source of life, but the bringer of death, the sea's terrible power is symbolized by ᚱ. This rune warns that a great cleansing is at hand. Something you depend on is on the verge of being washed away; relinquish it with grace.

If ᚱ predicts the flood, its reversal tells you to get on the Ark quickly. Those who ignore the deluge do so at their own peril.

ᛝ *(ing)*: Ing is the ancient Germanic god of fertility, and his rune foretells no namby-pamby metaphoric birth of ideas, but an explosion of plain old sex, with accompanying love, lust, and energy. ᛝ is, more than anything, a sign of making. Its influence is felt physically more than mentally.

Luckily, ᛝ can't be reversed.

ᛟ *(odal)*: Literally, this rune means "our land," though it is more commonly translated as "native land." In a rune spread, it symbolizes your past, the place you came from, what you already have. You can read ᛟ as a call to remember your past and your family ties or as a prediction of a forthcoming inheritance (which can be defined as something you receive from the past). Most people prefer the latter, although the former is more likely.

ᛟ upside-down advises you to attend to your family. You have separated yourself too much from your origins.

ᛞ *(dag)*: This, the final rune, represents day, which, like the Sun, was a potent force in the icebound north. ᛞ is an indicator of health, strength, and good luck. It implies triumphant achievement and perhaps even victory over another. There is an old Scandinavian tradition that ᛞ confers invisibility (probably derived from the blinding light of day): mark anything you want to hide with this rune.

CASTING THE RUNES

In ancient times, runes were read by the tribal priests in a somber ceremony. Decked in long robes marked with runic symbols, the wise man or woman would gather up the twenty-four rune tiles and then scatter them across the ground. Whichever runes landed face-up were then interpreted. Though comprehensive, this method is rather inconvenient, not only because you inevitably lose at least one of your tiles, but also because it provides too much information. A rune has a more general meaning than, say, a tarot card; for that reason, the rune caster must establish strict parameters for the reading. The first, and most important, step is to establish the issue you want the rune spread to address. The more specific your question is, the more effective the runes will be in suggesting the correct path. Questions such as "Should I accept the job offer?" or "Is my relationship over?" are much more conducive to runic consultation than "Tell me what's going to happen in my life," which will result in a vague and fairly useless reading.

THE THREE-RUNE SPREAD

Even the early Germans themselves must have found that casting twenty-four runes was a bit inefficient, because the Roman historian Tacitus, writing in the first century A.D., noted that the "savages" selected three runes for divination. This must be the ancestor of the three-rune spread that is the standard for modern rune casters.

Once you have established the subject about which you which to consult the runes, you are ready to construct your rune spread. No matter what kind of runes you have—stone, wood, or cardboard—they are best stored in a pouch or bag. This is not only convenient but also facilitates a faithful reading because it keeps you from seeing—

and subconsciously demanding—a particular rune.

Meditate upon the question or issue at hand. Once it has filled your consciousness, reach into your pouch and pull out a single rune. Remember to set it down exactly as you first see it. If you get the blank back side of a rune, simply turn it over as quickly as possible. Above all, don't try to unreverse a reversal. Repeat twice more, setting the tiles in order from right to left (runes were written in that order).

The first rune (on the right) identifies the situation. Usually, the rune will express an aspect of the problem that you have never considered before. Do not discard its interpretation merely because it does not dovetail with what you already know. In my experience, runes offer a singularly elemental evaluation of the forces at work in any issue; unsentimental clarity is their forte.

The second rune (in the middle) reveals what is being brought to bear on the situation. Commonly, this is the conflict—people generally don't consult the runes unless there is a conflict—or the element that is holding you up.

The third rune (on the left) tells you what action—or, occasionally, inaction—is called for. It provides your runic instructions, which, though they are not elaborate, are also not simple.

A three-rune spread I ran across some months ago provides a nice exemplary reading, partly because the chosen runes, which seemed inappropriate at first, ultimately proved to be quite revealing. A young man had spent nearly eight months in his parents' home caring for his father, who was ill. He was trying to decide if it was time for him to leave and get on with his life. The following rune spread appeared:

(3)   (2)   (1)

The first rune seemed the most puzzling. How could his current situation be seen as a gift or reward? When he thought about it further, he realized that he was repaying the years of parenting he had received and that this time with his father was irreplaceable. X, remember, is very concerned with the issue of reciprocity. It heartened the querent to think of himself as a receiver as well as a giver.

↑ was less strange at first—the son certainly saw himself as withstanding discomfort with strength, but its position seemed odd. How was this characteristic in conflict with the situation? Then he began to understand that his defensiveness and rigidity were standing in the way of truly accepting the gift he was receiving. His anxiety about his independent life and career were separating him from the valuable experience of being with his father.

As the course of action to be taken, ♦ advised patience and assured the young man that he would, in the fullness of time, embark on new adventures. He was encouraged to have faith that his current situation was a necessary part of his development, and he was advised that he should not force its termination.

The useful counsel of this rune spread was ignored by the querent, who moved to New York to pursue his career. His father died shortly thereafter (✝ hints at this possibility), and the young man regretted his decision to leave.

THE FIVE-RUNE SPREAD

The three-rune spread is adequate for most issues. If, however, you find yourself confronted with a complex problem that involves not one choice, but several, you may want to use a five-rune spread. The structure is the same—draw one rune at a time and lay them horizontally from right to left—and the first three runes have exactly the same significance that they do in the three-rune spread. The fourth rune represents the road not taken. Some runologists call it the Sacrifice Rune, because it shows you what you will have to give up when you take the correct course of action advised by the third rune. The fifth tile bears the rune of the future, for the five-rune spread not only suggests a plan, it also tells you what will happen when you follow it.

TALISMANIC RUNES

In addition to their divinatory function, runes may be used singly or in pairs as talismans. The warning against using runes lightly is especially salient with regard to magical purposes—be very careful with the power you are about to release. You make a talisman by painting or carving the rune (or runes) on a piece of wood. If you use paint, it should be some reddish color, to emulate blood. After the paint has dried, wrap the wood in cloth and store it in a dark place for nine days (if it's an emergency, nine hours

WILL'S CIGARETTES.

MAGIC NAILS.

Containing a mishmash of runes and magic symbols, magic nails were regarded as lucky charms in the construction of new houses and boundary markers.

will do, but the charm will be less effective). As you prepare to use the talisman, trace a circle three times around the rune symbol with your finger and meditate on your motives. A talisman can be worn, carried, or hung on a wall. To combine the forces of the runes, you may bind two runic amulets together with straw or a strip of leather. If your talisman's purpose has a limited duration, it is important to turn it off when you are done. To defuse a talisman, slash the rune diagonally with a knife.

ᛉ is often carved into hidden beams or hung inside the chimney of a house. It protects the home from thieves and marauders.

ᛗ is also often used inside the home. Carved into a wooden beam or door, it will ward off psychic attackers.

ᛚ bound with ᚠ combines natural power with commanding communication, ensuring academic success.

ᚠ reversed and bound with ᚺ is an effective curse.

ᚢ combined with ᚱ keeps your car from breaking down on long trips.

ᛈ bound together with ᚷ is a charm for attraction.

HARUSPICY

Prediction from the entrails of animals, aka haruspicy, is an ancient system that went out of fashion about two thousand years ago, much to the relief of the world's sheep and goat populations. In the haruspicial heyday of the Roman Republic and Empire, battalions of animals were sacrificed to the divinatory cause. Haruspicy is derived from a very early form of fortune-telling called hepatoscopy, or "liver-gazing," particularly popular among the Babylonians and Etrurians, who believed that it had been bestowed upon them by one of Jupiter's grandsons, Tages.

Both hepatoscopy and haruspicy proceed upon the same basic principles. Following the ritual sacrifice of some largish animal—sheep, goats, calves, and bulls were preferred—the haruspex slit open its belly to inspect its entrails. Even in the multi-organ exegesis of haruspicy, the liver was key; the pattern of its veins and the variation of its colors were examined and interpreted according to their resemblance to the signs associated with the gods. The gallbladder, too, was important. A particularly swollen gallbladder foretold military triumph; deflated, it predicted disaster.

The Romans were originally suspicious of haruspicy, seeing it as just the kind of backwoods divination you would expect from an Etruscan. They preferred their native form of divination, augury, or prediction by omens. The problem was that their omen of choice—the flight of birds—was unwieldy, and, as time went on, the Romans turned to haruspicy. Generals in the midst of battle, especially, needed a quick method of consulting the gods and found entrails most convenient. In the last years of the Republic, a haruspex was included on the staff of every commander-in-chief and was habitually consulted on military strategy.

Entrail reading remained a popular form of fortune-telling in the early days of the Roman Empire, not merely for military decisions but for the resolution of political issues and even domestic problems. However, it was always regarded as a somewhat déclassé method of divination. The installation of Christianity as the state religion in 391 dealt a mortal blow to haruspicy, though the patient continued to thrash about for centuries. Around 580, Bishop Gregory of Tours was scandalized to discover that a Frankish king had disemboweled a goat in order to decide whether to combat or flee an enemy. The last Visigoth haruspex probably read his last liver in the eleventh century.

CHARM SECRETS

BINNER CHICAGO

Charm Secrets was published by a Milwaukee soap manufacturer around the turn of the century.
Notwithstanding the Gypsy seeress and the talisman she presses into the palm of the ingenue, the
primary charm secret advocated by the text is frequent washing.

TALISMANS

Sometimes, mere knowledge of the future is insufficient. On occasion, we must take events into our own hands, and then we are obliged to turn from divination to sorcery—specifically, to talismans and spells—to create a future that meets our requirements. *Do not employ these techniques lightly.* The consequences of misused magic are more dire than you might think. The parlor practitioner tends to assume that disbelief somehow defuses the power of the chosen spell: "A death spell! How absurd. I know! I'll cast it on my chemistry teacher! Maybe she'll get a cold, ha ha ha . . ." Ha ha, indeed. You may not know what you're doing, but the spell does. Leave it alone unless you really need it.

Talismans and spells work in different ways. The former is primarily defensive, warding off psychic or physical attack. The latter is primarily offensive, in the sense of working the caster's will on the castee. In the spirit of optimism, let us first investigate the talisman. The talismanic impulse is an ancient one. Excavations in the pyramids of Egypt and the ziggurats of Mesopotamia have turned up numerous examples, usually in the form of small metal or stone fragments carved with signs. More simply still, precious stones, whether set in jewelry or jingling around in your pocket, always have magical properties: pearls remedy headaches; diamonds, placed in the mouth, cure habitual lying and anger (in addition to ensuring the success of dieting); emeralds curb lasciviousness and megalomania and strengthen memory; rubies promote general good health, providing particular protection against plague and poison, and draw money to their bearers; sapphires bestow peacefulness, good humor, and piety while warding off scorpion bite; and topazes neutralize poison.

Planetary talismans, all the rage in sixteenth-century Europe, varied wildly in magical and material density. Most commonly, since each planet has dominion over a different day of the week, the average talisman-bearer simply donned a new planetary

FIGURE 11.

talisman each morning. Just such a set of talismans appears in Figure 11, each day's medal modestly inscribed with the figure of its planetary ruler. The eighth talisman of this set (lower left), which comes from an undated French manuscript called *La Clavicule de Salomon,* can be worn on any day. Around its rim are etched the words *Super aspidem et basiliscum ambulabis et conculcabis* (you shall walk upon asps and basilisks and trample them under your feet). Presumably, the striped egg with legs in the center of the medal represents the squashed basilisk.

For those who feel that they could use more assistance during the week, the nineteenth-century magician Papus created a catalogue of signs, seals, and symbols for each of the planets, including the *gematria* for the mystic names associated with each, as well as its magic square (a magic square is a palindrome of numbers; all rows, columns, and diagonals add up to the same total). Each planet's catalogue culminates in a grand *Figure synthétique,* a compendium of signs that Papus suggests engraving on the back of your planetary talisman to double its power. Figure 12 shows the *Figure synthétique* for Mercury.

Papus is a stellar source for useful talismans and charms. If you wish to make yourself invisible—as who, on occasion, has not?—Papus offers the following instructions:

You must make a little figure resembling yourself from yellow wax, in the month of January, in the day and hour of Saturn [i.e., on Saturday at 5 A.M. or 5 P.M.], and with a needle, you must engrave underneath and on top of the head the following characters. [characters] [You may need to decapitate your figure to achieve this. If so, replace the head on the body.] Quickly, you must write, on a small strip of the skin of a tree frog that you have killed in the dog-days [i.e., August], with the blood of the same frog, these words: HELS, HEL, HELS, and these characters. [characters] Next, hang the figure by one of your own hairs in the arch of a cave at the stroke of midnight while burning appropriate incense and reciting the following words: *Maturation, Mulatto, Beret, Not, Venibbet, Mach, et vos omnes, conjuro te figura cerea per Deum vivum, ut per virtutem horum caracterum et verborum me invisibilem reddas, ubique te portavero mecum. Amen.* Once it is permeated with incense, the figure must be enclosed in a small pine box. Each time you wish to enter or leave someplace without being seen, you simply place the box in your left pocket and repeat these words: *Veni ad me nunquam me derelinquas ubicumque ivero.*

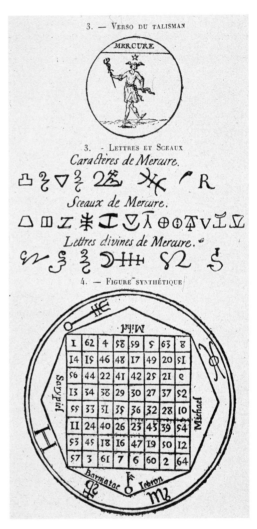

FIGURE 12. *From Papus's* Traité élémentaire de magie practique, *1893.*

Less time-consuming are the following two talismans, the first (Figure 13) against sudden death and accidents causing sudden death on Saturdays, and the second (Figure

FIGURE 13.

FIGURE 14.

14) for success in gambling. Simply engrave them on suitable metals (gold, silver, and tin are preferred) and carry them around until needed. At that point, finger them surreptitiously and imagine your desired outcome.

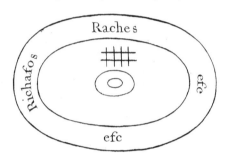

FIGURE 15.

A powerful and malignant charm comes from an eighteenth-century guide to religion. Tucked in between pictures of rosaries and the medal of Saint Benoit is a medal that causes blindness (Figure 15). This must be deposited on the eyes of the intended victim, which makes it difficult to employ for all but the most intimate of friends.

The same source offers us a rather anemic-looking rendition of the renowned Hand of Glory (Figure 16), a combination spell and talisman that stupefied and froze all observers and was therefore much in demand by thieves, who could simply wave the hand in front of their victims and then rob them at a leisurely pace. The Hand of Glory is much more difficult to manufacture now than it was in the eighteenth century, as the first ingredient is "the right or left hand of a felon who is hanging from a gibbet beside a highway," according to the anonymous author of *Secrets merveilleux de la magie naturelle et cabbalistique du Petit Albert*. Once you procure the hand, you are to squeeze it tightly in a funeral pall and pickle it for two weeks in zimat, nitre, salt, and long peppers. Lay it in full sunlight until it is nice and dry. Then make a candle from the fat of a gibbeted felon (it doesn't have to be the same felon), virgin wax, sesame, and ponie, and use the hand as a candlestick. Everyone you encounter will be struck dumb and motionless. Or would be, if only we knew what zimat and ponie were—the lack of these crucial yet mysterious substances is the only thing standing between us and stupefaction.

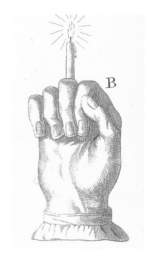

FIGURE 16.

Spells are often easier to deploy than talismans, because they are primarily verbal. For instance, it's a snap to make the victim of your choice rip off all his clothes and dance wildly. All you need to do is write the word *Frutimiere* on virgin parchment in bat's blood, and then lay the parchment on a stone over which a mass has been said. Put the parchment in the threshold of a door through which your chosen one must pass, and then sit back and watch the show.

Since bat's blood is likely to be the most difficult ingredient to obtain for this spell, you don't want to let it go to waste. To make an enemy go into convulsions, use the same procedure as above, writing the palindromic

```
S    A    T    O    R
A    R    E    P    O
T    E    N    E    T
O    P    E    R    A
R    O    T    A    S
```

on parchment in bat's blood.

Most of the love spells advocated by antique texts are designed to produce the complete submission of the female object to the desires of the male subject. I do not know whether they are efficacious in the other direction. The most common love spell of the seventeenth century was quite simple: The man was to lure the woman of his choice into private conversation, look deep into her eyes, and recite, *"Kaphe, kasita, non kapheta et publia filii omnibus suis."* Immediately, she would be his to command.

Good old Papus does not concern himself overmuch with love, but he deigns to include a few such spells in his *grimoire.*

Take some of your own blood one Friday in the springtime and dry it in a little pot. Mix the aforesaid together with two testicles of a hare and the liver of a dove. Reduce the whole to a fine powder and see to it that the woman upon whom you have designs swallows at least a half-dram [about an eighth of a teaspoon]. If it has no effect the first time, you may repeat the process three more times, and you will be loved.

With your fortune assured, your health preserved, your enemies vanquished, and your beloved captivated, you should feel that you have enough margin to return to the stately halls of divination.

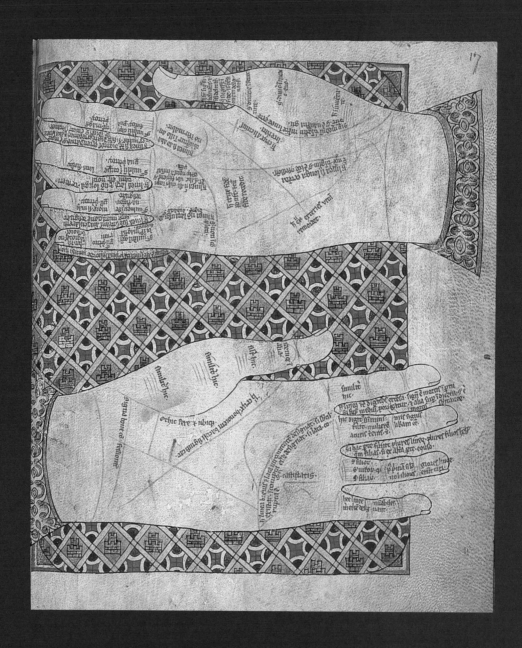

An illumination from a thirteenth-century manuscript on palmistry.

CHIROMANCY

God seals up the hand of every man
that all men may know his work.

Job 37:7

We've all got the image somewhere in our heads: the wizened old Gypsy (with turban) bends over an outstretched palm and, after several agonizing minutes, announces, "You will soon make a long journey." Sad to say, this pronouncement is not palm reading, it is a wild guess (there is no line devoted to travel).

Palmistry has more to do with states of mind, of character, and of development than with the places you will go or the amount of money you will make. Palmistry (which is also known as chiromancy) is a tool for divination, certainly, but the object of its divining is *you:* your creativity, your ambition, your talent, your intuition, your dedication, your passions—in short, all the things about you that will constitute your fate.

Palmistry itself is a somewhat misleading term. The palm is just one source of information; the real chiromancer reads the hand as a whole, looking first at its general shape, then at the fingers, then at the lines and lumps (called *mounts*) that furrow and swell the palm. Accordingly, then, we will begin with the six hand types; move along to the four fingers and their leader, the thumb; and, finally, learn the signs to be found in the palm's mounts, lines, and marks.

Undoubtedly, your first question will be, Which hand do I read? The answer is easy: read the dominant hand (i.e., usually the right). The nondominant hand can be interesting, as it reveals the baseline character and situation of the querent, but it tells you more about where the subject started from than where she is going, which is revealed in the dominant palm. As one

Above: A 1907 postcard illustrating the Line of Health: "When this line lies straight down the hand and is not very well defined, or if entirely absent, it signifies Good Health." The possessor of this hand is obviously doomed.

palmist says, "The nondominant hand shows what you have been given, and the dominant hand shows what you will make of it."

But how can this be? you ask. The lines in your hand are simply and eternally *there*. How can they accommodate the changing course of events? The lines can't just change, can they? Strangely enough, they can and they do. They bend; they develop offshoots; circles, stars, and boxes appear. Sometimes entire lines are etched or erased in the space of a few months. If you keep an eye on your own dominant hand for even so short a span as six weeks, you'll be surprised at the number of changes you will notice.

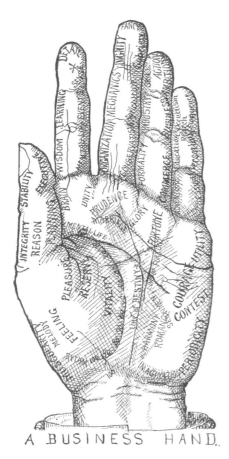

"A Business Hand" is just a polite way of designating a Square Hand. The rather unusual attributions labeled on this chart are the work of the imaginative Holmes Merton, author of Descriptive Mentality from the Head, Face, and Hand.

THE SHAPE OF THE HAND

There are six basic hand types, but you must bear in mind that the platonic ideal of any of these shapes is rarely to be found in the real world. Most hands are a mixture—a Square Hand may display two Conic fingers, for example—and should be read as such. As characters are complex, so are hands, and however great the temptation, you cannot interpret a primarily Square Hand as you would a completely Square Hand.

THE ELEMENTARY HAND is thick and strong and inflexible. The palm dominates the hand, and the fingers are short and sausagey. Only a few heavy lines appear on the Elementary palm, which belongs to a brutal and instinctual character. The great nineteenth-century palmist Cheiro declared snobbishly that "such people are violent in temper, passionate but not courageous . . . They possess a certain low cunning, but it is the cunning of instinct, not reason. These are people without aspirations; they but eat, drink, sleep, and die."

THE SQUARE HAND is, as you might suspect, square. The palm flares out into a square above the wrist and forms an even edge at the base of the fingers. Even the fingertips are blunt and squared off. The Square Hand is sometimes called the Useful Hand, because it generally belongs to a practical, efficient, orderly character, someone who can get things done. Square Hands respect authority and eschew passion for reason. They are not temperamental, but they are tenacious; there is nobody in the world more determined than a Square Hand going about his business. These are definitely the people you want in your workplace.

THE SPATULATE HAND can be alarming at first sight. Spatulate fingertips, instead of tapering to dainty points, do the opposite; they flare out like shovels or, well, a spatula. The hand itself flares too; a true Spatulate Hand is very broad at the wrist or at the base of the fingers. The Spatulate Hand is wildly energetic, imaginative, and active; its fingers want to move and dig and explore. The

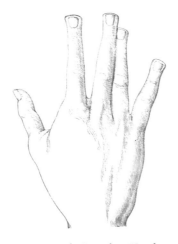

An excessively Spatulate Hand from Les Mystères de la main.

only problem is follow-through: Spatulate types are so restless that they have a hard time finishing their many projects. At their best, Spatulate characters are bold explorers and innovative problem solvers. At their worst, they are chronically discontent and inconsistent.

THE PHILOSOPHIC HAND is a rarer type, especially in this dark era of instant gratification. It is long and lean, with bony fingers, long, narrow nails, and particularly knotty knuckles. This is the hand of a seeker after wisdom, a true intellectual. The Philosophic Hand will probably not be rich or given to dramatic impulses, but she will be thoughtful, extremely analytical, even visionary. The Philosophic type finds her best outlet in academic, artistic, or religious realms, where she uses her brain power judiciously and benignly. In politics, the Philosophic type can be positively frightening.

THE CONIC HAND belongs to a less rigorous character. Altogether the hand forms an ellipse, with a rounded palm and conic, slightly pointed fingers. It is generally medium-

A very strange version of the Idealistic Hand as it appears in the nineteenth-century parlor palmist's guide Les Mystères de la main, *by Adolphe Desbarrolles.*

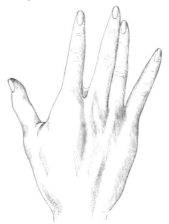

sized, though the fingers may be fairly long, and it is often found in combination with other hand shapes. In its pure form, the Conic Hand reveals an artistic temperament; its possessor has strong emotions and is particularly sensitive to the aesthetic quality of his surroundings. Conic types are responsive and instinctual—sometimes too much so. When the Conic Hand is soft and flexible, it denotes a person with a quick, impulsive, generous nature who may move from enthusiasm to enthusiasm without ever really landing anywhere. A firmer, thinner hand supplies the necessary sense of purpose and discipline to realize some of the grand visions that the Conic mind dreams of.

THE IDEALISTIC or POINTED HAND is the rarest type of all. It is the Botticelli hand, long, narrow, and delicate, with slender, tapering fingers and oval nails. It reveals a dreamy, almost otherworldly nature, drawn to the poetic, the spiritual, and the transcendent. These people are extremely sensitive and intuitive, but they are also fragile and impractical. Though their gentleness and natural grace make them lovable, you can never ask them to run to the store for some bread or show up at a specific time. The possessors of Idealistic Hands often have a somewhat melancholy outlook; this can be exacerbated by the feeling that they are useless and good for nothing. So it is best to accept them as they are, rather than scolding them for their lack of pragmatism.

The most notorious palmist of the late nineteenth and early twentieth centuries was Cheiro (pronounced "Chi-ro"), the nom de palm of Count Louis Hamon, who was born in France in 1866. A man of many hats, Cheiro ran a profitable champagne export business, was a fellow of the Royal Geographic Society, and somehow wound up in Hollywood in the 1920s, writing movie scenarios. However, his greatest fame came from his work as a palmist and psychic, and he must certainly have possessed a profound intuition, for despite a complete misunderstanding of the theory of chiromancy and some of the most ridiculous line interpretations of all time, he managed to be a remarkable palm reader. His book, *Cheiro's Language of the Hand,* which went into twenty-eight editions, is divided into two sections. The first outlines Cheiro's baroque theory of palmistry, containing such pearls as this method for identifying a murderer: "The line of head may or may not be out of its proper position. It will, however, be set higher than usual across the hand, but will be very long and thin, denoting the treacherous instincts. . . . Such are the hands of the skilled artists in crime." The second section is much more interesting; it is a series of thirty-six palm prints, some of them belonging to such luminaries as Sarah Bernhardt (though a close inspection reveals that our friend Cheiro has drawn a few extra lines in ink upon her hand) and some of them to nonentities. It is in the interpretations that accompany these images that we can see Cheiro's real skill. In June of 1911, for example, he wrote in a note to a nervous client, "I see no reason to go back on what I said . . . any danger of violent death to you must be by water and nothing else." The poor man trundled off, satisfied that he would not be set upon by thugs, and went down with the *Titanic* a year later.

Cheiro seems also to have been a powerful hypnotist. There are stories galore: he is said to have saved a young anarchist from the firing squad by bribing the soldiers to use blanks and hypnotizing the putative victim into a coma until he was safe in his coffin at the funeral, at which point he rose again. In another episode, Cheiro was in the process of being robbed at gunpoint when he hypnotized the robber, momentarily paralyzing him. The robber was instantly convinced of the error of his ways—as who wouldn't be?—and reformed.

THE FINGERS AND THUMB

The thumb is your most important finger. Just as our opposable thumb is what distinguishes us (and a few apes) from the other beasts, so the thumb provides the crucial definition of character. Flexibility, rather than shape, is the key factor in thumb interpretation. There are flexible thumbs, inflexible thumbs, and a whole range of mobility in between. An extremely supple thumb can be bent 90 degrees or more away from the hand. An inflexible thumb gets stuck at around 45 degrees. The former reveals exactly what you would expect: a flexible nature, open to new ideas, not bound by convention. Such a character is broad-minded and giving but often yields to the opinions of others rather than sticking to her own. The more inflexible thumb shows a harder nature, resistant to outside influences and opinions, highly directed and determined (some would say pig-headed).

The thumb's phalanges also bear investigation. The top phalange, containing the nail, is associated with the will, the bottom phalange, with logic. The longest of the two will show which element has the greater influence on the personality of the querent. Beware the thumb with the bulbous tip—it reveals a nasty, brutish nature.

On to the fingers:

The index finger is known as the *FINGER OF JUPITER* and is related, in a greater or lesser degree as the finger is more or less long, straight, and strong, to the subject's stance toward the outer world. It is the finger of career, ambition, adaptability to surroundings. A short Finger of Jupiter—that is, an index finger that is shorter than the third finger—is a sign of a retiring, unambitious type. Such a set of digits most often appears on the Idealistic Hand, which is, as we have learned, the hand of the unworldly dreamer. A long Finger of Jupiter—longer than the middle finger—denotes a dominating, ambitious, even ruthless character. A long Jupiter is often called "the Napoleonic finger," a complete misnomer, as Napoleon had an extraordinarily short index finger, with a corresponding inferiority complex (see page 152).

The middle finger is the *FINGER OF SATURN* and is a source of great confusion to palmists everywhere. Each has a different theory about its interpretation, most of them hovering around an association with issues of balance and harmony. Think of it this way: the thumb and index finger relate to the subject's manner of acting in the outer world; the third and little finger reveal the subject's interior world and emotional character. The Finger of Saturn, then, is the sign of the balance between these inner and outer worlds; it represents the querent's ability to mediate between the intellect and the emotions. This plays out in a predictable way: a supremely long or short Finger of Saturn is a sign of instability, excessive length indicating an overly conscious, unemotional, but deeply responsible character, and a somewhat stubby finger representing a person who experiences the world emotionally and intuitively. A distinctly bent middle finger denotes imbalances (the ancient chiromancers were quite specific—a bent Saturn equals intestinal disorder—but now we are not so categorical).

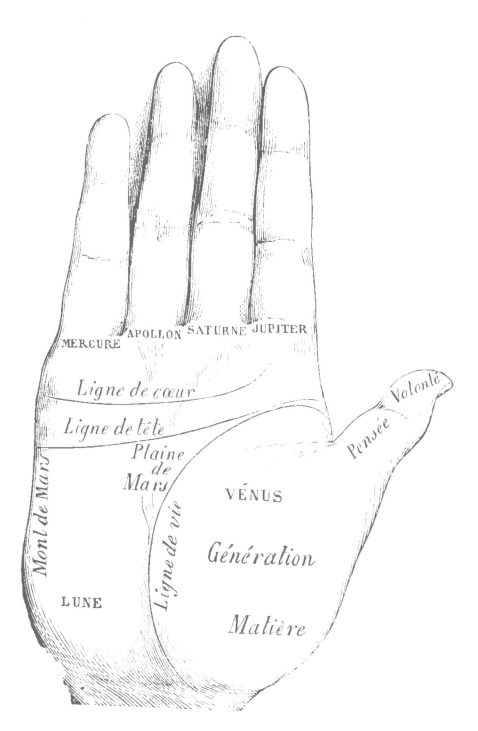

FIGURE 17. *A French chart showing the Life Line* (ligne de vie); *the Head Line* (ligne de tête); *the Heart Line* (ligne de cœur); *and the mounts of Mars, Venus, and the Moon* (lune).

The third finger has always been associated with the Sun. It is called the *FINGER OF APOLLO*, and it signifies the querent's level of creative and emotional energy. This energy may be artistic, or it may be the energy with which the subject experiences his emotions. For instance, an excessively short Finger of Apollo signifies a subject given to histrionic outbursts, an emotionally volatile person. Grotesquely long Fingers of Apollo manifest the opposite: an introvert, unable to extend his emotional connection beyond himself. A nice, middle-of-the-road Finger of Apollo suggests a subject who is able to embark upon and sustain emotional involvements without too much Sturm und Drang. A frustrated artist will have an attenuated Finger of Apollo, reflecting his dwindling creative energy. A productive artist, whose creating is in balance with his intake, will have a strong, straight Finger of Apollo.

The little finger is called the *FINGER OF MERCURY*; it is concerned with sexual matters and the querent's ability to participate in intimate relationships (including the parent-child relationship). Some palmists designate it as the finger of communication as well, but this seems redundant, for what is communication but the essential element of intimacy? Accordingly, it is not length or strength we look for in the Finger of Mercury, but its relationship to the other fingers. A Mercury separated from Apollo by a larger space than that between the other fingers manifests a chronic difficulty with intimacy. If an isolated Mercury appears with a large Mount of Venus and an unbroken Girdle of Venus (see Figure 17, page 148, and Figure 18, page 159, respectively), major sexual problems may be diagnosed. If the little finger is set into the hand at a much lower point than the other fingers, it manifests a basic alienation and inferiority complex with regard to intimate matters. It is both telling and pathetic that to the repressed Victorians, a little finger crooked away from the activity of the rest of the hand was considered to be the height of refinement. A Mercury severely bent toward Apollo signifies a liar.

THE MOUNTS

A quick survey of the palm's seven mounts will be sufficient, as they are subsidiary in importance to the lines and are best used to discern predilections and tendencies. The most obvious mount is *THE MOUNT OF VENUS*, which is the fleshy lump at the root of the thumb. As the name implies, this area is related to love—the higher and more pronounced the lump, the greater the capacity for love and pleasure (although you've got to watch out for the grossly distended Mount of Venus, which means exactly what you would think). A flat Mount of Venus betokens a more cerebral, less bodily type.

THE MOUNT OF THE MOON appears directly opposite the Mount of Venus and, accordingly, represents more ethereal realms, such as imagination, idealism, romance, and the spiritual. An enlarged Mount of the Moon expresses a dreamy character, and it rarely appears on the pragmatic Square Hand.

The mounts that appear beneath each of the fingers embody the attributes of that finger: a large *MOUNT OF JUPITER* denotes an independent, forceful attitude toward career; a pronounced *MOUNT OF SATURN* reveals a serious nature, a flat mount shows a lighter type; a developed *MOUNT OF APOLLO* shows a warm and responsive character coupled with a strong disposition to take center stage; the *MOUNT OF MERCURY* shows mental and sexual energy.

There are three *MOUNTS OF MARS*, all elusive. They are ranged across the middle of the hand. One is above the Mount of Venus, one is above the Mount of the Moon, and one is supposed to be smack in the middle of the palm, though I have seen this one only rarely. All of these denote energy. The one above the thumb shows outward energy—the larger it is, the more aggressive the subject. The central mount shows powers of resistance and generation. And the mount above the Moon shows interior restlessness.

THE LINES

Here is where real divination begins. Until now, we have been reading the general character of the hand. In shifting our focus to the lines, we will still be analyzing character, but in the manner of Heraclitus, who said, "Character is fate." The lines of Heart, Head, Life, and Fate will show how character plays itself out over time, which is the essence of predicting the future.

Everybody is familiar with the *LIFE LINE*, which curves around the Mount of Venus (see Figure 17). Amateur autopalmists may often be found staring intently at their Life Lines, trying to calculate when they will die. Actually, the date of death is quite difficult to figure out from the Life Line; even the alarming spectacle of an abrupt break in the line usually denotes a trauma rather than The End. The line begins under the Finger of Jupiter and swoops around the Mount of Venus, ending toward the wrist. If you divide your Life Line into ten equal lengths (begin with a mark on either end, bisect the length in the middle, bisect the ensuing lengths in the middle, and so forth, until you have ten marks), each length represents about seven years. This will give you an approximate time frame for the events you see on your Life Line, but beware of an overemphasis on schedule—you could be off by about seven years in any prediction.

More salient is the appearance of the line itself. As I mentioned above, a break in the line can indicate a severe illness or an accident, but equally worrisome is the generally weak line or the chained line (i.e., a series of small links constituting the line). Since the Life Line reveals energy and life force, such weak lines show low vitality and a disposition to illness and torpor.

If the Life Line begins above the Head Line, from the Mount of Jupiter, it indicates that ambition and career will rule the life. If Life runs alongside or together with the Head Line, the energies will be directed by the head, and your querent may tend to have a shrewd and intellectual character. However, a Life Line that emerges far below the Head Line denotes a subject whose brain imposes no restraint on his energies. Such a fellow may be impulsive and uninhibited, but he'll never win at chess.

The usually pagan fingers have been assigned to the holy family and some saints in this nineteenth-

Marie-Anne-Adelaide LeNormand was the eighteenth-century version of Palmist to the Stars. Born in obscurity in 1772, she manipulated the upheaval of the French Revolution to her advantage and had the incredible luck to become the chiromancer of Josephine de Beauharnais, a young widow who had the incredible luck to become the Empress Josephine, wife of Napoleon Bonaparte. Mademoiselle LeNormand knew a good thing when she saw it, and she paid tender attention to the palm of Madame de Beauharnais, making predictions of such complexity that the rather vapid Josephine was obliged to request a number of return visits, to make sure she had gotten it all straight. So convinced was Josephine of the genius of Mlle. LeNormand that she persuaded Napoleon himself to submit to a reading. Mlle. LeNormand made it worth his while by finding so many signs and portents in his palm that a lesser man would have collapsed under the strain: "Seen from a distance, the hand of Napoleon Bonaparte seemed brutal and unattractive, but on examining its interior, one felt oneself suddenly gripped by keen emotion. There one saw to what planet or what sign of the Zodiac every part of this hand was subject. Everything was shown there, even to the marks proclaiming the hero and conqueror. . . . I declare that the hand of Napoleon is the universal book, that it will be centuries, perhaps, before this book is reproduced."

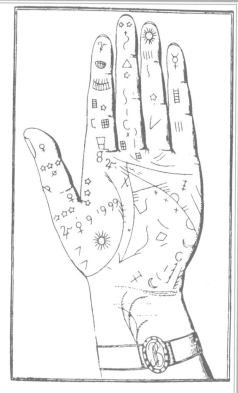

Napoleon Bonaparte's left hand, according to Mlle. LeNormand.

In 1807, Mlle. LeNormand had the tactlessness to foresee in the Emperor's palm his intention to divorce Josephine. Napoleon pooh-poohed the prediction, but on December 11, 1809, he had her arrested and detained for twelve days while he concluded his divorce. Mlle. LeNormand should not be pitied, however; this confirmation of her skill made her the most sought-after seeress of her time.

Some people seem to have two Life Lines. This is always a positive omen, as it implies double vitality and double protection. The outer line is the one you should read as the Line of Life.

THE HEAD LINE begins, usually with the Life Line, under the Mount of Jupiter, and runs outward across the hand to the Mount of the Moon (see Figure 17). We can think of it metaphorically as extending from the realm of outer life represented by the Fingers of Jupiter and Saturn and the thumb, toward the more interior realms of the Finger of Mercury and the Mount of the Moon. The common perception is that the longer the Head Line, the brainier the subject, but this is too crude. As with so many things, size is less important than intensity. A long Head Line, stretching across the palm, simply expresses a wide field of understanding. If the line is straight, ending well above the Mount of the Moon, your subject will have a powerful but practical intellect, probably in conjunction with strong rational powers and an impressive ability to concentrate. A well-defined Head Line that slopes down into the Mount of the Moon reveals a character just as smart, but more imaginative and artistic. A short Head Line, terminating under Saturn, say, implies only that your querent has a limited range of understanding; she may be profoundly intelligent within her field as long as the line is well-marked and powerful.

A chain on the Line of the Head expresses either wavering concentration or a severe taxa-

A French palmistry manual.

tion of the mental powers (to predict such an episode, use the dating system described for the Life Line). Contrary to popular belief, a break in the Head Line does not reveal that you're about to go nuts; it usually just means that you will reorganize your thinking in a dramatic way. Traditionally, a Head Line that swoops all the way down to the wrist, following the Life Line, has been seen as a strong predictor of suicide. This seems too unqualified, but such a Head Line would certainly reveal a character with deep difficulty in differentiating between reality and imagination.

Moving in the opposite direction to the Head Line is *THE HEART LINE*, which is born underneath the Finger of Mercury and reaches across the palm toward the Finger of Jupiter (see Figure 17). This makes sense, as the emotional energies represented by the Heart Line move from the subconscious, interior world to the conscious, exterior world. The line of the Heart represents the quality and depth of the subject's emotions, and a strong, smooth Heart Line betokens strong affections and a smooth course of love. A telling aspect of the line is where it ends up: if it terminates between the Fingers of Saturn and Jupiter, a healthy interest in sex is denoted. If the line ends farther down on the hand toward the Head Line, the subject is sexually cooler and more intellectual in his approach to love.

A heavily chained Heart Line expresses a complicated and difficult romantic life. Actual breaks in the line foretell powerful emotional upheavals and upsets, such as broken hearts and sexual shocks. Small branches off the line in the area of Mercury represent extracurricular affairs or, at least, a propensity to them. A series of breaks or an extra-ordinarily weak line may indicate problems with the organ of the heart itself.

If you are lucky, you will never encounter a *SIMIAN LINE*. A true Simian Line—so called because it appears on gorilla palms—is the fusing of the Head and Heart Lines into one thick string crossing the hand. It signals a depraved and willful nature, and it appears with astonishing frequency in the hands of criminals. As you might guess, a Simian Line represents a catastrophic conflation of desire with reason, which is the essence of psychosis, and, at the very least, it makes for an intense personality. It appears in about six percent of the population.

THE FATE LINE is the most erratic of the major lines of the palm; it begins where it will, measures anywhere from half an inch to a good seven inches, and is alto-gether absent from about twenty percent of hands. This imperious line may be found, when it decides to show up at all, in the center of the palm, running vertically, some-times toward Apollo or Jupiter, but most often to the Finger of Saturn. The Line of Fate represents the subject's sense of direction and purpose, her motivation and predispo-sition to solve problems. It is intimately related to career and the subject's way of work-ing in the world. A short or missing line does not necessarily mean that your querent is lazy or unemployable; it may simply express a character that prefers to work alone, a nonconformer. At the other extreme, a Line of Fate that runs from the wrist bracelets (the horizontal lines that mark the bottom of the hand) straight up to the Finger of

The sixteenth-century chiromancer Bartolomeo Cocles called this double Line of Intuition "a double Mercurian line" and wrote that it signified a "loquacious, presumptuous man."

Two extra Life Lines—these are always helpful, even if they are truncated.

This hand is notable for its robust rascettes (the bracelets that appear on the wrist), which denote vigor and health.

Saturn implies a directed, confident, even somewhat dictatorial type. If the Line of Fate lurches over to the Mount of Jupiter, you may expect a highly ambitious—and probably highly successful—character. If it ends in Apollo, fame—though not fortune—may be foretold.

It is particularly interesting to note the variance between dominant and nondominant hands with regard to the Fate Line. The nondominant hand, reflecting the innate, essential character of the querent, will usually have a much weaker, more disrupted Line of Fate. Many children are born with no Fate Line and then develop one abruptly after the age of twenty—the age when people begin to define and pursue their goals.

Less important but still informative are the subsidiary lines to be found in some palms. It is important (and often difficult) not to mistake the *LINE OF APOLLO* for the line of Fate. The Line of Apollo runs down vertically from the Finger of Apollo, sometimes paralleling the Fate Line and sometimes seeming to replace it altogether (if the Fate is short or missing). However, the Line of Apollo usually ends farther up the palm than the Line of Fate begins. It is a different entity altogether: the Line of Apollo is entirely concerned with the gratuitous forces of creativity and talent; it has nothing to do with the sober hard work expressed in the Fate Line. The Line of Apollo may appear as a scattering or crisscrossing of lines. We all know this type: blessed with many talents but so unfocused as to be unable to develop any one of them.

THE GIRDLE OF VENUS, which runs in a semicircle across the Mount of Jupiter and Saturn, is a reiteration of sensual interests. It is usually linked to intense sexuality, but it may, in a hand with an undistinguished Mount of Venus, simply indicate a lusty, energetic nature.

This, as you might suspect, is the hand of a miser.

Such a bulging Life Line is good news; its abrupt halt is not.

A pronounced Fate Line indicates a driven, even bossy character. Watch out for anyone with a thumb this big.

ALLERS FAMILJ-JOURNAL

N:r 34. 16 aug. 1927.

Pris 30 öre.

Handens Geografi

är läran om handytans upphöjningar (berg), fördjupningar (dalar) och linjer (floder) samt om de karaktärsegenskaper dessa röja, sammanställda med handens och fingrarnas form i dess helhet.

Handens geografi har intet att göra med kiromanti eller konsten att spå med ledning av linjerna i handen, — den försöker endast tyda det språk, som vi se i handens berg, dalar och floder. »Säg mig med vilka du umgås, så skall jag säga dig, vem du är!» säger ordspråket. »Visa mig dina händer, så skall jag säga dig, vem du är!» säger handgeografen. Inne i tidningen finner man en illustrerad artikel om det intressanta och underhållande ämnet »Handens Geografi».

A 1927 Swedish magazine on palm-reading.

THE LINE OF MERCURY, which rises out of the Fate Line and reaches to the Mount of Mercury, is also known as the *LINE OF INTUITION.* Clairvoyants and witches always have this line; it is one way to tell the charlatan from the genuine article. *THE RING OF SOLOMON* is a very rare mark that runs in a semicircle under the Finger of Jupiter. It denotes a being who is not merely intuitive but an adept, a powerful psychic master.

Contemporary palmists have dubbed the little horizontal line between the Mount of Mercury and the Line of Heart as the *LINE OF AFFECTIONS.* It and its branches are supposed to reveal how many children you will have, but since it seems to indicate that everyone in the world will have three children (or one spouse and two children, depending on how the large central line is being interpreted), I have discarded its definition as an ersatz explanation for a line that appears on almost every palm. I'm inclined to believe that this little line means nothing.

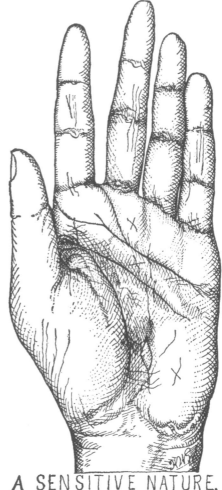

A SENSITIVE NATURE.

An Idealistic Hand bedecked with several inauspicious crosses. If the subject doesn't die violently, she will go insane. Perhaps both.

Odd Marks and Extras

We have already learned that any double line is a positive sign, strengthening and protecting the area represented by the line in question. A line that forks is also positive; a fork imparts a greater range or double nature to the line. A Head Line that ends in a wide fork, for example, shows that the subject's intellect has both a practical and an imaginative element. The only unwelcome fork is on the Life Line, where it betokens an actual splitting off, indicative of an accident or severe illness.

Little lines branching upward are generally benign and denote the influence of the line, finger, or mount they point to. Lines branching down are malign and show a depletion of the strength of the line or an unfortunate turn of events.

Stars are bad and crosses are worse. A star always reveals an explosion of some sort. Usually, explosions are negative events, but if a star appears on the Mount of Apollo, it means a sudden flush of celebrity. There is an old tradition that a star on the Mount of Saturn is the mark of murder; in recent years this has been muted to the point where such a star merely implies a terrible fatality. Small comfort. Crosses are the most ominous signs of all. They express danger, disappointment, and catastrophic change (rest assured that what is meant here is a freestanding cross, not merely a small line crossing a major line). On the Mount of Saturn, a cross means your querent will die violently; on the Mount of Apollo, it indicates a terrible fall from grace, financial mortification, or decrease of talent; on the Mount of Mercury, it portends suffering due to deception; on the Mount of Mars (any of them), it foretells that enemies will undo your querent; on the Mount of the Moon, it prophesies a fatal surrender to the imagination; and on the Mount of Venus, it promises a destructive love affair or sexual attachment. If you have a cross on your palm, you should probably stay in bed (alone) until it goes away.

The caption to this magazine cover reads: "You have both a deep sensitivity and a rare courage. Your heart line is admirable. You could be either a great poet or a great leader."

Islands, like chained lines, reveal difficult episodes in the realms to which the lines pertain. Crossbars express obstacles and problems that must be overcome. Squares are beneficent—they offer protection and preservation. Grilles (otherwise known as "the pound sign") denote obstacles, particularly obstacles that arise from the querent's own character.

Now that you have the essential tools of palmistry, inspect your own hands. You will find both confirmations and revelations in what you see there, but you must be sure to look at yourself and your palms honestly. If you see a star on your Fate Line, it's no good pretending it's really a square—a star will out. This applies when you're reading others' palms, too. But remember—your hands change constantly: an abrupt break today can become an upward offshoot next month.

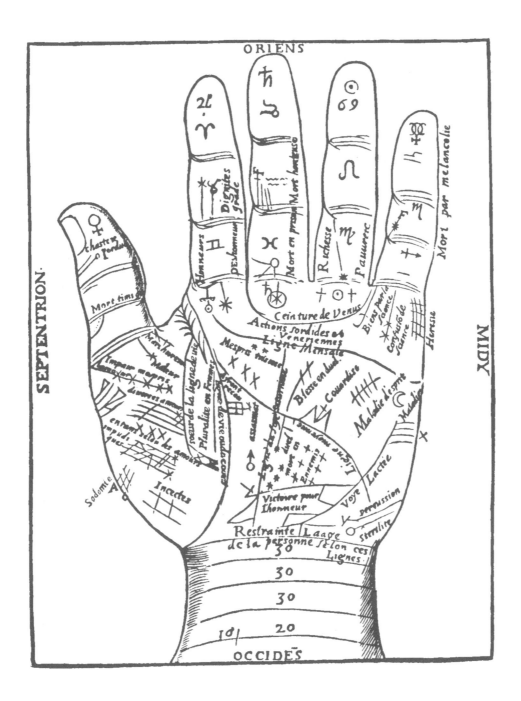

FIGURE 18. *A wildly active palm from a seventeenth-century manual by the curious curate Jean Belot. The chart predicts sodomy, incest, imprisonment, and death by melancholy.*

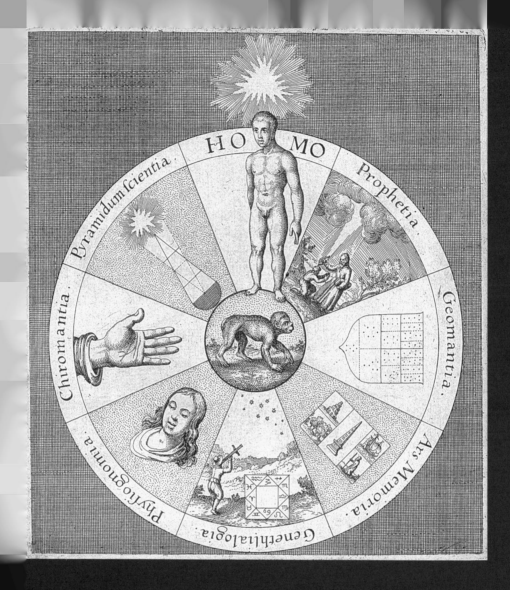

Robert Fludd considered geomancy one of the great divinatory systems available to humankind and, therefore, a sign of the divine hand in nature. This illustration, from Utriusque cosmi majoris et minoris historia, shows that geomancy is the equal of such arts as prophesy, chiromancy, and memory. The latter was a complicated mnemonic philosophy developed by—surprise!—Fludd himself.

GEOMANCY

Originating in North Africa in the ninth century, geomancy was a method of divination practiced by reading random marks drawn in the sand, which North Africans certainly had no shortage of. By the late twelfth century, when the practice attracted the attention of European mystics and established itself as one of the fundamental Western divinatory systems, it was translated in the notably less sandy halls of Europe into a system of reading marks made on paper. From the Greek *gaia-manteia*, meaning "earth-seeing," oracular geomancy is sometimes mistakenly associated with Chinese feng shui (commonly mistranslated as "geomancy"), an unrelated system of landscape and household arrangement meant to maximize the beneficial flow of universal Tao energy, a mechanism of luck influence rather than future prediction.

Geomantic genealogists trace the system to the millennium-old Egyptian and Muslim south Mediterranean divinatory practice of *khatt al-raml* ("lines in the sand"), in which the diviner posed a question in rhymed Arabic and then drew and erased a series of lines, creating geomantic trees from the odd or even number of lines remaining (see Figure 19). The system was carried by Islamic conquest and by camel trade across Africa to Ghana and Nigeria, where its symbols were incorporated by the Yorubas in their Ifa divinatory technique. With the Arab invasion of Spain and the subsequent translation of Arabic texts into Latin, geomancy became, after astrology, the most popular form of divination in Europe among the educated (hoi polloi were still gazing into entrails). Mystic, magician and sometime con-man Cornelius Agrippa introduced a new wrinkle to the system in the sixteenth century by integrating geomantic figures and the astrological houses and so cornered the European divinatory market. Geomancy, astrological and otherwise, remained popular until the eighteenth century's increasing enthusiasm for the rational diminished it and other divinatory arts to drawing-room entertainment. A pair of geomantic texts bogusly linked to Napoleon surfaced in the nineteenth century (Napoleon was "in"), and one, *Napoleon's Book of Fate,* also fashionably rooted in Egyptology, became enormously popular throughout Europe. At the same time, geomancy was adopted by the influential mystic society the Order of the Golden Dawn, thereby attracting some serious occult interest and making the period something of a geomantic renaissance. Modern practice has come to emphasize the astrological aspects geomancy acquired in its European conduct, but the technique needs no such ornament—geomancy is substantially the same system practiced by ninth century desert nomads.

THE READING

The essence of geomancy is the manufacture and reading of a series of sixteen figures. The best thing about it is that it requires very little equipment to deploy: a pen and some paper will suffice. The worst thing about it is the arduous process of deriving the sixteen figures. At a certain point, you will find yourself surrounded by several hundred

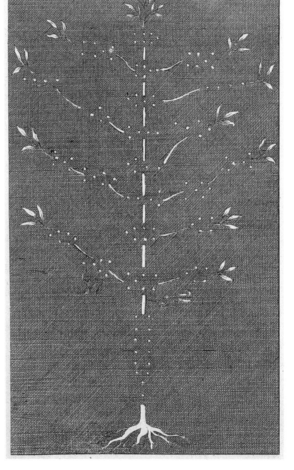

FIGURE 19. *An Arab geomantic tree. Note that the derivation of the figures seems entirely different from the Western method.*

dots. But do not repine; they will eventually lead you to illumination.

You must begin with a question. Once derived, the figures offer qualitative interpretations, which are less suited to yes or no questions than to questions about the prospects for or outcome of certain actions. The reading begins by framing your question in this way (e.g., "What are my chances for a happy marriage?"). Then you begin to generate the answer by making sixteen rows of a random number of marks on a sheet of paper. Avoid counting while doing so—just quickly make a line of dots and stop when you feel like it. After you have made sixteen rows, count the dots in each. You are interested only in whether the number of marks in each row is odd or even: mark a single dot next to each row containing an odd number of dots and mark two dots for an even number. Thus, at the end of stage one, you will have a column containing sixteen rows, each line containing one or two dots.

The following is an example:

. . . .	=	10	=	. .
. . . .	=	12	=	. .
. . . .	=	7	=	.
. . . .	=	14	=	. .
. . . .	=	14	=	. .
. . . .	=	9	=	.
. . . .	=	9	=	.
. . . .	=	18	=	. .
. . . .	=	14	=	. .
. . . .	=	15	=	.
. . . .	=	16	=	. .
. . . .	=	11	=	.
. . . .	=	15	=	.
. . . .	=	14	=	. .
. . . .	=	13	=	.
. . . .	=	16	=	. .

At this point, you probably—and quite reasonably—assume that you have made the necessary sixteen figures. HA! You have only just begun. Count off the first four rows from your column of sixteen rows of dots.

. .
. .
. .
. .

There is one figure. Count off the next four rows. There is a second figure. Repeat until you have four figures. Each of your sixteen figures is composed of four rows of either one or two dots, and your random marks on paper generate only the first four figures of your reading, the "Mothers."

. .   . .
. .   . .
. .   . .
. .   . .

The rest of the geomantic household will be created from these initial four through a recombination of the Mother dots.

Mark your four Mother figures in order across the top of a sheet of paper. A sequence of four "Daughter" figures are then derived from the Mothers by the following means: the top rows of the four Mother figures become, in order, the four rows of the figure of the first Daughter; the second rows of the four Mothers become the second Daughter, etcetera.

HEINRICH CORNELIUS AGRIPPA

A man of his time, Agrippa's restless personality was well-suited to the intellectual and spiritual ferment of the sixteenth century. He was, variously, an occult scholar, military strategist, linguist, court astrologer, alchemist, theologian, historian, demonologist, doctor, lawyer, faith healer, financial advisor, magician, and secret agent. Famous and infamous in the royal courts and universities of western Europe, he was the subject of folklore even during his lifetime (Goethe is known to have drawn on Agrippa's exploits in creating the character of Faust).

Born Heinrich Cornelis in 1486, in Germany, our hero latinized part of his name to the more scholarly Cornelius and assumed the phony noble title Agrippa von Nettesheim because he felt it his due. Moving throughout Europe, he lived by his wits, working for the Pope and then the rival Emperor as opportunity arose, occasionally founding a secret society in order to exploit its members. On the grift, it's not surprising that between his royal and Papal gigs Agrippa did a stint in debtor's prison. He died in 1535, after some of his enemies found and tortured him so severely that he survived only a few weeks after his release.

Like his persona, Agrippa's writing made brilliant and sometimes conflicting use of available material. His most famous work, the four-volume *Occult Philosophy,* is a synthesis of Neoplatonic, Christian, and Kabbalistic belief that postulates that all living and inanimate objects have spiritual aspects, which, considered together, compose a universal spiritual soul that is synonymous with God. This soul component reveals itself the magical properties of plants, animals, and metals, some conventional (magnets attract iron), and some not so conventional (consumption of mule urine is a surefire female contraceptive). According to Agrippa, the study of such "magic" is meant only for the initiated, that is, men like himself and those lucky enough to be admitted to his secret societies. The book defends study of the natural world's magic properties as a means of knowing God's work. Agrippa's *The Uncertainty and Vanity of the Sciences and the Arts,* written sixteen years later, chucks all that for the singular certainty that God may be known through His word alone—the magnets and mule urine suddenly mere clutter.

Agrippa's main treatise on geomancy is in the fourth, posthumously published volume of *Occult Philosophy.* His method considered the numerological and symbolic meanings of geomantic figures in relation to the positions of the planets and astrological houses at the time of the reading, the figures serving as raw material for an astrological interpretation. Although sincerely intentioned (Agrippa was capable of sincerity), the system allowed shifty mystics to produce instant horoscopes without troublesome calculations or textual consultation—a boon for the spiritual entrepreneur, and, in that, perhaps an appropriate legacy.

$$\begin{array}{ccccccccc}
\cdot\;\cdot & + & \cdot\;\cdot & + & \cdot\;\cdot & + & \cdot & = & \cdot\;\cdot \\
\cdot\;\cdot & & \cdot\;\cdot & & \cdot\;\cdot & & \cdot\;\cdot & & \cdot\;\cdot \\
\cdot\;\cdot & & \cdot\;\cdot & & \cdot\;\cdot & & \cdot\;\cdot & & \cdot\;\cdot \\
\cdot\;\cdot & & \cdot\;\cdot & & \cdot\;\cdot & & \cdot\;\cdot & & \cdot\;\cdot
\end{array}$$

(Daughter #1)

These figures are recorded below the Mothers. The four "Nephews" are then derived in a slightly different manner. The marks of the first two Mothers are added together row by row to compose the first Nephew: if the sum of the first rows of the two Mothers is odd, the first row of the Nephew is one mark; if even, two marks.

$$\begin{array}{ccccc}
\cdot\;\cdot & + & \cdot\;\cdot & = & \cdot\;\cdot \\
\cdot\;\cdot & + & \cdot & = & \cdot \\
\cdot & + & \cdot & = & \cdot\;\cdot \\
\cdot\;\cdot & + & \cdot\;\cdot & = & \cdot\;\cdot
\end{array}$$

(Nephew #1)

The rows of the second Nephew are the sums of the rows of the third and fourth Mothers. The third and fourth Nephews are derived from the Daughter figures in the same fashion, and the four Nephews are recorded below the Daughters. The four Nephews are combined in the same way to derive two "Witnesses," and these are combined to create the "Judge," the ruling figure of the reading. If you have not by this time gone blind or mad or both, you are the happy recipient of the answer to your question— see the list that follows for the interpretation of your Judge figure. In a clear reading, you will need only consider the implications of the Judge as it applies to your question. A more nuanced interpretation may consider the opinion expressed by the Judge in light of the opposing influence of the two Witnesses. If the querent seeks guidance through a process rather than a simple answer, the geomancer may consider the significance of the order of the four Mother figures, as they generate the chronology of unfolding events. If and *only* if all of these interpretations still prove inconclusive, a "Reconciler" figure may be derived by adding the Judge to the first Mother, row by row, in the same way that the Nephews are created. The

Heinrich Cornelius Agrippa von Nettesheim.

Reconciler is a last resort and is to be considered with the utmost seriousness; those who consult the Reconciler simply because they are not satisfied with the Judge's decision are said to find poisonous reward.

THE INTERPRETATION OF THE FIGURES

The following definitions apply to all figures, whether Judge, Reconciler, or Mother.

 Puer: The Boy; son, slave, bachelor, employee, male youth; inquisitive but also rash; beardless; perhaps yellow or callow; aggressive and inconsiderate; an unknown enemy; considered a negative sign except in matters of love and war, where callow aggression is appropriate. Associated with Aries and the planet Mars.

 Puella: The Girl; daughter; wife; youth; beauty; nurse; grace; love but also deceptiveness; both purity and false appearance (the saint-slut dichotomy). Associated with Libra and the planet Venus.

 Amisso: Losing, Lost; removal; failure; powerlessness; defeat, dispersion; sadness; ruin in love or finance; but: escape or freedom for those imprisoned. Associated with Taurus and the planet Venus.

 Albus: White; white-haired (wise); wisdom; clear thought; spiritual advancement or elevation; calm, peaceful; serenity; profit; aspects of beauty. Associated with Gemini and the planet Mercury.

 Populus: The People, Assembly; community; gathering; reunion; without order (real or imagined); news, rumor and gossip; democracy. Associated with Cancer and the Moon.

 Fortuna Major: Great Fortune; good luck, fate, chance, or lot; security; health; happiness; light and flame; glory; union; success. Associated with Leo and the Sun.

 Fortuna Minor: Lesser Fortune; good but not great luck; received assistance; protection; nomadic success; voyage; solitary endeavor and benefit. Associated with Leo and the Sun.

 Conjunctio: Conjunction, Union, Marriage; recovery of loss; alliance; relationship; renewal; gathering; public recognition; sympathy; participation; hope; friendship and love. Associated with Virgo and the planet Mercury.

 Rubeus: Red; attention, stop; passion; vice; temper; rage and power; violence, and warfare; excitement and stimulation; anger and murder; blood and fire; traditionally a highly negative figure. Associated with Scorpio and the planet Mars.

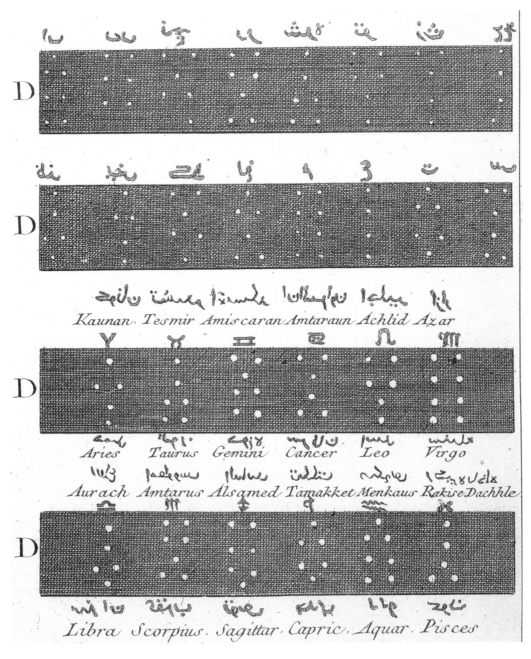

Kaunan Tesmir Amiscaran Amtaraun Achlid Azar

Aries   Taurus   Gemini   Cancer   Leo   Virgo

Aurach Amtarus Alsamed Tamakket Menkaus RakiseDachhle

Libra Scorpius. Sagittar. Capric. Aquar. Pisces

This chart, appearing in an eighteenth-century tome on magic and religion, is described by the author as "The secrets of Arab geomancy." However, the labels associating geomantic figures with astrological signs make the whole enterprise suspicious, both because the link between geomancy and astrology was European and because the labels are incorrect.

*I*fa divination is a sophisticated west African variant of geomancy central to the Yoruba culture in Nigeria. Also practiced in parts of South America and the Caribbean, its techniques are incorporated in Voodoo, *Santería*, and Creole religious practices. A rich and imaginative system, *Ifa* uses geomantic symbols (generated by either a handful of palm nuts or a string of cowrie shells) as reference keys to an immense pool of related stories, myths and rituals, held only in the memory of the divining priest, called *Babalawo* (Father of Secrets), who devotes his life to the art of their interpretation. In *Ifa*, the familiar geomantic figures are rendered in pairs called *Odu*. Like pairs form the sixteen major, most powerful *Odu*, considered individual spirits with wills of their own. Mixed pairs form another 240 minor *Odu* for a total of 256 possible outcomes, each with its own history, fables and resonance. In *Ifa* mythology, the fathering spirit (*Ifa*) has withdrawn from the world to live in heaven, leaving chaos, but also leaving the *Odu* as a means to find order in his absence. The trickster god *Elegba*, by causing trouble, gives believers the opportunity to consult the divine *Odu* for advice, and he offsets his mischief by passing on their prayer and sacrifice to the appropriate god or ancestor.

The *Babalawo* and the querent sit before an idol of *Elegba*, and the querent, without revealing his trouble to the *Babalawo*, whispers his question to a ritual shell or coin and places it on a divining tray sprinkled with wood dust. The *Babalawo* taps the tray with a wand to invoke the *Odu*. Then, holding sixteen smooth pine nuts in his left hand, he transfers as many as he can in one grab to his right. If two nuts remain in his left hand he draws a single mark in the tray's dust; if one nut is left, he draws two parallel marks—a reversal meant to trick the trickster *Elegba*. Any other outcome is discounted. When the process has been completed successfully eight times, the *Odu* has been conjured as represented in the marks in the dust: a pair of four-line geomantic figures. The *Babalawo* then recites the stories associated with the *Odu*, asking questions about the querent's life and informing his reading with their answers.

Acquisitio: Acquisition, Acquiring; profit; possession and money; investment; financial success; benefit, riches, and power; grasp, grip, and seizure; a light spirit; traditionally a positive figure. Associated with Sagittarius and the planet Jupiter.

 Carcer: The Prison, Cell; confinement; binding and restriction; egotism and lies; sadness; public humiliation; authoritarian exertion; despair; but conservation, preservation of secrets, protection and insulation; in itself a neutral figure dependent on circumstance. Associated with Capricorn and the planet Saturn.

 Tristitia: Sadness, Sorrow; misery; melancholy; damnation; condemnation; poverty; death; shadow and obscurity; inflexibility; but for some reason considered a good sign for pregnancy. Associated with Aquarius and the planet Saturn.

 Laetitia: Joy, Happiness; delight; grace; freedom from restraint; health; laughter; beauty; acquisition; generosity; goodwill and accord; peace. Associated with Pisces and the planet Jupiter.

 Caput Draconis: The Dragon's Head; entrance, entry; crossing a threshold; introduction by marriage; the beginnings of spiritual development; the heavens. Associated with Capricorn and the planets Jupiter and Venus.

 Cauda Draconis: The Dragon's Tail; exit; termination; illusion, fraud; danger; bad magic and bad karma; the underworld; specific loss; but also the way out; a sign suggesting a change of direction. Associated with Scorpio and the planets Saturn and Mars.

 Via: The Way, the Wanderer; journey; direction; solitude; dispersion; news; a guide; a successful trip; but a hearse; a sign dependent on circumstance. Associated with Cancer and the Moon.

I.ᵉ Maniere de tenir la
Baguette.

This illustration, from Abbé de Vallmont's Physique occulte, shows
the most common method of holding "la Baguette." However,
according to the Abbé, there are some devotees who balance the
rod on the backs of their hands and some who march along holding the rod by both ends, which seems odd.

RHABDOMANCY

or Dowsing

In addition to prediction, another great divinatory goal is the retrieval of missing objects, lost people, and, best of all, precious metals. Rhabdomancy, more commonly known as dowsing, is the art of finding resources—and humans—by using a divining rod.

This semimagical skill has been around for thousands of years, though it probably reached its apex of popularity in Germany in the sixteenth century, when it was vigorously employed to prospect for mines. The divining rod itself is undoubtedly derived from the sorcerer's wand, but it is a much more democratic instrument—almost anyone can use one. The technique is equally foolproof. According to an eighteenth-century French dowser and, incidentally, abbot, nothing could be simpler:

> A forked branch of hazel, or filbert, must be taken, a foot and a half long, as thick as a finger, and not more than a year old . . . The two limbs of the fork are held in the two hands, without gripping too tight, the back of the hand being towards the ground. The point goes foremost, and the rod lies horizontally. Then the diviner walks gently over the places where it is believed there is water, minerals, or hidden money. He must not tread roughly, or he will disperse the clouds of vapours and exhalations which rise from the spot where these things are and which impregnate the rod and cause it to start.

Contemporary dowsers are less rigid with regard to the brand of tree necessary for the divining rod: ash, willow, and apple branches are now permissible, and some dowsers even countenance plastic. The physics are inexplicable, but the results are inescapable: the divining rod does indeed lurch upward—sometimes quite violently—as it passes over buried spring and minerals.

Rhabdomancy was denounced as the work of the devil at various points in history, but it has been employed almost continuously in Europe since the Middle Ages (practical benefits outweigh the maledictions of the church every time). The French were particularly keen to assert the benign, God-fearing attributes of *la baguette,* as they call the divining rod, and so were the chief innovators in its development as a policing tool. In 1692, a peasant named Jacques Aymar used his divining-rod to track down the murderers of a local wine merchant. His forked stick bobbed up and down dramatically at the murder site and then led Aymar through town, over the Rhone, and all the way to Lyons, where he found a hunchback who confessed to taking part in the deed. Upon the publication of this detective story, judicial rhabdomancy became all the rage in France. In early America, dowsing had the purely pragmatic function of locating well-water, but it is now used by oil and gas companies to find caches of those resources. During the Vietnam War, dowsing was practiced to find land mines.

IN THE CARDS

Playing cards have been a perennial source of advice about the future. While the more serious seekers of wisdom should consult the tarot (see next chapter), those who are pressed for time can read their fortune using an everyday deck of cards. Note, though, that playing cards are best used for simple questions, such as "Does he love me?" Red cards are positive, and black are negative. A one is yes; two is no; three is more; four is completion; five is creation; six is the body; seven is the mind; eight is work; nine is trouble; ten is eternity. Court cards are fairly obvious: Jacks are young men and apprenticeship; Queens are women and fertility; Kings are older men and power. The suits may be applied as follows: Hearts are love; Spades are troubles; Clubs are sudden events; Diamonds are wealth.

Playing card divination is not overburdened with rules. In fact, there aren't any. But most people lay out three cards to deduce their answer, and particularly scrupulous types declare that the color of the first card laid out defines the overall tone of the reading (positive or negative).

The fortune-telling cards pictured here—an elevated version of a playing card deck—were published as an inducement by an early twentieth-century cigarette manufacturer. The small scenes they sport, alternately evocative and mystifying, were apparently meant to assist in the interpretation of the cards.

Une Fabricante
de Cartes à jouer

1. Baquet avec couleur à bruiner, 2. Le pinceau à bruiner.
3. Les Patrons, 4. La Feuille de cartes. appelée l'Image.
4. Les Planches portant les gravures. des N.os 7. 8. 9. 10.
5. Le Bâton contre lequel on frappe le pinceau, 6. La Brosse à coller.
7. La Feuille à coller. 8. Le Pinceau pour la peinture.
9. Le Plat sur lequel on prend la couleur avec le pinceau.
10. La Brosse pour appuyer, 11. Le Planoir, 12. La Feuille de carte à aplanir.

It is not mere whimsy that causes me to place tarot at the end of this divinatory opus. The position is dictated by the nature of the system, composed as it is of symbols adopted, adapted, and kidnapped from every other brand of Western fortune-telling. Simple in method and hair-raisingly complicated in meaning, tarot provides a good return on serious study. The more you know about astrology, numerology, the Kabbalah, Theosophical color theory, Neoplatonism, Christian theology, thaumaturgy, ancient Egyptian religious cults, Rosicrucianism, early modern European social structures, and the history of magic, the more information you can extract from the symbols that appear on each of the tarot cards. But if, like most people, you know nothing of those subjects, do not despair. Tarotian meanings are remarkably elastic and variable. Unlike astrology, which has maintained its rules and characterizations for centuries, the tarot is redefined every time a new deck of cards is published (which is to say about every twenty minutes). Though this makes for interpretive chaos, it also gives tarot a vitality and responsiveness unmatched by any other method of divination.

The tarot deck is made up of seventy-eight cards. There are fifty-six minor arcana cards, which are divided up into four suits that are ancestors of our current playing card suits. Like regular playing cards, each suit contains aces and the numbered cards two through ten. However, the tarot court consists of King, Queen, Knight, and Page, as opposed to the King, Queen, and Jack of playing cards. The Page corresponds to the Jack, but the Knight was dropped altogether from the playing card deck. The tarot suits are Cups, Swords, Wands (sometimes called Clubs or Scepters), and Pentacles (sometimes called Coins), and they are the antecedents of, respectively,

Above: Strangely costumed girls reading fortunes with playing cards. From a 1908 postcard.

Hearts, Spades, Clubs, and Diamonds. Here the analogy with playing cards should be dropped, for it will lead us only towards the quagmire that is the history of the derivation of tarot. Onward. In addition to the minor arcana, there are twenty-two major arcana cards in the tarot deck; each is named as well as numbered. They are

	The Fool
I	The Magician
II	The High Priestess or The Popess
III	The Empress
IV	The Emperor
V	The Hierophant or The Pope
VI	The Lovers
VII	The Chariot
VIII	Justice
IX	The Hermit
X	The Wheel of Fortune
XI	Strength
XII	The Hanged Man
XIII	Death
XIV	Temperance
XV	The Devil
XVI	The Tower or The House of God
XVII	The Star
XVIII	The Moon
XIX	The Sun
XX	Judgement
XXI	The World

Such a list always seems tidy and authoritative, but this one is neither. Almost every card's name has been the subject of heated debate at one point or another. Some adepts refuse to use any but the Italian names. Some denounce the title of "Magician" for the first card, preferring "Thimble-rigger," "Juggler," or "The Pagad" (an Egyptophiliac designation). The dignity of "The High Priestess" endows the third card with one meaning, but the mockery of "The Popess" gives an entirely different one. Of the maelstrom that howls about the subject of "The Tower" versus "The House of God," it is probably best to say nothing. However, the controversy of the titles pales in comparison to the controversy of the sequence. As you doubtless observed, the Fool, which appears at the top of the list, has no number. In the fifteenth and sixteenth centuries, he seems to have been a wild card, but later, he was interpreted as the twenty-second card or as an unnumbered card positioned between the twentieth and the twenty-first cards. Arthur Edward Waite, who developed what is today the most commonly used tarot deck, the

Rider-Waite deck, placed the Fool at the beginning of the deck, before the first card, and numbered him zero. Even more radically, he transposed the eighth and the eleventh cards, Justice and Strength, for reasons that were at best obscure and at worst frivolous. Almost every other deck keeps them in their original places. All of this may seem like mere academic shillyshallying, but it is critical to the understanding of tarot, for one of the few universally accepted principles of the system is that the sequence of the major arcana cards reflects the journey of the soul.

Each of the many participants in the battle claims that history is on his side (I use the pronoun advisedly). Indeed, it seems to be an article of faith that "original" means "true," and the object of each tarot interpreter is to find evidence that his reading, name, or sequence appeared in one of the fifteenth- or sixteenth-century decks, preferably the Marseilles pack, which is the granddaddy of our current tarot decks. I hold an opposing opinion, that the cards have accumulated meaning through the centuries of their existence, and, though I do not approve of decks that mix tarot with entirely unrelated systems—the Javanese Puppetry Tarot, for instance—I believe that a wealth of meaning is superior to purity for its own sake.

Page of Swords, copy of Gringonneur card, c. mid-fifteenth century. From Les Cartes à jouer du quatorzième au vingtième siècle.

Another reason not to get too het up about the cards' pedigree is that nobody knows what it is: "The precise origin of tarot cards is obscure." "The origins of the tarot remain a mystery." "Any history of the tarot cards can be little other than an extended commentary on human credulity, duplicity, inventiveness, ignorance, and superstition." The little we can say without being credulous, duplicitous, or inventive is that the oldest known European tarot cards were painted by Jacquemin Gringonneur in 1392 to disperse the gloom of King Charles VI of France. There are seventeen cards in the Bibliothèque Nationale that were long thought to be members of this deck, but they are probably impostors. One of the oldest decks that is still in existence is the beautiful Visconti-Sforza deck, which was created in the middle of the fifteenth century for the Duke of Milan on the occasion of his marriage. The Tarot of Marseilles, composed at the end of the fifteenth century, was the first deck to display the iconography and design structure that are used in today's tarot decks.

And so it went for three and a half centuries. Decks were published with varying numbers of cards, varying names, and varying purposes. The same cards were used for games and for cartomancy, and nobody thought much of it. Then, in 1775, Antoine Court de Gebelin upset the applecart by declaring that the tarot was, in fact, a relic of ancient Egypt, a book of sacred mysteries transmitted to Europe by North African holy men in the first century. He avowed the cards (which he called the Book of Thoth), when properly deciphered, would unleash the secrets of Egypt upon the moral wasteland of France and usher in a wiser era. Coincidentally, France was experiencing a bout of Egyptomania in the late eighteenth century. With Court de Gebelin's assertion, tarot became the height of fashion, and sphinxes and ankhs became a permanent part of its repertoire of symbols.

Knight of Pentacles, from a 1708 Spanish deck of playing cards.

The next revolution came from the barbershop of M. Alliette, who decided to spell his name backward and become a cartomancer. As Etteilla, he published an excessively idiosyncratic deck that reordered and renamed the cards to suit his own somewhat fragile sense of logical progression. The Tarot of Etteilla was the first to offer reversed meanings for cards that appear upside-down, an element that has become a fixture in most readings, though not in mine.

The great Papus, the nineteenth century's master of debilitating spells, was also a scholar of the tarot. He was much concerned to establish connections between the Kabbalah and the tarot, particularly by corresponding the twenty-two major arcana trump cards with the twenty-two letters of the Hebrew alphabet, which, remember, are integral to the structure of the Tree of Life. Papus further asserted in his *Tarot of the Bohemians* that the philosophy of the tarot was embodied in the word *ROTA*, arranged in a wheel, which corresponded, he believed, to the four letters of the Divine name—Yod, He, Vau, He—also known as the Tetragrammaton. The complexity of Papus's algorithm deserves a detailed discussion, but we must merely note that Papus was certainly on to something, for the symbolic and graphic resonance between tarot and the Kabbalah is undeniable. The deck that most completely embodies Papus's theories is Oswald Wirth's, which employs the Hebrew letter related to each trump in the design of the card.

The synthesizer of all these strands was the redoubtable Arthur Edward Waite, who had his fingers in numerous occult pies. Waite was one of the original members of the Hermetic Order of the Golden Dawn, a Rosicrucian offshoot whose stated objective was to "prosecute the great work: which is to obtain control of the nature and power of my own being." Accordingly, the members of the Golden Dawn were initiated into the secrets of ritual magic, astral travel, the Kabbalah, scrying (looking into an object to see the future), the tarot, alchemy, geomancy, and astrology. With this background, it is easy to find the source of Waite's philosophy of the tarot: "The Tarot embodies symbolical presentations of universal ideas, behind which lie all the implicits of the human mind, and it is in this sense that they contain secret doctrine, which is the realization by the few of truths embedded in the consciousness of all." Linguistic hypertrophy aside, Waite was describing the tarot as an artifact of what Jung later called the collective unconscious. In Waite's view, the tarot was a vehicle for World Mind, expressed in a language of symbols that every viewer had the ability to identify and interpret without knowing that he had it. Of course, like all good occultists, Waite disagreed violently with all previous explications of these symbols, and, to settle the matter effectively, he designed an entirely new tarot deck. Painted by Pamela Coleman Smith, the deck now known as the Rider-Waite deck was innovative in providing pictorial minor arcana cards. Whereas most decks simply represented the Four of Wands with a picture of four wands—requiring the reader to gape at them until memory served— the Rider-Waite deck supplied an illustration of the divinatory meaning. And a very pretty one, too; the deck is notable for its agreeable, pre-Raphaelite-but-not-too-cheesy aesthetic.

Queen of Wands, Rider-Waite deck.

The next major development in the tarot was Aleister Crowley's 1944 Thoth deck, which renamed and reordered the tarot to induce a more symmetrical sequence. A black magician with an erudition almost equal to his estimation of it, Crowley included symbols from a wide range of occult and religious traditions in his deck, which, unfortunately, I find so generally overwrought as to be entirely unusable for divination.

In the past twenty-five years, there has been a great resurgence of interest in the tarot. Inevitably, popularity has led to product, and the world is now awash in tarot decks for every possible taste and political affiliation. With a few exceptions, these new decks are descendents of one—or all—of the decks I've mentioned.

Despite the claims of their creators, there is no "correct" deck. Almost any deck will serve, and the tarotier-in-training may as well use attractiveness as her primary criterion in selecting a pack, for the first task of the novice is to

THE WICKEDEST OF THEM ALL

The Hierophant, from Crowley's Thoth deck.

Aleister Crowley, the impresario behind the Thoth deck, cultivated wickedness from tenderest youth; even his mother regarded him as the Antichrist. While in college, he dabbled in occultism of various squalid ilks, and in 1898, he was admitted to the Hermetic Order of the Golden Dawn, from which he was expelled after attacking one of its founders, Samuel MacGregor Mathers, with astral vampires and ghosts. During this period, rigorous yogic practices allowed Crowley to recall past lives as Queen Elizabeth I, Cagliostro, Eliphas Levi, and Egyptian priest Ankh-fa-n-Khousu.

A philosopher of magic as well as a practitioner, Crowley codified his theories into *The Book of Law,* in which he expounded his Law of Themela: "Do what thou wilt shall be the whole of the law." This, Crowley explained, meant that you were permitted to do what you must, but nothing else. Crowley himself followed this law at his infamous Sicilian villa, the Sacred Abbey of the Thelemic Mysteries, where orgies and magic rituals were the order of the day. Persistent rumors about human sacrifice led that old moralist Mussolini to banish Crowley from Italy in 1923. He spent the next two decades writing, taking drugs, and getting sued. He came to a wretched end, living on the dwindling proceeds of his increasingly incoherent and unread books, and died in 1945.

Personal flaws aside, Crowley was undoubtedly the most accomplished magician of the twentieth century, and unlike the nineteenth century's Eliphas Levi, whom he considered his spiritual forefather, he did not shrink from utilizing the spirits and powers he summoned. An adept in most of the western magical and esoteric branches of knowledge, he synthesized much occult information in his teachings and publications.

study the cards thoroughly, and if the cards are pleasing to look at, so much the better. My sole opinion on the matter is that decks with pictorial minor arcana cards are easier to begin with. Aside from this, let inclination be your guide.

LEARNING THE CARDS

We will soon embark upon an exegesis of each card of the tarot deck, but it is important to begin with a general introduction to the symbolic language of the system. Even the simplest card contains a multitude of signs. Some are explicit, residing in the card's colors and images, and some are implicit in the connotations of the card's number and element. All of these entities contribute to the meaning of the card, though certain factors may or may not be germane to a particular reading (more of this anon).

Let us start with the minor arcana suits: Cups, Swords, Wands, Pentacles.

Cups are the suit of the emotions and the instincts. Their element is the water held in the cup, which betokens the unconscious. In a formal spread, cups generally represent love and relationships.

Swords are the suit of challenges, intellect, perception, and the penetration symbolized by the sword. Their element is air, the symbol of mind and thought, and their divinatory implication is that of conflicts and trials.

Wands are the suit of change, life force, and growth. The wands themselves are symbols for the growing trees from which they were taken. Their element is fire, and in a spread, they connote a new opportunity, a change, or the querent's energy level.

Pentacles are the suit of materiality in both the sense of physical being and the sense of money. The Pentacles are clearly meant to depict money, and the five-pointed star that appears in the center of each coin is a magical symbol that denotes man's ability to shape his world. The element of the suit is earth, and its divinatory meaning is that of money, business, and career.

The sequence of each suit from ace to ten represents a progression from inception to completion, but it is a somewhat waltzy progression rather than a beeline. The significance of numbers on tarot cards is similar to their numerological meanings:

Ones, or aces, represent new beginnings or opportunity. They are always positive.

Twos signify the active, positive principle of the One joined by an opposing factor—the balance of opposites.

Threes denote creativity, the product of the paternal One and the maternal Two, as well as commitment to the opportunity presented.

Fours signal stasis, with attendant peril (stagnation) or pleasure (respite).

Fives present the test of the midway point. All Fives are striving to attain goals in the face of unmet expectations and unforeseen problems.

Sixes symbolize a new balance attained.

Seven is a mystical number announcing the interjection of irrational forces, such as luck, into the situation at hand.

Eights imply some kind of ordeal or evolution.

Nine is the number of initiation—the test necessary for the achievement of Ten.

Tens are the symbols of completion.

The figures of the court cards represent various stages of life and character. The Page is youth, just beginning his or her spiritual journey. The Knight shows the

Clockwise, Page of Wands, Knight of Swords, Queen of Cups, and King of Pentacles, D'Este cards, fifteenth century.

character working in the service of an ideal or toward a goal. The Queen represents receptive power, the character who does not have to do anything to possess power. Kings symbolize active, forceful authority; each is the ultimate embodiment of his suit and has learned all the lessons of the cards that precede him. One of the court cards is selected to represent the querent in every reading (I will explain the method of selecting this card, called the significator, later); other court cards that appear in a reading usually symbolize a person in the querent's life. Accordingly, each of the court cards has its own character.

The colors that appear on the tarot cards are rich in meaning. The colors maintain their traditional significance no matter what use they are put to. However, one designer may choose to use a given color in one way, a second designer in another, depending on how they want the cards to be interpreted. Thus, for example, a figure cloaked in red in one tarot pack may be cloaked in yellow in another, which will radically alter the meaning of that card.

Red signifies life force, aggression, sexuality, and martial energy.

Blue is passive and receptive. It is particularly associated with the female principle and with water.

White denotes purity.

Green symbolizes fertility, growth, and success.

Orange is the color of change and rebirth, as well as sexual energy.

Yellow represents spirituality and the spiritualized life force.

Black is, as usual, the color of death.

Much has been made of the graphic significance of the cards; that is, whether this card's composition is square or that card's composition is circular. This generally dissipates into a passionate defense of one deck over another, as the compositions vary from deck to deck. Bah, I say. As with colors, shapes carry the same meaning whenever they appear:

Circles represent wholeness and unity.

Triangles denote transcendence, movement from the physical to the spiritual.

Squares are figures of the material world and the four elements.

Lemniscates, which look like sideways figure eights, signify the resolution of opposing forces, also and by extension, infinity.

Now that you have been introduced to the symbolic grammar of the tarot, you must move on to learn the meanings of each card. You will progress swiftly if you simply pay close attention and look to the card for evidence of its meaning. Once you become mildly familiar with the whole sequence, you will see connections and resonances among the cards that will aid your memory and add depth to your interpretations. Rest comfortably in the assurance that you will never know everything there is to know about the tarot.

Contrary to most guides to the tarot, I will discuss all four representatives of each number together, rather than the whole sequence of each suit, for this is both more revealing and easier to remember. Unless otherwise noted, all interpretations are based on the Rider-Waite deck.

THE MINOR ARCANA

Whereas the major arcana cards symbolize a querent's spiritual position, the minor arcana cards display the matter of her ordinary, sensual life. One expert has said that the major arcana shows us our destiny and the minor arcana shows us our will. It is one of the predicaments of humanity that these two forces are often opposed, and it is one of the goals of a good tarot reading to reconcile them.

ACES

Ace of Cups suggests that the querent is being offered an opportunity to love and be loved. It is critical to recognize that the new relationship comes without stipulations and is freely given. The querent must allow himself to be guided in this matter by spirit and intuition.

Ace of Wands shows that something is about to begin. There is a surge of energy, a growth spurt, a fresh start. New alternatives are popping up, and anything could happen. In a spread, the Ace of Wands usually appears with messenger cards that reveal the nature of the change at hand.

Ace of Swords predicts that the querent will face an unexpected challenge, which she can see as an opportunity to use her mind and her power. Through its symmetry, the card reminds the querent to strive for balance. This card may also portend forceful triumph.

Ace of Pentacles tends to imply that a new job opportunity is on the way, but it may be more broadly interpreted to mean that energy and external circumstances are coming together. The querent is also warned by the gate and distant mountains that the path to success is long and arduous.

TWOS

Two of Cups depicts a balanced love relationship, in which the active and passive forces are both expressed. The winged creature above the figures indicates that the relationship transcends the individuals.

Two of Wands shows that the querent's energy is being tempered by the needs of others. As he learns how to compromise, he will find a sign that will guide him to the correct choice.

Two of Swords reveals a querent who is maintaining a balance by resting between two opposing forces. She is achieving this equilibrium only through stasis, through ignoring her own feelings. Some action must be taken soon.

Two of Pentacles signifies that the subject has successfully juggled opposing duties, but she is being trapped by her own competence. This card usually represents someone who is working too hard to make up for others' deficiencies.

THREES

Three of Cups is a call to celebrate the ripening of love through time. The querent should form a creative culture with his friends.

Three of Wands suggests that the querent watch carefully and wait for his destiny to come to him. He is well prepared and well equipped, and this will serve him in good stead, but for now, he must be patient.

Three of Swords is an abysmal card, portending discord, betrayal, and disillusionment. It represents the lesson that lovers must learn before they can grow, that of loving unconditionally even when they receive no love in return.

Three of Pentacles denotes a period of apprenticeship. The querent is learning his craft and building his reputation. It is a sign that work is proceeding well.

FOURS

Four of Cups shows that the querent, settled in a number of stable relationships or withdrawn into herself, is ignoring a new possibility for emotional satisfaction. She may have decided that the devil she knows is better than the devil she doesn't know. She is probably wrong about this.

Four of Wands can be construed rigidly as foretelling a marriage, but it should be seen more broadly as an indication that two independent characters will produce an efflorescence of creativity. This card urges the querent to accept the freedom that fosters such a renaissance.

Four of Swords is known as "the hermit's repose." It suggests that the querent needs a period of peace in which to contemplate recent upheaval. In other words, she should go on vacation.

Four of Pentacles reveals a character who maintains balance by controlling every aspect of life. The querent is imprisoned by her image of herself and possessed by what she owns—she is receiving no new ideas or energy.

FIVES

Five of Cups is the Hamlet card, picturing a character so immobilized by past failures and betrayals that he can't take the opportunities being offered to him. The querent is wallowing in the past; he needs to come to terms with his mistakes, even if they were dreadful.

Five of Wands shows the mock battle, the minor power struggle in which various opponents are testing one another and displaying their own prowess. This card suggests that the querent should strive to be less irritable.

Five of Swords depicts reckless authority and disregard for others. The querent is being tempted to intimidate other people for the pleasure of it, and though he might well succeed in winning all the swords, or money, or acclaim, he will ultimately be the loser. The card implies that he should develop some compassion. Everyone hates a gloater.

Five of Pentacles displays poverty, both of material goods and of spirit. Although the querent may not have everything he wants, or even needs, his spiritual development is in his own hands, and he must take responsibility for it.

SIXES

Six of Cups has moved beyond the failures of Five and portrays a querent who is open to new relationships or to rediscovering an old one. The querent should attempt to maintain her honesty and open heart instead of succumbing to fear and dissimulation. She should try to be as childlike as possible.

Six of Wands is a card of success after struggle. The querent has triumphed in the mock battle, and her former adversaries cluster below the equestrian figure in admiration and homage. The querent must remember that her success bequeaths responsibilities, which are symbolized by the horse, always an emblem of service and work in the tarot. The green cloak on the horse shows that the work will be fruitful.

Six of Swords is an ambiguous card. On one hand, the swords that cluster around the huddled figure represent troubles that will not disappear, no matter how far the querent flees. On the other hand, the figure—and by extrapolation the querent—is being ferried to smoother waters. The suggestion is that though the querent's suffering will not be assuaged, she should take comfort in knowing that she has a protector. (There is, however, a tradition that this protector is not alive, which some may find less than comforting.)

Six of Pentacles represents the essence of material balance. Those who have must give to those who don't to create a balance of energy. This may foretell a sudden cash infusion, but equally, it may be an exhortation to the querent to lead a life of greater moral or physical equilibrium.

SEVENS

Seven of Cups is a card of delusion. It displays a silhouetted figure looking intently at a cloud of illusions he has conjured up and cast upon his partner. The querent is making the terrible mistake of expecting the world from his loved one—riches, security, beauty, spiritual fulfillment, success, even evil—and he is in danger of believing his illusions are the truth. Emotionally, the querent is out of his depth; it is imperative that he take a deep breath and try to distinguish reality from his fantasy.

Seven of Wands is no mock battle. The querent's opposition is not now merely cosmetic but deep-seated. He must exhibit self-control even as he pursues what he knows to be the correct path. This card may hint that the querent is too defensive.

Seven of Swords is the card of the sneak. The silver-tongued thief making off with the swords may represent the querent, who is trying to get away with something; or it may represent someone in the querent's life who is in the process of ripping him off.

Someone, at any rate, is trying to steal power, information, and reputation. However, the truth will out.

Seven of Pentacles represents an overcommitted figure, someone with too many irons in the fire. The querent must focus his energies. The neglected irons will simply grow cold; they will not die. He should concentrate on what's working.

EIGHTS

Eight of Cups depicts the figure who is prepared to distance herself from an unsatisfying emotional life. The symbol of the fused moon and sun connotes active accompaniment to what is known subconsciously. The querent is ready to strike out on her own to fulfill her emotional needs.

Eight of Wands betokens rapid—even reckless—change. Chaos reigns, and though such wild activity may be positive, the querent has no guarantees as to the character of the outcome.

Eight of Swords is a bad omen for women. The figure is trapped and helpless, her life force suppressed by her troubles. The querent must remember that simply walking away is an option; freedom is more readily available than it appears. The message holds true for a man, too, though the card may also represent his manner of treating the women in his life.

Eight of Pentacles represents the satisfactions of work well done. Though the querent may not be rich, she grows in the mastery of her craft. This card prophesies a great deal of personal satisfaction and sense of worth from career. Workaholics often receive this card.

Left to right: Page of Cups, Rider-Waite deck. Knight of Wands, from a 1708 Spanish deck of playing cards. Queen of Pentacles, Rider-Waite deck. King of Cups, from a 1708 Spanish deck of playing cards.

NINES

Nine of Cups shows the jolly buffoon. The figure sits within a circle of Cups, well fed and happy, and yet lacking any real intimacy in his many friendships. The card constitutes a warning against superficiality and self-absorption.

Nine of Wands displays the fruits of Eight's radical change: anxiety. A lot of things are out of the querent's control, and though he is doing the best he can, he must learn to trust his helpers. The card tells us that one form of initiation is being given more than we can handle as a test.

Nine of Swords is utterly stifled, unable to express himself or his desires, frustrated, enraged, and despondent. This is the dark night of the soul.

Nine of Pentacles shows a figure rich in the fruits of her work and contented in her garden. This is a character who has reaped peace and profit from solitude and now must decide whether to engage with the world. Something is trying to get produced, but the querent is uncertain whether she wants to proceed. Women who are deciding if they want to have a baby often get this card.

TENS

Ten of Cups is a paradisical vision of domestic bliss. The card portends great familial love and contentment but reminds the querent that these blessings are given from above rather than created by human will.

Ten of Wands takes Nine of Wands to the end of the road. The querent is completely bewildered, at her wit's end. Her life is a chore, and she rushes blindly into the future because her view is totally obstructed by the number of things she's bearing. The card advises the querent to drop everything. The burdens are often related to worries about one's children.

Ten of Swords depicts a prone figure pierced from stem to stern with swords. It's better than it looks, however, because it represents the end of the line. Everything that can go wrong has gone wrong. The failure is complete. The querent needs to get up, move on, and never come back. Despite the visuals, the querent herself is not dead; what is dead, rather, is the desire that got her into all this trouble in the first place.

Ten of Pentacles is, again, the result of the test of Nine. It shows that the cycle of energy is completed by the family. Lonely productivity can be gratifying, but this card reminds us to ask what we were put on earth for. If the querent has no family, this card may betoken a successful business partnership.

Right top: Page of Pentacles, Rider-Waite deck.
Right middle: Knight of Cups, from a 1708 Spanish deck of playing cards.
Right bottom: Queen of Swords, Rider-Waite deck.

PAGES

Page of Cups shows a young character embarking on a journey of the emotions; the card is a direction to the querent to listen to his intuition regarding a new relationship.

Page of Wands is a messenger from a higher intelligence. The querent's consciousness will be awakened by strange tidings. As a significator, it indicates a person of great energy.

Page of Swords represents a fierce creature. The card exhorts the querent to use her brain to avoid being victimized by sexuality. She faces some sort of sexual confrontation.

Page of Pentacles is a scholar, applying his mind to his work. The querent's energies should likewise be spent on his work.

KNIGHTS

Knight of Cups is following his heart. The querent is receptive to love, yet aware that armor is necessary. Girded with his intuition, he seeks love. Alternately, this may mean that a lover is searching for the querent.

Knight of Wands symbolizes change or movement. It can even mean that the querent will soon move house.

Knight of Swords dashes forward on a charger. Accordingly, the querent must battle powerful obstacles. He must stay on course, no matter what opposition, self-doubt, or bad karma he encounters.

Knight of Pentacles is a more stolid sort. His horse is a work horse, and he is weighted down by his heavy black armor. He is patient, even plodding, and his efforts will ultimately be met with success. This card also tells the querent that her instincts are good.

QUEENS

Queen of Cups is full of emotion and loving intelligence. She may even be visionary, for her intuition is so strong that it is tantamount to extrasensory perception. Additionally, this card bespeaks a woman who is not afraid of pleasure.

Queen of Wands is simple and straightforward, comfortable with change. Active and experienced, she can accomplish a great deal and adapt to many circumstances. She is connected to other realms through her pragmatic understanding of the structure of the world.

Queen of Swords is a strong and powerful woman. She is also, by choice or fate, lonely, and yet she doesn't hide from being alone. Though she doesn't feel connected to other people, she is deeply involved with her own intelligence and spiritual life. Reflective, penetrating, and subtle, she represents a very intriguing character.

Queen of Pentacles is a paragon of fertility. Extremely capable in the physical world, she is surrounded with abundance and uses her energies in practical and productive ways. She is very attuned to her surroundings and wise to the ways of nature.

KINGS

King of Cups is the quintessential lover. This can go either of two ways: If well aspected (that is, surrounded by benign cards), the querent may be open, emotional and communicative. If badly aspected, he may be an insincere womanizer. Traditionally, the King of Cups is regarded as the father of the Fool, the card that commences the major arcana.

King of Wands is a master of change and growth. He is active, honest, impulsive, and easygoing. Comfortable with change, but not with problems, he acts quickly and generously.

King of Swords is the apotheosis of power. You do not mess with the King of Swords because he will not be deceived and he will gain retribution. He is intelligent and educated but no maverick. Unless he is very malignantly aspected, the King of Swords is on the querent's side.

KING of SWORDS.

King of Pentacles is a creative force. With lots of energy and lots of ideas, he is also stubborn, independent, and willful. He controls his own dark side—a predisposition to greed and lust—and he generally controls other people as well. Rich in things that matter, including money, he may represent a mentor in the querent's career.

THE MAJOR ARCANA

Much ink has been spilled in the service of the idea that the major arcana represents the path from spiritual infancy to spiritual completion. Most writers of the tarot attempt to show how each card embodies this or that milestone on the freeway of life. While I believe that, in general, the sequence of the major arcana describes a progress toward enlightenment, I do not believe that each card represents an equivalent advance on that path. Instead, I see the major arcana cards as a series of reminders and warnings to those who would understand the forces at work in their lives, or even as a kind of philosophical machine for understanding the ramifications of their choices. Some scholars regard the major arcana as a representation of the karmic proposition; the

Above left: King of Wands, from a 1708 Spanish deck of playing cards.
Above right: King of Swords, Rider-Waite deck.
Right: The Fool, Rider-Waite deck.

cards a subject receives reveal the goals toward which she must work in this incarnation. This is interesting, but not as compelling as the more quotidian interpretation. We all—or almost all—experience life as a mixture of conduct and consideration. Primarily, we just wake up and do our jobs and worry about money, sex, and calories, but occasionally, we lift our heads to reflect upon our moral direction, intellectual development, and spiritual choices. Character is not fixed, except in the movies, and most thinking people attempt on some level to evolve—this can be as simple as resolving not to get mad at the cat or as complicated as renouncing desire—and the major arcana cards are a commentary on and a guide in this evolution. As the minor arcana represents what you are doing, the major arcana represents what you are meaning.

No matter what tarot deck you use, every major arcana card is rich in symbolism. A whole book could be written—and probably has been—on the Hanged Man or the Moon or the Magician. But a fixed definition of their symbols presents only a portion of their meaning, because the cards are meant to be read as part of a spread, and their significance varies in combination with other cards. For example, the Devil and the Magician together evoke a world of self-delusion that is not apparent in either card independently. However, in the interests of practicality, I will offer the traditional fixed meaning of each of the major arcana cards. The last section of this chapter will contain a sample reading in which the influences of the cards upon one another will be considered and explained.

THE FOOL

Casting myself into the arms of A. E. Waite, I place the Fool before the first card, for he so clearly represents embarkation. Absolutely unprotected, holding nothing but the white flower of purity, the youth sets off on his journey, unaware that he is about to tumble off the edge of the precipice. He is the very type of bootless freedom, but actually, he is not free because he is still bound to the earth. This is reiterated by the little dog who leaps at the Foolish heels; he is a figure for carnality, and his attempts to draw his master back are both positive—he will save the Fool from imminent catastrophe—and negative—the imminent catastrophe is what the

Fool needs in order to become airborne. There is a long-standing tradition that the Fool's satchel contains wisdom and understanding; though the packet remains sealed, the legend teaches that these qualities are the possessions of the Fool.

Divinatorily, this is considered a positive card, indicative of a life choice at hand. The querent will probably take the right path for all the wrong reasons.

THE MAGICIAN

I must admit that Waite seems to have missed the boat on this one. His Magician, cloaked in Merlinesque robes, belted by the ouroboros and crowned by the lemniscate, is an adept, a lightening rod transmitting energy between the higher and lower spheres. Sad to say, this is an interpretation utterly at odds both with the traditional meaning of the card and with its position. Much more usually, the Magician is a dissembler, a fraud whose only inkling of wisdom is that he knows he's a fraud. Typically, the table on which he performs his magic tricks—for us, the readers of the card—is set with dice cups and coins and a penknife. In his hand, he holds a little stick. Look closely, for these are primitive versions of the minor arcana's Cups, Pentacles, Swords, and Wands; they signify the Magician's potential mastery of the forces that rule the world, a potential that he ignores in favor of minor theatricality. The Magician encapsulates the human condition all too well: distracted by trifles and small pleasures, we fritter away our time on Earth, ignoring the germs of the divine that we carry within us. The divinatory meaning of the card is essentially a positive interpretation of its symbolism: it announces potential, intelligence, the capacity to understand hermetic secrets. Equally it warns against the absorption of the spirit in superficial affairs. Occasionally the card may represent a person who is trying to dupe the querent.

THE HIGH PRIESTESS

The High Priestess is the incarnation of receptive feminine wisdom. The card is generally chockablock with symbols of the female—water, the Moon, fruit, flowers, and pomegranates are some of the usual adornments—and the central figure of the Priestess is usually swathed in veils and enclosed by some sort of screen, a stand-in for the womb. The implication is clear: this card represents passive wisdom. Not actively seeking, but nonetheless knowing the secrets of the ages, the Priestess exhorts the querent to listen, to be quiet, to observe what will be revealed. This exhortation may refer to occult truths or to the querent's manner of life.

THE EMPRESS

Close upon the heels of the passive, receptive understanding of the High Priestess, we find the Empress, who expresses the active, fertile aspect of feminine wisdom. The Empress represents living from the point of view of the heart, a being devoted to creating and loving. Usually crowned with a three-tiered coronet of stars that symbolizes her attunement to celestial power, the Empress transmits the divine energy she receives to the world around her. The archetype of creativity, the Empress does not simply hold on to the information she receives; she casts it abroad. She is mother incarnate, and it is wise to remember that because of this, the real power to make is in her hands. She may not rule the world, but without her, there is no world to rule. Consequently, though she is a figure of Venus, she can also be a figure of Kali—the one who makes can also destroy. This is the duality that renders all mother figures frightening as well as comforting. Unsurprisingly, the Empress represents the querent's mother in a formal reading. Alternately, she may portend fertility if well aspected, or dissipation and overindulgence if poorly aspected.

THE EMPEROR

If the Empress signifies the power to create, the Emperor signifies the power to stabilize. He consolidates power by eliminating what is superfluous and retaining only what is true. This is a very simple and extremely difficult concept, because it wears the same clothes as plain old brute force (hence the armor). However, the Emperor's goal is not destruction, but the embodiment, in institutions as well as individuals, of the truth. He is a reminder that flesh is not the enemy of spirit but its equal. In a reading, this card is usually an instruction to get real. In addition, the Emperor may be a representation of the querent's father or of a mentor. If he shows up with the Empress in a spread, it means that the querent has met his or her match.

Left top: The Magician, D'Este cards, fifteenth century.
Left bottom: The High Priestess, from an early nineteenth-century French cartomancy deck.
Above right: The Empress, from the "Soprafino" deck by F. Gumppenberg, mid-nineteenth century.
Above left: The Emperor, copy of Gringonneur card, c. mid-fifteenth century. From Les Cartes
à jouer du quatorzième au vingtième siècle.

THE HIEROPHANT

The Hierophant has two meanings, both relating to instruction. It is clear that the central figure, the Hierophant himself, is graphically related to the High Priestess, but in this case, as the incarnation of masculine wisdom, he teaches truth rather than simply holding it within himself. In this card, too, we usually see acolytes, the humble recipients of his revelations. Herein lies the dual significance of the card: in some cases the Hierophant suggests that the querent must teach what he knows to others. In a far greater number of cases, the card suggests that the querent has something important to learn. In the Waite deck, the two students stand on either side of the papal throne; they represent two attitudes toward learning. One will use the knowledge he has received correctly, and the other will use it foolishly. The card urges the querent to accept that he has much to learn, yet he has complete responsibility for the manner in which he uses the information he receives.

THE LOVERS

It is hard to divest oneself of the belief that this card signifies an impending love affair. It would be so gratifying if this were true. The world's tarot readers would be able to tell their clients to go home and put on some nice underwear, and everyone would be happy. Unfortunately, the card is about discrimination and choice, which are certainly prerequisites for love but are not quite as charming as the fairy godmother scenario. The card shows the character who has learned to resist the inclination to charm. Charm, ease, luck—these are the enemies of correct choice, which tends to be arduous and sometimes even unappealing. The male and female figures stand before each other—sometimes they are pictured nude, to emphasize that they have nothing to hide—and hovering above them is a sun-enveloped angel who represents and sanctifies their freedom from the dull sublunary world of desire and carnality. The older decks portray the male figure flanked by two women, between whom he is obviously choosing. There have been many arguments about which of the two female figures constitutes the right choice, but whichever one it is, this old version stresses the true matter of the card: the triumph over animal nature that makes true love endure. In a reading, the Lovers are a positive sign that the querent is able to achieve the higher consciousness (that is, the union of conscious and unconscious mind) necessary to accept and create a love relationship. In other words, the querent is ready to get what he or she really wants.

Top: The Hierophant, D'Este cards, fifteenth century.
Bottom: The Lovers, Rider-Waite deck.

THE CHARIOT

The seventh card marks the conclusion of a sequence that begins with the Magician. We have been dealing here, in a peripatetic way, with issues of reconciling our consciousness—which, let's be honest, is just a nice way of saying our will—to the idea that we must obtain access to the higher world of superconsciousness. The Magician, remember, has only an inkling of the forces he bandies about; the Empress and the Emperor embody and direct creation; the High Priestess and the Hierophant urge us to acknowledge and approach the secrets of the wise; and the Lovers offer an exemplary wise choice. With the Chariot, we find that the will has relinquished its throne. The charioteer, crowned and holding a scepter that symbolizes the link between the higher and lower worlds, stands in his cart, ready to proceed. But, in a decidedly rare unanimity, there is no version of this trump card in which the charioteer hold the reins, and this detail is the key to the card. The chariot is steered by divine, rather than human, will and can therefore meet with no obstruction. Waite whacks us over the head with this concept by depicting the cart pulled by two sphinxes.

Divinatorily, this is an excellent sign: having learned the lesson of self-control, the querent is now on the right path. No second-guessing the itinerary, no attempts to control fate are allowed. The querent's current direction is correct.

JUSTICE

It seems strange to move from the Chariot, which congratulates the querent on his good sense, to Justice, which questions it. This card suggests that the querent needs to deliberate; it is, in fact, a visual representation of a decision being made. The figure of Justice generally carries a sword, which, as we know from the lower arcana, is the sign of challenges. Justice is not easily attained. In a formal spread, Justice commands the querent to be decisive, to stop pussyfooting around. Further, it advises the querent to consult the ideals of justice, equality, and harmony in order to make the correct decision.

Top: The Chariot, from an anonymous Parisian deck, seventeenth century. Note that in this version, the cart is pulled by the swans.
Bottom: Justice, from an anonymous Parisian deck, seventeenth century. Justice is not only blind but two-faced.

THE HERMIT

The Hermit, too, is a fairly straightforward card, portraying the necessity of maintaining one's ideals even in the face of rejection or ostracism. It tells us that the approval of society is not nearly as important as the search for self, which is the quest of the Hermit. As we saw with the minor arcana, Nine is the number of initiation, the step before completion (though the way the major arcana depicts completion is fairly mind-boggling), and, as the trump reveals, hermitism is both the means and the end of the initiation process.

Note also that as one of the few major arcana cards in which the figure moves to the left, the Hermit symbolizes the necessity of scrutinizing one's past. Appropriate contemplation and understanding of the self will generate detachment, that most useful of spiritual qualities.

The Hermit has two divinatory meanings, and they are related. Either the querent needs to spend some time alone learning to be comfortable with herself, or she needs to integrate a past event into her consciousness before she can progress.

THE WHEEL OF FORTUNE

One of the most complicated and fascinating cards of the major arcana, this trump is a visual manifestation of the idea that all of us are the fools of fortune. In the Sforza deck, shown at right, the king at the top of the wheel is quite literally made an ass by blind luck, who stands at the center (I can't imagine that this card was very popular with the Duke of Milan, for whom the deck was made). Though he holds the orb of earthly dominion, donkey ears sprout from his head. Equally fortuitous and gratuitous are the respective rise and fall of two identical young men clasping the sides of the wheel. They are virtually indistinguishable, yet one ascends to the heights and the other

sinks to the depths. And the wise man, whose white robes signal his purity, is cast down in the dirt. Most commentators try to wrest satisfaction from the card by announcing that it depicts the wheel of karma and thus, that the cycle is meaningfully related to spiritual development. Waite places one of his sphinxes atop the circle and fills the wheel with occult symbols and the letters of the Tetragrammaton, suggesting that wisdom will bring freedom from the vagaries of fortune. This, to my mind, is base sentimentality. The point of the card is that life is unfair, the karmic cycle is a mystery we cannot hope to understand, our attempts at justice will be forever baffled by the caprices of fate.

When the Wheel of Fortune appears in a formal spread, I take the gloomy view that the querent is entering a period of instability or that something quite undeserved shall befall her (could be good, could be bad). Other readers find the opposite meaning: that the querent will see the fruits of former works.

STRENGTH

Here we see our old friend the lion, which is the symbol of Leo, which is ruled by the Sun, which is, in turn, a stand-in for the conscious mind. He is being tamed by a woman, as always associated with the Moon and hence with the element of water, symbol of the unconscious mind. Though the name of the card is Strength, it is not clear whose strength is being referred to. Obviously, the lion could tear the lady limb from limb; she is not stronger than the beast, just wiser. The woman teaches the lion to discard his animal nature—to go against nature—in order to change. The reconciliation of the conscious and the unconscious cannot be attained without self-control, which is the essence of strength.

The divinatory meaning of the card is that some weakness can and must be transcended by the querent. It most definitely won't be a fun little failing, easily discarded. No, getting rid of this one—a propensity to jealousy, say, or a need to have one's tastes validated by some outside authority—will require great force of character and self-love.

Left top: The Hermit, from an anonymous Parisian deck, seventeenth century.
Left bottom: The Wheel of Fortune, from the Pierpont Morgan–Bergamo Visconti–Sforza deck, mid-fifteenth century.
Above: Strength, from the "Soprafino" deck by F. Gumppenberg, mid-nineteenth century.

THE HANGED MAN

The Hanged Man has been subject to every possible interpretation throughout the centuries, but all scholars agree that the figure himself is an enlightened character. Contrary to every expectation, he never appears discomfited by his situation. Indeed, he is often depicted with a halo around his head. Furthermore, his posture is the precise reverse of the figure in the final major arcana trump, who represents the World Soul. The implication is that just one whirl would give him access to enlightenment. The Hanged Man is totally surrendered to truth, egolessly aware of truth, and in this

THE HANGED MAN.

way he overcomes his outward circumstances, but he is nonetheless stopped, bound, held up. The divine will is, for some reason, suspending the power that should be his. He dangles from a frame of lopped-off trees; these could be the remains of the Tree of Life or they could simply be a gibbet. (It is interesting to note that upside-down hanging was a punishment for debtors in sixteenth- and seventeenth-century Europe.) We may deduce that our hanging man owes even more than he has already given; accord-

ingly, I interpret the card as a call for further surrender. A querent who receives this card will experience delays, problems, or hang-ups. The trick to surviving these setbacks is not to wallow in self-pity but to cultivate patience and reverence for the methods of the divine.

DEATH

Here we are, at the Death card, which is not as bad as it looks. In some ways, Death is the answer to the Hanged Man. Suspended as he is, the Hanged Man is visually and figuratively reminiscent of a cocoon. Death is emergence from the old cocoon of the body in order to begin a new incarnation. Most querents find this terrifically ominous, but in the world of tarot, death is merely transformation. The card is yet another exhortation not to take the honors and rewards of this world too seriously, for all will be mowed down and reborn without regard to worldly stature.

In a spread, the Death card means that something is about to come to an end, but it also points to the beginning of a new cycle, which in the Waite deck is symbolized by the Sun rising in the east.

Top: The Hanged Man, Rider-Waite deck.
Bottom: Death, Oswald Wirth deck.

TEMPERANCE

After we have been flattened by Death, Temperance seems to offer some comfort. Actually, this card is telling us how to live our larval life out of the cocoon. It shows, graphically, the entry of spirit (water) into matter (cup). The subconscious mind is being directed by higher consciousness into the cups of consciousness. What does that mean? It means that the querent should use her experiences to temper and modify her life. This may be as straightforward as Stop drinking so much, or it may be as oblique as Stop fretting about the fate of the world and direct your attention to an individual who needs you. Balance is the issue.

THE DEVIL

In contrast to the Death card, this one is as bad as it looks. The Devil card represents humanity's enslavement to its desires, and it portends a period of self-destruction and torment in its recipient's life. As in Dante's *Inferno*, the figures in this card have chosen their chains. They all have, in fact, the ability to escape from their prison any time they wish, simply by removing their shackles, yet they prefer their predicament. The Devil is a divine force—after all, he began his days as Lucifer—but he is not autonomous. He must have compliant subjects in order to work his will.

The appearance of the Devil card in a spread usually indicates unhealthy attachments or bad habits on the part of the querent, but it may also suggest a forthcoming bout of self-loathing, the most poisonous form of the destructive impulse.

THE TOWER

Ugh. The Tower is worse than it looks. Those who do not learn the lesson of the Devil are condemned to experience God's rage, represented by the Tower. In other words, those who reject the opportunity to free themselves from their weaknesses are, in essence, rejecting the divine spark within themselves. This is tantamount to despair, the greatest of all sins. The ego that rejects grace gets it in the end, but it's painful, and this is what's depicted in the Tower. The proud, man-made structure, a figure for man himself, is utterly destroyed by the purifying rage of God in the form of a lightning bolt from heaven. Repeated failure to learn the lessons that our life is trying to teach us and stubborn refusal to integrate

Top: Temperance, copy of Gringonneur card, c. mid-fifteenth century. From Les Cartes à jouer du quatorzième au vingtième siècle.
Middle: The Devil, Oswald Wirth deck.
Bottom: The Tower, from the "Soprafino" deck by F. Gumppenberg, mid-nineteenth century.

our inner being with its outer manifestation will inevitably result in the annihilation of everything we depend on.

There is really no way to soften the blow in a reading: catastrophe is imminent. The querent may be able to avert it by correcting her failings and exerting some self-control, but it's not likely.

THE STAR

After the catastrophe of the Tower, the Star offers regeneration and recovery. This card is laden with mystical symbols, which makes it both reassuring and difficult to read. The great central star is thought to be Sirius, fiery harbinger of the dog days of summer. In the Waite version, the female figure pours her healing waters both into the pool of the unconscious and onto the soil of consciousness, creating, in effect, a circle of replenishment. All of the elements are represented in the card—fire is figured by the stars—which emphasizes the comforting message about the self-generating and eternal cycles of time and nature. The card reminds us of the harmonious state of prelapsarian man, when the four elements existed in perfect balance within every being, and there was no sickness, fear, or destruction.

The Star is an extremely promising card, though what, exactly, it promises is a bit vague. Its recipient may expect a period of restoration and creativity. If the querent has been sick—particularly if that sickness was related to an addiction—the Star foretells recovery.

THE MOON

This is one of my favorite cards, though it is much reviled by some interpreters. Throughout the preceding major arcana trumps, the unconscious has been figured as the source of creativity, and its reconciliation with the conscious depicted as an essential factor in spiritual evolution (particularly in Temperance and the Star). Here, the tarot reveals the dark side of the subconscious. The Moon, which is both the Sun's symbolic antithesis and its creation (after all, the light of the Moon is actually the light of the Sun), presides over the waters that always represent instinctual mind. But all is not sweetness and light down there. In the Waite deck, creeping out of the stagnant water is a crayfish, the sign of all the primitive nastiness we hold within us. On the shore, two animals howl at the moon—the dog, symbol of carnality (compare his role in the card of the Fool), and the wolf, who, as a wild dog, betokens the untamability of desire. I simply cannot agree with scholars who believe that the Moon represents material, earthly life (it just seems so darn counterintuitive), but I do agree with their conclusion that the card symbolizes the fearsome forces that keep us from enlightenment, which requires that we investigate all that is loathsome within us (what Jungians call the shadow). Unpleasant as the process of inventory might be, the goal of the tarot is to reconcile the dark side of the Moon with the valuable elements of the subconscious, not to eliminate them.

In a reading, the Moon predicts an unbalanced view of reality, a dangerous discovery of hidden forces, or uncomfortable memories. It is important for the querent to remember that the Moon symbolizes distorted vision rather than the truth. If the Moon is the first card in a reading, it means that the querent's understanding of the issue at hand is twisted. She should be advised not to let her imagination run away with her.

THE SUN

The jolly old Sun is usually depicted beaming down on two youths (though Waite eliminates one in favor of making the other an actual baby) in the nineteenth card. The relationship to the Moon is clear: just as we must become reconciled with our primitive natures to be whole, so does the full Sun of spiritualized life render us primitive—childlike—again. In short, consciousness is reborn through accepting the shadow *and* accepting the spirit. The point is that when your inner and outer life are joined together, you don't get to just keep on being the same old you. Becoming an integrated and evolved consciousness can be disconcerting.

Obviously, though, this is a positive card. Clearly rebirth under the Sun is not such an arduous process. The new being is protected by the wall that always encloses the figures on this card, which symbolizes the internal nature of the happiness that the card represents. This card predicts great success for the querent, but the reward will be in the realm of the personal. It is the success of becoming enlightened rather than of winning the lottery.

Left: The Star, D'Este cards, mid-fifteenth century.
Top: The Moon, from an anonymous Parisian deck, seventeenth century. Though this version displays few of the usual figures associated with the Moon, the stunned expression of the central character conveys the meaning of the card beautifully.
Bottom: The Sun, Rider-Waite deck.

JUDGEMENT

The wisdom of the tarot is nowhere more apparent than in this card's position. It is the tendency of western minds, formed as they are by literary models, to assume that rebirth is, like death, the end of the story: "She became good and lived happily ever after. The end." The tarot knows that this is not true: you may be reborn, you may be enlightened, but you have to live your enlightenment. You have to be enlightened while you clean the closet. Judgement reminds us that we live in a struggle between material and spiritual existence all the time. So we don't escape judgement simply because we have been reborn. Equally, we don't escape the requirement to use our judgement. We cannot assume that spiritual evolution makes us infallible.

Traditionally, this card has been interpreted as a sign of impending legal triumph. This seems suspiciously superficial, and later exegetes have concluded that it is a sign that the querent is supposed to support, or elevate, her community. Still others suggest that it shows the querent transcending past experiences to begin a new course. The latter seems to relate most closely to the meaning of the card.

THE WORLD

Finally! Total liberation! Freedom from the world! Freedom in the world to be enlightened! The World depicts a self whose ego is integrated with the unconscious, whose inner being is unified with outer activities, and whose spiritual purpose is realized. Such a being does not live a reactive life but is joined to all the elements of the world. As I mentioned earlier, the figure in the center of the card (thought by many interpreters to be a hermaphrodite, the fusing of Hermes with Aphrodite) is the graphic reverse of the Hanged Man. No longer hung up, no longer attached to the earth by gravity, she is in perfect balance, her wand the manifestation of her power to work in both the spiritual and the material world.

Obviously, the world portends great success and joy to its recipient. It implies a long journey happily concluded and a well-deserved reward.

Top: Judgement, from the "Soprafino" deck by F. Gumppenberg, mid-nineteenth century.
Bottom: The World, Rider-Waite deck.

Reading the Cards

Now, finally, we come to the crux of the biscuit: the tarot reading. As I mentioned earlier, it is fruitless to memorize the cards individually; the reason for this is that their meanings are best revealed in the context of a spread, where their significance evolves in harmony with their environment and with one another. Consider the Hermit, whose sternward posture is associated with dwelling in the past. That interpretation does not hold if he is placed opposite the Hierophant, for instance, in which case, his look indicates a conflict between instruction and independence. By themselves, the definitions are a pile of shards; in the context of the spread, they become a mosaic of meaning.

I will offer instructions for laying out and reading the Celtic Cross spread, which is the most commonly used arrangement, but you should bear in mind that there are almost as many spreads as there are decks, some composed of as few as four cards, some that use nearly every card. A few expert tarotiers and numerous amateurs simply make up an arrangement as they go along; this I find weak-kneed, but some experimentation with various spreads is valuable in order to help you select the one that best suits you and your querent.

Tarot readers are split pretty evenly on the subject of which cards to use. Some use the whole deck and some use only the major arcana. Some use the major arcana and the court cards of the minor arcana. I am scornful of the major-arcana-only types; they imply, like Henry James, that daily life and moral life are completely separate, when we all know that this is not true. Willingness to write in library books is just as valid a moral indicator as willingness to remain enslaved to desire. The minor arcana shows the way we spend our time (I suppose you could say that the major arcana shows the way time spends us), and it is therefore a crucial element of any reading. Furthermore, certain concrete questions cannot be well answered by the major arcana alone; to the question "Am I going to be fired?" the major arcana responds, "It doesn't matter." Querents tend to find that less than satisfying.

There is much fussing among experts about the appropriate attitude with which to conduct a reading. Some of this is reasonable. The system is predicated on the idea that the cards selected for a spread are uniquely suited to the querent and the query. The cards are thought to respond to the emotional transmissions of the querent and the reader by means of a sort of echolocation: what the emitter gives out, she receives back again. Obviously, if the tarot reader releases untoward and inappropriate vibrations, it's going to blow the circuit. The reader should strive for sympathetic detachment; that is, she should be sympathetic to her querent but detached from the outcome. A reader pulling for a particular answer can destroy a reading, which is why it's best to avoid throwing the cards for your loved ones, particularly on questions you feel strongly about. However, it is not necessary to achieve a trancelike state before you embark. There's no way you can subtract yourself out of the equation, so don't even try.

Most tarot readers keep their cards in some sort of special container—a silk wrap or wooden box—in order to reduce the number of vibrations they take in. This is probably wise. At the very least, don't let idlers and babies fool around with them, as people without superegos are notoriously virulent conductors. Never let anyone else read from your cards.

The Celtic Cross layout—so named because the reading makes a circle around a cross-formation of cards—is composed of one significator card placed in the center of the spread and ten other cards set out in the order you see in Figure 20.

The significator card represents the querent, as well as one of the thorniest issues in the study of the tarot. Some tarotiers allow the querent to select his own significator card by choosing the card that most appeals to him or seems most germane to his question. This method may be appropriate when the querent knows nothing about tarot, but even the slightest knowledge of the cards creates an unfortunate predisposition to select happy or artistically agreeable significators, which, to my mind, rigs the reading.

Even worse is the correlation between significator and physical appearance, though this method is much employed by otherwise respectable readers (in this technique, only the court cards are used). "For a blond querent with hazel eyes, choose the Queen of Wands." Yuck.

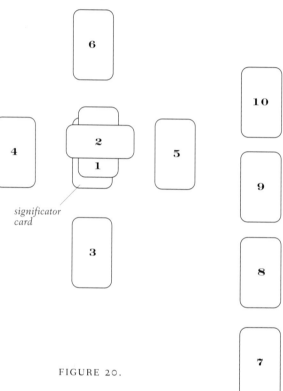

significator card

FIGURE 20.

And besides, what if the querent dyes her hair?

My own method of selecting the significator corresponds court card to querent via astrological sign. Adult males are Kings, adult females are Queens, children are Pages. The obvious question is, What's the demarcation between childhood and adulthood? The answer is: sex. But of course, you can't go around asking people if they've done it yet, so take an intelligent guess.

As you will recall, each suit of the minor arcana is associated with an element: Swords with air, Wands with fire, Cups with water, and Pentacles with earth. As you may not recall—it was many pages ago— each astrological sign is likewise associated with an element: Aquarius, Libra, Gemini with air; Sagittarius, Aries, Leo with fire; Scorpio, Cancer, Pisces with water; and Virgo, Taurus, Capricorn with earth. Therefore, you select a significator based on the shared element: a Virgo woman would be the Queen of Pentacles, an Aquarian man is the King of Swords, etcetera. Remove the significator from the deck and place it in the center of a table.

The ritual of shuffling is very important, for it is here that the querent's vibrations are unleashed upon the cards. Shuffling should take place before the querent has voiced his question, but he must ruminate upon it. Once the querent has thoroughly shuffled the cards, he must cut the cards into three piles using his left hand and toward his left. The reader then picks up the piles in the opposite direction. At this juncture, the querent tells the reader his question, and she then lays out the cards, face up, as pictured in Figure 20, beginning, of course, with 1, which should be placed over the significator card.

1. The first card, that which covers him (the querent as symbolized by the signifactor), represents the general situation of the querent regarding the question asked. It is the foundation of the reading.

2. The second card, that which crosses him, is the crossing card, which shows the forces opposing the situation.

3. The third card, that which is below him, represents the past or what the querent already knows or understands about the situation.

4. The fourth card, that which is behind him, shows the influences from the recent past that still play into the current situation.

5. The fifth card, that which is before him, signifies events in the near future.

6. The sixth card, that which crowns him, represents events in the distant future.

The four cards that are lined up next to the cross formation provide supplementary psychological and spiritual information. Their degree of bearing on the query is to be determined by the reader and the querent.

7. The seventh card reveals what the querent fears, how he is separated from enlightenment and happiness.

8. The eighth card represents the querent's position in relation to his family and friends and the attitude of his community toward him or toward the issue at hand.

9. The ninth card shows the querent's hopes for himself.

10. The tenth card reveals the outcome.

It is incumbent upon the reader to make a narrative from what she sees. The cards supply the bones, but the reader supplies the connective tissue. This is a most difficult element to keep in mind as a beginning reader; often you'll find yourself overwhelmed by the quantity of information presented in a spread and unable to weave it into a coherent whole. Practice is the key to success in this regard. Another problem is learning how to be the bearer of bad tidings. There is no way to avoid telling people what you see, but you will soon realize that the reading itself is a way around the disaster at hand. It is a warning that brings options with it. The tarot cards do not present the querent with an irrevocable future; they show the probable outcome of a certain series of events or behaviors. If those events or behaviors change, so, too, will the outcome.

A SAMPLE READING

Isabel, a thirty-six-year-old woman, had gone through a devastating breakup over a year before our reading. She was at the time of the reading involved with a new partner, Ted, whom she liked but did not love. Her question was, "Will I ever meet someone I want to spend the rest of my life with?"

The significator: Isabel is an Aquarius; hence, she is represented by the Queen of Swords. This in itself is telling, as the Queen of Swords is a strong woman who walks alone. Though others find her intriguing, she feels less connected to them than to her interior life.

1. The first card was the Page of Wands, probably in this instance representing Isabel's relationship to Ted, who was a much less complicated man than Isabel's previous lover and therefore less Kinglike than Pagelike. The emphasis on the sexual side of their relationship rather than the emotional is also an attribute of the suit of Wands.

2. The crossing card was the Death card, which alarmed Isabel unduly. Clearly, though, this referred to the death of her earlier love affair, the memory of which had impelled her into the situation with Ted. Indeed, the misery of that breakup had created a whole new defensive structure in Isabel with regard to relationships.

3. The third card, representing the distant past, was the Ace of Pentacles. This referred to Isabel's relationship with Ted, which she regarded somewhat in light of a business opportunity when they met. He offered a respite from bad memories, and she took him up on it.

4. The fourth card, signifying the recent past, was the Eight of Swords, a veritable illustration of being stuck in a lie. Having realized that despair had created the relationship in which she now found herself, Isabel felt powerless to change, unable to extricate herself from her false situation with Ted for fear of falling once again into despair. But, as is always true for the recipient of the Eight of Swords, the best remedy is simply to walk away.

5. The fifth card, representing events in the near future, was the Ten of Cups. It was tempting to say to Isabel that she was going to settle into domestic bliss any minute now, but this was a canard if I ever saw one. What this card emphasizes is the *vision* of domestic bliss: the family looks to the sky to see their happiness, and like the rainbow upon which the cups are arranged, their happiness is ephemeral, bestowed from above rather than created below. I believe that in Isabel's case, the domestic harmony displayed in the card was her own vision for herself, in its most insidiously charming aspect, rather than a prediction of imminent love and marriage. It was precluded, by its position and lack of connection with the other cards, from being the happy ending itself. It was much more likely to represent an obsession with happy endings and a corollary delusion that a happy marriage was the only possible positive conclusion for her. It was salient to observe that this was the sole Cup card in a layout devoted to a question of love and intimacy. Isabel's emotional life was in no way leading her toward the completion depicted in this card, and the dangerous aspect of its appearance was

This 1906 postcard was one of a series featuring this smirking Gypsy and her happy-go-lucky client experimenting with a variety of divination systems.

THE GYPSY SPREAD

Complex questions, particularly those regarding ongoing processes, may require more cards in order to generate an answer. An alternative to the Celtic Cross is the Gypsy Spread, which probably has nothing whatever to do with Gypsies. Twenty minor arcana cards are selected at random and combined with all twenty-two major arcana cards. The resultant pack is dealt into six stacks containing seven cards each; these are then spread into rows. Cards in the first row show the influences of the past on the query. The second row shows current influences; the third, external influences; the fourth, impending influences. The fifth row reveals future options pertaining to the situation, and the sixth row depicts the outcome.

TWO-MINUTE READING

In dire emergencies, you may perform a three-card reading. Prepare as you would for a Celtic Cross spread and lay out three cards. The first card is tantamount to the situation card, the second card is the crossing card, and the third predicts the outcome.

the possibility that she would leap into an ill-conceived marriage to obtain a mirage of happiness.

6. The sixth card, showing the future development of the issue, was the Four of Swords, otherwise known as the hermit's repose. This did not bode well for a lifelong relationship, but it did foretell that Isabel would come to find contentment and restoration in being alone. This card also served as a signal that her relationship with Ted was coming to an end.

7. As the representation of what separated Isabel from happiness, the Hanging Man was, as he usually is, utterly apropos. Not only was Isabel hung up on a man—her former lover—she was also dependent on the idea that a man was going to provide meaning to her life: the dream of the perfect man dangled before her like a carrot on a stick. In a larger sense, too, the Hanging Man showed that Isabel was stuck, held up from pursuing her goals as an individual, by an inability to expand her vision and

develop a satisfying life on her own. Even the Hanging Man's peaceable demeanor was appropriate to Isabel's situation, for she was perfectly content, on a day-to-day basis, with her life and her connection with Ted. It was only when she began to reflect on the larger picture that she knew she was not getting where she wanted to be.

8. The eighth card, signifying the attitude of Isabel's family toward her, was the Lovers. This seems odd, and at first I thought it might simply indicate that she was the product of a particularly harmonious union—which can be enough to skew anyone's romantic ideals. However, sober reflection engendered a different reading, and I asked Isabel if her family thought she was too picky about her partners. She confirmed that this was true. The card's emphasis on discrimination is integral to its meaning in this spread; Isabel had been frequently criticized for "wanting the world" and "being too demanding" with regard to relationships. It is important to realize that though the card in this position reveals the querent's position in his or her family, it in no way implies that the family is right. In this instance, the Lovers, a card about the necessity of truthfulness in the choice of a partner, knows better than Isabel's family what she should do, as it holds within it an exhortation to be demanding—of oneself as well as one's partner.

9. The Knight of Pentacles, in the ninth position, indicates Isabel's hopes for herself, which at the time of the reading were not very high. She felt that she was condemned to an arduous search for the right partner, slogging over hill and dale on an increasingly exhausted horse. She supposed that she would be successful in the end,

Irish cartomantic colleens, from a 1911 postcard.

as the Knight of Pentacles is, through perseverance rather than grace. Even the Knight's heavy and unornamented armor is symbolic of how Isabel's past relationships had made her defensive and guarded.

10. The outcome card was, of all things, the Wheel of Fortune. Though it did not predict the ending Isabel wanted, it warned her of imminent instability and offered some serious spiritual advice. All of Isabel's energies were being absorbed in the issue of relationships; she was virtually unable to devote her time to anything else. The Wheel of Fortune was telling her to step back from that issue and consider her life as a whole. There is no aspect of life that does not change, the card was telling her, and the ultimate wisdom is to extinguish your attachment to specific outcomes.

Clearly, the answer to Isabel's question was negative, at least for the period of time covered by the reading (which I take to be about nine months, unless otherwise indicated by the issues covered). The sixth card revealed that she was going to spend time alone, though this would by no means be an unpleasant time. The column of the four final cards, which always signifies the spiritual or moral ramifications of the issue, was unanimous in its opinion that Isabel's best path was to abandon her dependence on the idea that a man was going to be the key to her happiness. Indeed, the Wheel of Fortune suggested that she learn that there are no keys to happiness, that we are caught in a cycle of incarnation whose motives we can never hope to comprehend.

Though Isabel's cards are, of course, particular to her situation, they display a typical range of signals. It would be rare to find such a love-related query answered by a spread composed exclusively of Cups, but the near-absence of Cups was important in Isabel's reading. The appearance of anomalous cards presents a challenge to every reader, but experience teaches a respect for the ways of the cards. Tarot is a wily divinatory system; it knows what it means, and though you may be inclined to throw up your hands at an inexplicable plethora of Wands in a question about finances, it is better to stop and search for a reasonable explanation (stock-market crash).

As each card resonates against the others in a given spread, its implications multiply, and its symbolism becomes richer and deeper. Alone of all Western divinatory systems, tarot's dramatis personae replicates the complexity of the human psyche. We are both the Fool and the World and everything in between. With a combination of magic and tact, the tarot suggests that we will find the correct path in the wake of our Foolishness.

PICTURE CREDITS

Pages 2, 8, 13, 15, 53, 62, 64, 69, 154, 155, and 160: Courtesy of Special Collections, Stanford University Libraries

Page 6: The Metropolitan Museum of Art, Rogers Fund, 1960 (60.30). Photograph © 1982 The Metropolitan Museum of Art.

Pages 18 and 19: Charles Walker Collection, Images Colour Library

Page 33: Courtesy of the Library of Congress

Page 58: Yale Center for British Art, Paul Mellon Collection

Pages 60, 114, 119, 153, 156, 158, 198 (bottom), and 199 (middle): Mary Evans Picture Library

Pages 67, 108, 110, and 112: Getty Research Institute, Research Library

Page 76: Fine Arts Museums of San Francisco, Achenbach Foundation for Graphic Arts 1963.30.24

Page 84: Scala/Art Resource, NY

Page 87: Fine Arts Museums of San Francisco, Achenbach Foundation for Graphic Arts purchase, 1985.1.63.7

Page 91: Fine Arts Museums of San Francisco, museum purchase, Achenbach Foundation for Graphic Arts Endowment Fund and Emge Funds, 1987.2.108

Pages 93, 94, 98, and 100: Byzantium Archive

Page 96: Christie's Images/Bridgeman Art Library, London/New York

Pages 116, 118, and 121: Courtesy of Marlene McLoughlin

Page 117: Hulton Getty Picture Collection/Tony Stone Images

Pages 124, 125, 126, 127, 128, 129, and 130: Courtesy Christopher Stinehour Design

BIBLIOGRAPHY

Adrienne, Carol. *The Numerology Kit.* New York: Plume, 1988.

Agrippa von Nettesheim, Heinrich Cornelius. *Occult Philosophy: Or, Magic.* New York: AMS Press, 1982.

Bascom, W. *Ifa Divination: Communication Between Gods and Men in West Africa.* Bloomington: Indiana University Press, 1969.

Blum, Ralph. *The Book of Runes: A Handbook for the Use of an Ancient Oracle: The Viking Runes.* New York: St. Martin's Press, 1993.

Bohme, Jakob. *The Works of Jacob Behmen, the Teutonic Theosopher.* Edited by William Law. London, 1764.

Campion, Nicholas. *The Practical Astrologer.* Bristol, England: Cinnabar Books, 1993.

Cardano, Girolamo. *La Métoposcope de H. Cardan.* Paris, 1658.

Cocles, Bartolommeo della Rocca. *La Physionomie naturelle, et la chiromance.* Rouen, 1698.

Dee, John. *A True and Faithful Relation of What Passed for Many Weers between Dr. John Dee (a mathematician of great fame in Q. Eliz. and King James, their reignes) and Some Spirits: Tending (had it succeeded) to a General Alteration of Most States and Kingdomes in the World.* London 1659.

Desbarrolles, Adolphe. *Chiromancie nouvelle: Les Mystères de la main, révélés et expliqués.* Paris, [1870].

Fludd, Robert. *Utriusque cosmi maioris scilicet et minoris metaphysica, physica, atque technica historia.* [Francofurti], 1621.

Fontana, David. *The Secret Language of Dreams: A Visual Key to Dreams and Their Meanings.* San Francisco: Chronicle Books, 1994.

Fowler, O. S., and L. N. Fowler. *New Illustrated Self-Instructor in Phrenology and Physiology.* New York, 1859.

Freud, Sigmund. *The Interpretation of Dreams. The Basic Writings of Sigmund Freud.* Translated and edited by A. A. Brill. New York: Modern Library-Random House, 1938.

Gettings, Fred. *The Book of the Hand.* London: Paul Hamlyn, 1965.

———. *Tarot: How to Read the Future.* Stamford, Connecticut: Longmeadow Press, 1993.

Gray, Eden. *A Complete Guide to the Tarot.* New York: Crown Publishers, 1970.

Grillot de Givry, Emile. *Picture Museum of Sorcery, Magic and Alchemy.* Translated by J. Courtenay Locke. New Hyde Park, New York: University Books Inc., 1963.

Halevi, Z'ev ben Shimon. *Kabbalah: Tradition of Hidden Knowledge.* New York: Thames and Hudson, 1980.

Hamon, Louis. *Cheiro's Language of the Hand.* Los Angeles: The London Publishing Co., n.d.

Holroyd, Stuart, and Neil Powell. *Mysteries of Magic.* London: Aldus Books, 1978.

Indagine, Johannis. *Ioannes ab Indagine Introductiones apostelesmaticae in physiognomian.* N.p., 1603.

Isaacs, Ronald H. *The Jewish Book of Numbers.* Northvale, New Jersey: J. Aronson, 1996.

Kaplan, Stuart. *The Encyclopedia of Tarot.* Vol. I. Stamford, Connecticut: U.S. Games Systems, Inc., 1978.

Klossowski de Rola, Stanislas. *Alchemy: The Secret Art.* London: Thames and Hudson Ltd., 1973.

———. *The Golden Game: Alchemical Engravings of the Seventeenth Century.* London: Thames and Hudson Ltd., 1988.

LeNormand, M. A. *Mémoires historiques et secrets de l'impératrice Joséphine.* Paris, 1827.

Levi, Eliphas. *The History of Magic, Including a Clear and Precise Exposition of Its Procedure, Its Rites, and Its Mysteries.* 3rd ed. Translated by A. E. Waite. New York: E. P. Dutton and Co., 1930.

Lilly, William. *Astrologicall Prediction.* London, 1648.

Lineman, Rose, and Jan Popelka. *Compendium of Astrology.* Atglen, Pennsylvania: Whitford Press, 1984.

Lyons, Albert. *Predicting the Future: An Illustrated History and Guide to the Techniques.* New York: Harry N. Abrams, Inc., 1990.

McKinnie, Ian. *Fun in a Teacup.* Berkeley: Celestial Arts, 1974.

Merton, Holmes Whittier. *Descriptive Mentality from the Head, Face, and Hand.* Philadelphia [1899].

Papus. *Traité élémentaire de magie pratique.* Paris, 1893.

Parker, Derek, and Julia Parker. *Parkers' Astrology: The Definitive Guide to Using Astrology in Every Aspect of Your Life.* London: Dorling Kindersley, 1994.

Paul, Jim, trans. and ed. *The Rune Poem: Wisdom's Fulfillment, Prophecy's Reach.* San Francisco: Chronicle Books, 1996.

Piccart, Bernard. *Cérémonies et coutumes religieuses de tous les peuples du monde.* Amsterdam, 1739.

Raphael's Witch: Or, the Oracle of the Future. London, 1835.

Reading Tea Leaves. New York: Clarkson Potter/Publishers, 1995.

Schimmel, Annemarie. *The Mystery of Numbers.* New York and Oxford: Oxford University Press, 1993.

Schwei, Priscilla, and Ralph Petska. *The Complete Book of Astrological Geomancy: The Master Divination System of Cornelius Agrippa.* St. Paul: Llewellyn Publications, 1990.

Sheridan, Jo. *Teacup Fortune-telling.* N.p.: Mayflower, 1978.

Sibly, Ebenezer. *A New and Complete Illustration of the Occult Sciences: Or, the Art of Foretelling Future Events and Contingencies by the Stars.* London, 1784.

Skinner, Stephen. *Terrestrial Astrology: Divination by Geomancy.* London and Boston: Routledge and Kagen Paul, 1980.

Stephens, George. *The Old-Northern Runic Monuments of Scandinavia and England.* Vol. 2. London, 1867–68.

Tuchman, Maurice and Judi Freeman, eds. *The Spiritual in Art: Abstract Painting 1890–1985.* New York: Abbeville Press and the Los Angeles County Museum of Art, 1986.

Vallemont, abbé de. *La Physique occulte, ou, Traité de la baguette divinatoire.* La Haye, 1762.

Waite, A. E. *The Hermetic Museum, Restored and Enlarged: Most Faithfully Instructing All Disciples of the Sopho-Spagyric Art How That Greatest and Truest Medicine of the Philosopher's Stone May Be Found and Held.* London, 1893.

———. *Lives of Alchemystical Philosophers Based on Materials Collected in 1815 and Supplemented by Recent Researches with a Philosophical Demonstration of the True Principles of the Magnum Opus.* London, 1888.

Wasserman, James. *Art and Symbols of the Occult: Images of Power and Wisdom.* Rochester, Vermont: Destiny Books, 1993.

Wharton, George. *The Works of that Late Most Excellent Philosopher and Astronomer, Sir George Wharton, bar.* London, 1683.

Woods, Ralph L. *The World of Dreams: An Anthology.* New York: Random House, 1947.

ACKNOWLEDGMENTS

I would like to thank Christine Carswell and Sarah Malarkey for their astute and gracious editorial guidance, as well as Pamela Geismar for her aesthetic savoir faire, and Leslie Jonath for having the idea in the first place.

Robin Bromley, Karen Silver, Peter Lawrence, Sally Barrows, Benjamin Darling, Marijane Osborn, Morgan Atkin, and Stephanie Zappa provided help in one form or another, for which I thank them. Barbara Hodgson was unfailingly informative and generous throughout this project; her vision and good sense rescued me on a number of occasions, and I am grateful to her.

I am deeply indebted to Steve Mockus, who contributed the sections on geomancy and tasseomancy, in addition to undertaking a vast amount of research on obscure divinatory practices, all of which he completed with dispatch and élan. His assistance was incalculably valuable, and he has my fervent thanks.

And finally, I am grateful to Jeffrey Goldstein, who was sympathetic amidst tribulation.

INDEX

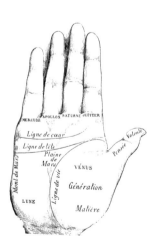

THE END